The Last Resistance

The Last Resistance

JACQUELINE ROSE

VERSO
London • New York

This edition published by Verso 2017
First published by Verso 2007
© Jacqueline Rose 2007, 2013, 2017

1 3 5 7 9 10 8 6 4 2

Verso
UK: 6 Meard Street, London W1F 0EG
US: 20 Jay Street, Suite 1010, Brooklyn, NY 11201
versobooks.com

Verso is the imprint of New Left Books

ISBN-13: 978-1-78663-075-9
ISBN-13: 978-1-78663-076-6 (UK EBK)
ISBN-13: 978-1-78663-077-3 (US EBK)

British Library Cataloguing in Publication Data
A catalogue record for this book is available from the British Library

Library of Congress Cataloging-in-Publication Data
A catalog record for this book is available from the Library of Congress

Typeset in Bembo by Hewer Text UK Ltd, Edinburgh
Printed in the US by Maple Press

for Ronit and Asher Tlalim

'The man who is the possessor of force seems to walk through a non-resistant element; in the human substance that surrounds him nothing has the power to interpose, between the impulse and the act, the tiny interval that is reflection.'

Simone Weil, 'The *Iliad*, or the Poem of Force', 1940

'The "inner world" . . . meets with a two-fold resistance; on the one hand, the incapacity to understand it, and on the other, a direct emotional rejection of it as unwelcome suggestion which is hardly rationalised by serious discussion.'

Joan Rivière, 'The unconscious phantasy of an inner world reflected in examples of literature', 1952

Contents

Preface

These essays were all written post-11 September and in the shadow of the worsening conflict in Israel–Palestine. They are published in the year that Israel's occupation of the West Bank and Gaza reaches its fortieth anniversary, an occupation that has now lasted longer in Israel's history than the period between the Declaration of Independence of 1948 that founded the state and the 1967 war which was when it begun. This has also been the time when America's plans for a new century have led to the maelstrom of Iraq. An illegal war, to which Great Britain is shamefully a party, and one of the longest occupations of modern history form the sombre backdrop to this book.

In this context two discourses or ways of thought make their mark, as they always have for me, against the darkness of the times. One is psychoanalysis, in its ability to uncover truths that would remain hidden, and to unsettle the most rigid forms of identity as they play themselves out across the stage of political life. The other is literature whose power to subvert the status quo receives new urgency when the dominant clichés and deceptions of statehood, whether here and in the US or in Israel, have reached such new and mind-numbing heights. Both psychoanalysis and literature appear in these essays as forms of resistance, which is the term that gives its title to the book. Resistance has of course another history, most famously in the struggle against the Nazis, whose genocide of European Jewry was the prelude to the founding of the Jewish state. It is one of the tragedies of the history examined in these pages that the nation intended to protect the Jewish people has become the agent of state violence against another people, the Palestinians, who find themselves engaged today in a resistance of their own. These forms of resistance are not the same, any more than what, or whom, they are fighting against. Across the world, resistance shifts its meanings and location. Whole destinies, only some of them touched on here, are contained in the mutations of this word.

The writers who people these essays – my travelling companions as I like to think of them – all open up the space of critical thought. They allow me, as I hope they will allow the reader, to think against the grim orthodoxies of our times.

Originally, these pieces had different audiences and destinations. The less formal, non-academic essays I have chosen to keep to their original format without notes.

I am enormously grateful to the *London Review of Books*, where a number of the essays were originally published, in particular, once again, to Mary-Kay Wilmers. Thanks also to Adam Shatz at *The Nation*, to Alex Scrimgeour at *Harper's* magazine, to Derek Johns, and to Tom Penn at Verso where I am delighted to be published once again. Other people have been of immense importance over the period the essays were written. I cannot now imagine writing without the support and insights of Sally Alexander and Marina Warner. Avi Shlaim brings his exemplary scholarship and clarity to everything he reads. I owe a special debt to the thoughts of scholar of Tibetan culture Ronit Tlalim, and to the dynamic creativity of filmmaker Asher Tlalim, new friends to whom, with much appreciation, I dedicate this book. And to Jonathan Sklar who reads me with such profound care. Queen Mary, University of London has continued to provide a free space of intellectual enquiry and unfailing support. The students of the course I have been teaching there over the past two years – 'Palestine–Israel, Israel–Palestine: Politics and the Literary Imagination' – have played a crucial role. I thank them. Finally, the strongest thanks are due to my daughter, Mia Rose, who continues to be the most vital presence of all, and the source of much joy.

Introduction

At a key moment in Irène Némirovsky's *Suite Française*, Lucile Angellier walks into the garden towards Bruno, the German soldier billeted in her house since the Occupation of France, with whom she has fallen in love. She has burdened her desire for him with the meaning of freedom. Not the superficial freedom to travel or leave her house, 'even though that would be unimaginably blissful', but freedom of the mind: 'I'd rather feel free inside – to choose my own path, never to waver, not to follow the swarm. I hate this community spirit they go on and on about.' Her illicit love will free her from a loveless marriage (her husband, who has kept a mistress for most of their married life, is at the front), from the grip of a cruelly vigilant mother-in-law, and, even more startling in the context of the Occupation, from the crowd – the community spirit pounded into her ears (*'cet esprit communautaire dont on nous rabat les oreilles'*). Lucile is resisting conformity, even if that means consorting with the enemy, even if it means rejecting the ethos of her community as it struggles to maintain its dignity and survive. In Occupied France, this is of course to turn the meaning of resistance on its head. For a moment, resistance degrades itself, descends a rung into vulgarity (as in 'will she resist his charms?'). But when the long-awaited encounter takes place, something erupts inside Lucile and she pushes Bruno away: ' "No, never!" she cried out. "Never!" Never would she be his. She was afraid of him. She no longer craved his touch. She wasn't depraved enough (or too young perhaps) to allow her fear to be transformed into desire.' At the final hour, resistance is spared contamination – although to say it is a close thing is an understatement. They were enemies 'in spite of everything', and what made them so were the 'secret movements of blood they had counted on to unite them and over which they were powerless'.

Resistance is the term that gives its title to these essays. For Némirovsky, at this crisis point in the novel, it is the blood that resists, halting Eros in its tracks as it tries its chance across enemy lines. A tinge of racial fantasy in her language does not detract from her genius in condensing into such a brief passage the strange permutations of resistance in our time. Resisting Bruno, Lucile becomes a true daughter of her nation, 'united with her captive land', although once more a 'prisoner', 'gagged' and 'bound' (she sacrifices her freedom in identification with France's darkest hour). At huge risk to herself, she will go on to protect a young Frenchman on the run after he has shot a German soldier. For many, resistance, as Resistance to Nazism, can only bear this meaning – only in that form does the term have its capital 'R': a word husbanded by history, sacred, eternally sequestered, whose meanings are exhausted by the moments of bravery and cunning of the Second World War. 'This word', Jacques Derrida writes, 'which first resonated in my desire and imagination as the most beautiful word in the politics and history of this country [. . .] charged with all the pathos of my nostalgia, as if what I would have wanted not to miss at any cost would have been to blow up trains, tanks and headquarters between 1940 and 1945.'

　　Némirovsky adds another dimension. In fact Derrida also laments the mutability of the term, comparing it to a lover with infinite, unsettling, powers of attraction. The second part of *Suite Française*, which Némirovsky entitles 'Dolce', is in no small part carried as a piece of writing by the growing passion of Bruno and Lucile (collaboration as erotic collaboration before anything else). It is also something of a scandal in itself to have called this section, even ironically, 'Dolce', as in 'life is sweet'. As readers we desire their desire. With Lucile, we enter into the heady excitement of fear, which she barely, if ultimately, resists. That is how narrative works. There is no way we can read her story and remain pure. Not sexually, not politically. In the space of a few days or weeks, we are buffeted from resistance as inner sexual freedom, to resistance as revulsion – in the blood – towards the German enemies of France. Since its publication in 2004, *Suite Française* has become famous. It was written after Némirovsky fled Paris for Issy l'Évêque, from where she was deported to Pithiviers and then Auschwitz, where she died on 17 August 1942 (more than sixty years later her novel was uncovered and transcribed by her daughter). Némirovsky's relationship to her Jewishness was deeply ambivalent. She converted to Catholicism in February 1939. After 1939, no Jewish characters appeared in her novels (although in a journal entry of 1940, she planned a novel for better times; 'Juif, la débâcle'). But from the centre of the crisis which still in so many ways defines our modern epoch, she shows resistance changing shape and shifting allegiance, as it plunges into the bloody depths of inner and outer worlds. Many of the essays that follow are about the legacy of that moment. But each one suggests in its different way that we cannot understand this history and its aftermath unless we are willing, while remaining on historical ground, to lose our bearings, and to enter – as all fiction requires – into the strangest pathways of the mind.

Sometimes resistance is simple, needs no gloss, as it will also appear in this book. For Marcel Liebman, who is one of my topics (Chapter 12), resistance was heady euphoria, light surging in a landscape for the most part unremittingly bleak. 'It was militants of the far left', he writes in *Born Jewish*, his memoir of Occupied Belgium, 'who, at the very start of the Occupation, decided to unite and plan for resistance' (they were used to being on the wrong side of the law). Every time the occupier went on the offensive, Jewish Solidarity of Charleroi convened to organise their response. Jews fleeing deportations in northern France were found jobs as factory workers, families who had received rounding-up notifications were visited and urged not to respond, and in the most remarkable coup of all, a bogus list was drawn up matching the real names of Jews to imaginary addresses on the outskirts of the city, sending the Nazis on a wild goose chase and depriving them of hundreds of their prey. At Malines on the first day of the Warsaw Uprising, a group of prisoners linked up with prisoners in the Dossin barracks, to sabotage the twentieth transport of Jewish deportees to Auschwitz.

Resistance in this shape dispenses with the equivocations of the world. 'As far as we were concerned,' Yitzhak Zuckerman writes in his *Chronicle of the Warsaw Ghetto Uprising*, 'the expected struggle had two aspects: first, not to hide, not to flee, but to fight. Second, not to be taken alive by the Germans.' When Zivia Lubetkin Zuckerman appears as a witness to the uprising during Eichmann's trial, she stands out for Hannah Arendt as almost luminous, hers as the 'purest' and 'clearest' account (at such moments the occasion shifted from show trial into something more like a mass meeting). Mostly, however, there was no chance of resistance. Arendt is enraged by the question regularly addressed by the prosecutor to each witness, except the Resistance fighters: 'Why did you not rebel?', not just because it acted as a smokescreen to conceal Jewish cooperation with the Nazis, but also because, in the words of Idith Zertal, 'rebellion was for her utterly impossible under the Nazi murderous terror, the realm of the very few and the very young'. We cling to these moments of resistance because they tell us that anything is possible in conditions where mostly nothing was. Hence the aura of the word, which dons the garb of the miraculous: 'To be sure those who resisted were a minority, a tiny minority,' writes Arendt after the testimony of Zivia Zuckerman, 'but under the circumstances "the miracle was," as one of them pointed out, "that this minority existed".' Inside the camps there were no miracles. As a child, Sara Roy – Middle Eastern scholar and daughter of Auschwitz survivors – came home one day from her *yeshiva* with a story of starving and emaciated children in a concentration camp who, after manna suddenly falls miraculously from the sky, go willingly to their deaths no longer hungry and thanking God (outraged, her parents withdrew her shortly afterwards from the school).

Two years ago, I was given Hannah Levy-Hass's *Belsen Diary 1944-1945* – published in German in 1979, English in 1982 – by her daughter, the Israeli campaigning journalist Amira Hass, who lives with the Palestinians in the Occupied West Bank today. From mother to daughter, this document bore witness, in one striking manifestation, to the journey – from the tragedy in Europe to the crisis in the Middle East – which is my pre-occupation here. Levy-Hass's diary, written from inside Belsen, is, amongst other things, a meditation on the capacity of thought. 'There was no sense in which I could resist in the camp,' she writes. 'All I could do was to try to remain human.' To read this extraordinary document is, however, even here to encounter a resistance of sorts: in her fierce refusal to accept the argument, notably of her co-Yugoslavian, Professor K., whom she visits in the sick bay, that morality does not apply in the camps, that, under such circumstances, matter has no choice but to dispose of mind. Instead, for her, life para-doxically becomes worthless the moment it will preserve itself at any cost. 'Is human life ultimately so precious that we can permit all these atrocities in order to preserve it?' (She is describing the lengths to which the inmates went in order to remain alive.) Survival cannot be its own end – this becomes a political as much as personal credo that she will carry forwards into the rest of her life. The horrors of the camps increase, rather than diminish, the necessity of another ethics. 'I am firmly convinced', she writes in March 1945, 'that those for whom ethical principles are fundamental laws, and to whom such laws have become second nature – a kind of human instinct taking the place of animal instinct – will not go under.' She also believes that only pure contingency saved her – she survived because she was so physically robust: 'Everything does indeed depend on one's health, on one's physical power of resistance [. . .] on it rests my ability to retain a sense of integrity and honour.' She insists it is not a personal achievement of her own.

These stories all seem like endpoints, in the face of which nothing remains to be said. Resistant to the Nazi destruction of thinking, they also seem to operate in the collective imagination as the point where thinking, whether out of respect, humility or fear of our own failure, is required to stop. To read the testimonies of Anton Zuckerman, Hannah Levy-Hass, and Marcel Liebman is, however, to be struck with how these tales cannot, and should not, be held to their originating moment, but instead become part of an ongoing history – if they didn't then they would be mere museum pieces, fossilised in awe. This is to deprive them of the future. 'The past lives in the present and in the future,' Zuckerman writes at the end of his memoir, 'if not, it has no meaning.' Ironically, against the very risk and wager of their narratives, they would have failed to survive.

One of the central questions of the essays that follow is how best to draw the line that runs from this history to Palestine. For many, including Zuckerman, the lesson of Nazism was the pressing urgency of a Jewish National Home. When members of the Resistance went to Anton Schmidt, the famous German who saved many Jews from deportation, he apparently told them that rather than transferring Jews from one part of Poland to another, they should be sent to 'Eretz Israel'. After the war Zuckerman was centrally involved in the emigration of the remaining Jews from Poland to Palestine, where he himself arrived, a year after his wife, in December 1947. Levy-Hass also makes her home in Israel: first returning to Yugoslavia at the end of the war, she leaves for the new state in 1948. Liebman stays in Europe, finally settling in England, where he becomes an outspoken critic of Zionism. This in itself suggests that the legacy of the Holocaust is more than one. Behind each of these stories, other stories are to be found that trouble the link between the genocide in Europe and the Jewish presence in Palestine. If that link is self-evident for Zuckerman, it is one of the hardest aspects of this history – hardest for him – that it was a link only partially recognised by the incipient nation. Lionised as a new Trumpeldor at the 1945 London Zionist Conference, he stands up and berates the delegates with their failure to come to Poland to help the survivors. When Moshe Sharrett asks 'How was it possible to get into Poland?' he simply replies: 'Isn't it as possible to get in as to get out?'. 'It was then that I knew there was a chasm between us – a broad chasm.' Later he will describe it as a 'psychological abyss'. 'Why', he asks, 'wasn't a single Ha-Shomer Ha-Tza'ir ("Young Guard") kibbutz established in Eretz Israel for the survivors? Because their leaders didn't believe in and were afraid of the survivors.'

If resistance gives the title to these essays, it is not, therefore, as an innocent term. For Freud, who plays a large part in what follows, resistance was a psychic reality that blocked the passage of the psyche into freedom. One of the mind's best defences, it cuts subjects off from the pain and mess of the inner life. If this seems counterintuitive, the history of Israel could be seen as providing a graphic illustration of how resistance can shift between its two poles. Zuckerman's story shows resistance picked up into the blood-stream of the new nation, as the survivors discover themselves both found and lost in their new home. Inaugurated in 1952, Israel's annual day of Holocaust commemoration was named the Day of Destruction and Hero-ism and placed as close to the date of the Warsaw Uprising as religious laws relating to Passover would permit. But when the Minister of Education and Culture, Ben-Zion Dinur, submitted to the Knesset in 1953 the Holocaust and Heroism Remembrance Law, whose purpose was to establish a memorial for every Jew slain, the one category not mentioned was the survivors, the only living people with a true memory of the event. This suggests that remembrance was conditional – Warsaw first, the survivors last, and least. As I argue together with Judith Butler in another of these essays (Chapter 14) – both of us indebted to the writings of Idith Zertal – trauma enters the national psyche in the form of resistance to its own pain. In fact the process can be traced back to the very earliest stages of the war. Shulamith Hareven, a distinguished Israeli writer little known in the English-speaking world, who will also appear in these essays (Chapter 2), is the author of a famous short story, 'The Witness', perhaps her best known. It tells the story of a young Polish boy who flees the Nazi massacre of his family to Palestine, and then tries to recount a tragedy for which the *Yishuv* accepts no responsibility and that it does not wish to hear.

The journey from Nazi Europe to Palestine is therefore not simple, although it is often presented as self-evident. To question it, or even to return to it and require that we reread it, is seen by many as breaking a taboo. And yet, as the Nazi shadow descended across Europe, Sigmund Freud and Arnold Zweig – whose 1930s correspondence is the subject of the opening essay – were already asking, as many of the essays to follow will ask, what would be the cost of that journey both for Jews in Palestine and throughout the world, and for the Palestinians whose displacement as a people would be its tragic consequence. Unlike Freud, Zweig will move to Palestine, only to be disillusioned by the rigidity that he sees taking shape all around him. One of his responses – at once part of and his answer to depression – is to write a novel about Jacob de Haan, critic of Zionism, who was murdered by Jews in Jerusalem in 1924. In his original con-ception of the novel – in the original reports of the murder – de Haan was murdered by an Arab for his homosexual relationship with a young Arab boy. Zweig's discovery of the truth forces him to confront the violence of a nationalism that will do anything, including murder, to preserve itself. 'I have established quite calmly', he writes to Freud in 1935, 'that I do not belong here.' (He finally leaves for what will become the GDR in 1948.) Confronting the imminent collapse of Europe, psychoanalyst and writer rehearse the options, go over the old and new ground, only to find each of them wanting: Europe in the grip of rising fanaticism, Palestine in the throes of an increasingly desperate and emboldened nationalism which brooks no argument and will only speak in one tongue. Zweig's final disillusionment occurs at a left demonstration of Paole Zion – Zionist

Socialists – who keep up the 'nationalistic fiction' that they cannot understand him when he speaks German.

There were analysts – Max Eitingon, Moshe Wulff – who emigrated to Palestine (the former to the objections of both Sigmund and Anna Freud). But in this dialogue between Freud and Zweig, psychoanalysis appears as a critique of national self-enchantment, of identities that harden like iron in response to the ills of the world. For Israeli analyst Eran Rolnik, author of the just-published *Freud in Zion* (*Osei Nefashot: Im Freud le'Eretz Yisrael 1918-1948*), psychoanalysis will always be at odds with a vision of pure or ideal selfhood since its question is always: 'Where am I most myself? In the places where I am most foreign, in my unconscious.' Freud, he also suggests, saw the Jews' choice of Palestine as an unwise attempt to revive an old love: 'the chances that such a love will work out are not very great'. Freud's interest in these questions may come as a surprise. Contrary to the more familiar stereotype, however, psychoanalysis has as much to say about our forms of collective belonging, about social, as about individual, life. As a Jew, Freud had found himself more than once the target of race hatred. He had every reason to turn his attention, as he did repeatedly throughout his life, to the question of what people do, for better but mostly for worse, when they bind themselves into a mass ('Mass Psychology' – one of his most important works on this topic – gives its title to another of the essays here, Chapter 3).

Both Freud and Zweig were subject to the cruel rigours of European nationalism. Although in 1935 Freud would express support for a Jewish home in Palestine, for the most part he remained deeply suspicious. For both of them, however, to see Jewish nationhood in Palestine as redemptive for the anti-Semitism of Europe was already in the 1930s a mistake. We start therefore at a turning point in the imminent catastrophe of the European Jews when Freud, along with hundred of thousands of others, is on the verge of becoming a displaced person. Like resistance, displacement has its psychoanalytic meaning, which points to the mind's infinite capacity to defend and dupe itself. People on the move carry with them the burden of a past that cannot always be recognised, a burden that shifts its shape, inciting new fears and dangers, as they arrive on uncertain shores. 'There are nine million of them today. There will be even more of them tomorrow and even more the day after,' writes Dorothy Thompson in her 1938 *Refugees – Anarchy or Organisation?* – on the eve of the *Anschluss* Freud recommended her book to Princess Marie Bonaparte, who was organising his exit from Austria. Today, such displacements are becoming the common currency of a ruthlessly globalised world. Thompson could also be talking about now: 'Wandering exiles, the innocent victims of economic and political persecution, their fate is probably the most pressing of humanity's problems.'

For Levi-Hass, the journey to Palestine after the war could only be made as a socialist struggling for the universal ethic to which her Belsen diary made its impassioned appeal. She went on to become a peace activist and feminist in Israel. Out of the anguish of her experience emerges an ethos that it is perhaps too tempting to see her as passing on to her daughter, winner of the World Press Freedom Prize in 2003, who steadfastly records the devastation of Palestinian life under occupation. 'Only if their search for an identity helps Jewish intellectuals to fight for a better future for the whole of mankind', Levy-Hass states in 1978 citing Isaac Deutscher, 'do I regard their search as justified' (the interview with Eike Geisel is published at the end of the English translation of her diary). Likewise Sara Roy lifts from her parents' experience in the camps, above all that of her mother and aunt, a universal ethic that poses the most radical challenge to Israel in its treatment of the Palestinians. For each of these writers, the disaster in Europe leaves a trace, an anxiety, which cannot be matched with uncritical belief in the virtues of state and nationhood, even while they recognise the pressing need of the Jewish people out of which Israel emerged. 'Obedience to a state was not an ultimate Jewish value,' Roy writes of her family, 'not for them, not after the Holocaust. Judaism provided the context for values and beliefs that were not dependent upon national boundaries, but transcended them.'

For Liebman, whose brother was deported to Auschwitz at the age of fifteen, Zionism, by claiming to speak for the dead Jews of Europe, would wrongly affirm Jewish identity as an absolute. Racism should be denounced; there should be no retreat behind the defensive barrier of being – and being only – a Jew (his memoir is dedicated to 'Jews and non-Jews' in their common struggle against Nazism). To demand that all or most Jews should emigrate to Palestine was to 'uproot' and 'maim', leaving the field to the enemy. The new nation was in danger of crushing the options of the next generation, and the generations to come, severing the link between Jews of the Diaspora and the Jews of Israel, between the Jews and other peoples.

Sometimes as the explicit focus, sometimes as backdrop, these writers form the cast of the essays to follow. Taking my cue from their stories, I would argue that to return anxiously and critically to this journey of the Jewish people, from a devastated Europe to Palestine – a Palestine still today in the throes of the crisis of that founding moment – is not to betray the legacy of the tragedy but to prolong some of its strongest ethical impulses.

If such complex, diverse histories people this collection, fiction is also its repeated refrain. When he wrote his novel, Zweig knew he had gone too far for his own comfort. Not just because he was ostracised (one of the *Verlatene*, or forsaken, as de Haan became), but as a result of his troubling identification

– he described the book as a form of 'self-analysis' – with both de Vriendt and with the young 'Arab (semitic) boy'. 'Semitic' in itself suggests an affinity, not often recognised, between the Jews and the indigenous peoples of Palestine, an affinity which the homosexual affair of the novel will then perform or bring dramatically to life. But Zweig's unease also speaks to another central preoccupation of these essays, and that is the power of fiction to make reader, as well as writer, enter pathways they had never, in their wildest dreams, intended to tread. We saw this at the beginning with *Suite Française*, when it was impossible not to be drawn into a potentially corrupting desire that runs counter to the best drift of history. It seems no coincidence, therefore, that when J.M. Coetzee, writing after 11 September, confronts the problem of evil in fiction, he also chooses a key moment in the history of resistance as his limit case. Elizabeth Costello, his fictional creation, finds the degrading portrayal of the execution of Hitler's would-be assassins in Paul West's *The Very Rich Hours of Count von Stauffenberg* obscene. Is there a danger, she asks, that the literary depiction of evil invites our unwitting complicity, makes it too tempting, attracts us despite ourselves? And yet, as I argue in my essay on Coetzee (Chapter 7), he can only make his point by inviting on our part the most intimate identification with Costello, even during moments that could also be described as obscene, where she recalls having been the object of sexual violence as a young girl; or moments where she finds herself, all too human, like the men on the verge of execution, subject to the depradations of her ageing, declining bodily self. Coetzee's essay is like a Russian doll: to read it is to find yourself making, at every stage, the very identification you least want to make, until finally, with no power of exit, you have been confined to the smallest, most suffocating place. The only way to warn against the power of fiction is to perform it, as Coetzee so brilliantly does here and elsewhere. But why, I would ask, if we need to understand the worst as well as the best of history, would you want to stop the mind from running away with itself?

For Walt Whitman, evil was an indispensable part of poetry. 'I make the poem of evil also, I commemorate that part also, I am myself just as much evil as good, and my nation is.' As we shall see in Chapter 10, the spirit of these famous lines makes its way into Michael Cunningham's novel *Specimen Days*. We will watch as their generous, unsettling, inclusiveness challenges the post-9/11 rhetoric of statehood that justifies its own violence by flinging all evil to the farthest corners of the earth.

Fiction appears here then as at once dilemma and opportunity. In this there is also a crucial political point. Going too far might be another way of making connections which the world, at its most obdurate, tells us that we

must not make (as between Jew and Arab, Semites both). In the writing of
David Grossman (discussed in Chapter 5), it often appears that the role of
writing – fiction but also non-fiction – is to push you right through what
should be the impassable boundaries of the mind. 'We will see the broken
forms in each other', one of his characters says to an unknown woman he
tries to reach through a string of letters. 'This is what I want right now. That
we will see the darkness in each other.' Grossman has never been wary of
acknowledging the darkness of his own nation, to which he retains total
commitment. In his speech at the Rabin memorial in November 2006, he
described that love as 'overwhelming', 'unequivocal' and 'complex'. Edward
Said praised him as one of the few Israeli writers willing to condemn the
Occupation without reserve. This shows in itself that love of Israel and
criticism of Israel are not, as so often suggested, incompatible (ambivalence,
one might say, is the true hallmark of love). But in a conflictual reality of
contested boundaries between peoples, where distance is so intensely
charged, to make such a crossing could also be described as a form of
political longing, whose meaning resides precisely in the revulsion it at once
encounters and must try, against the odds, to shed: 'I must enter the vortex
of my greatest fear and repulsion', Grossman wrote on his way to visit the
refugee camps in 1988. And then in relation to the Palestinian Israelis, Arab
citizens of Israel, in 1993: 'Make room for them within us. How does one do
that? It is precisely the thing that we, the majority, forbid them with such
deft determination.' The situation is not symmetrical – neither politically
nor psychologically. It is the Israelis who have the power, erect the barriers
(the checkpoints, today the wall), set the terms.

Grossman is doing much more than making a plea for understanding. He
is asking for the very forms of identification, of almost breath-to-breath
proximity, that pushed Zweig to the verge of breakdown, long before the
antagonism between Jew and Arab – or now Israeli and Palestinian – had
reached today's dreadful pitch. He is asking, as Said put it in one of his lesser-
known essays, that the two sides of the conflict enter into each other's
historical and ongoing pain. Not, for Said, although this should hardly need
stressing, as an alternative to justice, still owed to the Palestinian people from
the time that these essays more or less begin, but as the precondition for
justice to be achieved and as its most urgently required accompaniment. In a
recent interview in *Ha'aretz*, Yitzhak Laor, Israeli novelist, poet and
founding editor of the radical literary journal *Mita'am*, suggests that the
only way of saving man from 'the demand of obedience' is through a
sudden, intimate, 'close-up with pain'. 'We cannot', Said writes, 'coexist as
two communities of detached and uncommunicatingly separate suffering.'
This is strangely reminiscent of Simone Weil who observed in her wondrous

1940 essay 'The *Iliad*, or the Poem of Force', 'The variety of constraints pressing upon man give rise to the illusion of several distinct species that cannot communicate.' 'There is', Said wrote, 'suffering and injustice enough for everyone.' It is worth pausing here. No one has a monopoly of pain. The expression 'Jewish suffering', as opposed to the suffering of the Jewish people, or the Jews' history of suffering, is to my mind a mistake (the crucial difference between acknowledging the bleakest night of our history and staking a claim).

Said's 1997 essay 'Bases for Coexistence' is the only essay for which he received hatemail in the Arab press. It is because this strand of his thinking is so little known that it is my focus in the essay on his work included here (Chapter 11). But it is also because it makes a case, simple and yet I believe in need of constant repeating. Trying to understand, past the point of endurance, is not an obstacle to the world's enhancement. By shifting the templates, pressing enemies close, it might instead be the key to transforming the very forms of rigidity that make the world seem – more and more by the day – such an irredeemably frightening and dangerous place.

This is I believe true even when, in the case of the suicide bomber, which will also be my topic (Chapter 6), everything inside us recoils from the horror of the act. For many this would be the limit case. To empathise, to try imaginatively to enter into such an experience, is not, however, to condone. It is an attempt to grasp what, under intolerable historical circumstances, each and every one of us might be capable of. Today, Palestinian resistance to the Occupation takes up its place in the roll-call of meanings of resistance in our time, tragic endpoint of the history with which these essays begin. It was first watching 'the helpless terror of the Jews of France', and then 'what the Jews of Israel were passing on to the Palestinian people', that caused Carmen Callil the greatest anguish in her study of Nazi collaborator Louis Darquier. These words led to the cancellation of the launch of her book in New York. Even in anguish, the connection is taboo. Even when, as here, the suggestion is so clearly that the Jewish people are passing on their own pain (passing on pain would be the political opposite of entering the pain of the other). We are not allowed to acknowledge that the state intended to save the Jewish people has become the agent of policies which now place Jews in Israel and in the Diaspora at risk, as well as producing intolerable lives for another people.

When Cherie Blair spoke of the lack of hope that leads young people to blow themselves up, Downing Street apologised. When Liberal Democrat Jenny Tonge suggested that under similar conditions, she might become a suicide bomber herself, she was sacked from her front bench (in fact Ehud

Barak once said more or less the same thing). At moments like these, we are being instructed by the powers-that-be to block the sounds in our ears. Writing with reference to the South Africa of the 1960s Nadine Gordimer, who will also appear here (Chapter 9), described terrorism as the 'deadly logical outcome' of the situation: 'They felt useless as they were, and so became what they were not.' Terrorism, we are often told, is *sui generis* – without history, something deformed inside the actors that places them, and their culture (so the argument goes) outside humanity's reach. We need to ask, when we refuse the other psychic right of entry, even *in extremis*, what we are doing, not only to them, but to ourselves. 'How', asks Eyad El-Sarraj, psychiatrist and the founder and director of the Gaza Community Mental Health Programme, 'can you believe in your own humanity if you don't believe in the humanity of the enemy?'

If fiction plays a key role in what follows it is also for another reason: its powers to unsettle, like psychoanalysis, all idealised, official, rhetorics, whether of nationhood, race, religion or state – its powers of resistance, as one might say. In the course I have recently started teaching at Queen Mary, University of London – 'Palestine–Israel, Israel–Palestine: Politics and the Literary Imagination' – the mobility of poetry and fiction against the official language of statehood, the ability of literature to register the most complex layerings of political histories and identities, has given the students hope. This too is a sign of the times. These essays were all written after 11 September 2001, since when the terms of dissent both here and in the United States have dramatically shifted. 'War against Terror', 'Axis of Evil', these are just two of the phrases through which we are all invited, more or less on a daily basis, to stifle disquiet, ratchet up our inner violence, go to war. 'The man who is the possessor of force', Weil writes in her essay on the *Iliad*, 'seems to walk through a non-resistant element; in the human substance that surrounds him nothing has the power to interpose, between the impulse and the act, the tiny interval that is reflection.'

 In Israel, with the unqualified support of its Western allies, the 'War against Terror' has been hijacked to legitimate increasing harshness, not to say wholesale destruction, in the Occupied Territories, and in the summer of 2006, in Lebanon. As I write, it is at least on the table that there will be a strike by Israel against Iran's developing nuclear programme, defined as an existential threat to a nation that now acknowledges – or rather its Prime Minister acknowledged and then denied he acknowledged – itself to be a nuclear power. In response to the felt failure of the Lebanese war, it is assumed there will be another war. In 2007 the Occupation enters its fortieth year. At the *Limmud* Jewish cultural festival, in Nottingham in 2005, campaigning *Ha'aretz* journalist Gideon Levy pointed out that the time of the Occupation was now double (today, more than double) the time before the Occupation: between the 1967 war that inaugurated it and the Declaration of Independence of 1948. The Occupation can no longer be seen as a state of exception, a temporary and regrettable episode; it has become the reality of the nation. This has repercussions in the world of signs. 'Everyone is exposed to the way the army tells the story,' Laor comments, 'the world exists through the language of the army and the Shin Bet [Israel's Security Agency] and the prisons and the courts and the municipal inspectors and the newspaper and the school.' 'The State is the word [. . .] the greatest manufacturer of meanings is the State.'

All the writers discussed here belong to that tiny interval of reflection described by Simone Weil, the interval between impulse and act, shut down by force. This is true for Nadine Gordimer, one of the finest analysts of the ugliness of apartheid South Africa in the soul of the white man, whose critique now stretches to corporatism, in its brute hold over the new South Africa, and to US dominance of the struggle over nuclear capability – the insanity of living in an era 'where there are wars going on over who possesses weapons that could destroy all trace of it'. It is true of David Grossman, who has not muted a challenge he has been voicing for many years – to his own people: 'How do we continue to watch from the side as though hypnotised by the insanity, rudeness, violence and racism that has overtaken our own home?'; to the state: hollow, self-important leaders, lacking vision, with no memory of history, who seem to exist 'only in the minuscule space between two headlines of a newspaper or between two investigations of the attorney general' (again from his speech at the November 2006 memorial for Rabin). Echoing Weil, Grossman laments a fundamental lack of space, too rapidly filled with state clamour. In this atmosphere, writing fiction becomes an act of freedom, 'of self-definition in a situation that threatens literally to obliterate me'.

As much in their political as in their literary works, these are writers who resist the orthodoxy of the nation. But resistance in this form does not only come from the writer who explicitly takes up the voice of dissent. One of the last and surprising finds of these essays has been the literary writings of Ze'ev Jabotinsky, founder of right-wing Revisionist Zionism, whose novels and short stories express the profoundest disquiet about the iron-cast militancy that he did so much to create. In his heart, if not in his politics, Jabotinsky looked more ways than one. Even in the most fixed of identities, somewhere there will be a fault line (this is the fundamental premise of psychoanalysis). Zionism, as I argue in *The Question of Zion*, always knew the violence of its own path. Jabotinsky was one of the few Zionists to acknowledge this openly. But nostalgia for the road not taken, self-doubt, creep into his fiction. Although you would be hard-pressed to find it anywhere in the language of those leaders – Menachem Begin, Binyamin Netanyahu, Ariel Sharon and Ehud Olmert – who claim him as their inspiration.

Most of the writers in these essays are Jewish – the book is therefore a celebration of Jewish thought as it lays claim to the interval of reflection. This in itself should make clear that to criticise Israel is no self-hatred, but can arise out of a passionate identification with, and love for, the thoughts and words of Jews. Nearly all of them could be included under my final rubric 'men and women in dark times' – taken from Hannah Arendt's 1970 collection, *Men in Dark Times*. In this section, Edward Said, Marcel Lieb-man, Simone de Beauvoir and, finally, Gillian Rose are the writers who allow me to track one stage in the journey of their mind. Arendt's opening remarks to her essays have remarkable prescience for each of them, as they do for the world we are living in today. Dark times, no rarity in history, arise from 'credibility gaps' and 'invisible government', from 'speech that does not disclose what is but sweeps it under the carpet', from 'exhortations, moral and otherwise, that under the pretext of upholding old truths, degrade all truth to meaningless triviality'. Nonetheless, even in the darkest of dark times, we have the right to expect some 'illumination', the kind that comes 'from the uncertain, flickering and often weak light that some men and women, in their lives and works, kindle under almost all circumstances and shed over the timespan that was given them on earth'. Although only time will tell, she concludes, whether their light 'was the light of a candle or that of a blazing sun'.

January 2007

PART I

Zionism Inside-Out

1

The Last Resistance*

A Marrano is a Jew, forcibly converted to Catholicism in Spain or Portugal at the time of the Inquisition, who cultivates her or his Jewishness in secret. The Marranos cherish their identity as something to be hoarded that also sets them irrevocably adrift. Jacques Derrida liked to compare his Jewishness with theirs, because they do not belong, while still remaining Jewish, even if they reached the point where they 'no longer knew in what their Jewishness consists'.[1] Today, according to an article in *Ha'aretz*, descendants of the Marranos in South America are returning to their Jewish faith. They do not want to convert – they do not wish to repeat their history in reverse. But they do want to belong to an ancestral community that many of them, deep in the interior of the continent, have been quietly performing for more than 500 years in the rituals of family and domestic life (today, their journey is from the mountains and out of the interior, to the cities from the plains). They want the status of people 'returning to the religion of their forebears'.[2] An expert on the Inquisition at São Paulo University in Brazil describes one such descendant as carrying 'history in his flesh and blood'.[3] And yet there is also here a tragedy in the making. There is virtually no court to which they could declare their allegiance that is sure to be honoured by Israel should such a descendant decide to take what might seem to be the logical next step of their destiny and make the ancestral land of Palestine their home.

'Flesh and blood' suggests our most intimately held forms of allegiance. It brooks no argument one might say. And yet, as this story suggests, it can be contested, subject to the injunctions and restrictions of competing national identities and state laws. There is an irony here since Israel claims its allegiance to the land of Palestine precisely on the grounds of blood-transmitted descent. 'It is impossible to say', Freud wrote to the German author Arnold Zweig when Zweig had just returned from a visit to Palestine in 1932, 'what heritage from this land we have taken into our blood and nerves.'[4] Yet, if Israel founds its identity on the notion of return, it will not grant these Marranos citizenship, even while it converts Native Indian Peruvians and Catholic Croatians who claim no such historical affinity to Jewishness, in order to people the settlements.[5]

The term 'flesh and blood' is of course ambiguous. As well as the most intimate, visceral form of belonging, it also denotes flesh torn and blood spilt in times of war. If I start with the tale of the modern-day Marranos it is because it offers such an inflated, almost grotesque, version of the painful twists which flesh and blood are heir to. Derrida, I imagine, would have been truly horrified by this story. First as a type of betrayal – 'I feel myself the inheritor, the depositary, of a very grave secret to which I myself do not have access', he stated in the same interview in which he mentions the Marranos a few months before he died in 2004.[6] It seems unlikely therefore that he would have welcomed the attempt by these descendants to consolidate their identity and faith. But secondly, and no less, I think he would have been appalled to watch this yearning collide with the fierce and defensively drawn parameters of the modern nation state. Either way, our story suggests that flesh and blood, as intimate cherished belonging, cannot today escape – perhaps has never truly escaped – the fate of nations.

The Marranos stand for a form of identity that is at once precarious, creative and threatened. The question they pose – the question that frames this and many of the essays to follow – is: what does it mean to be 'one of a people' in the modern world? Throughout the 1930s, in his extraordinary correspondence with Arnold Zweig, Freud finds himself asking the same question. It carries with it, as we shall see, that of the future and destiny both of psychoanalysis and of the Jewish people.

In a letter to Zweig of August 1930, near the start of their correspondence, Freud expresses an uncharacteristic confidence in the future of psycho-analysis. 'I have never doubted', Freud writes, 'that long after my day analysis will finally win through.'[7] Overjoyed, Zweig reminds Freud in his reply of the 'bitter words of deep disappointment' Freud had uttered at their last meeting. 'I am now happy to learn', Zweig writes, that these words belonged 'more to a passing gloom in your feelings than to a Freudian judgement' – although no one is 'more entitled to feel this gloom than you [. . .] we are delighted to see it dispersed.'[8] But by the end of the same paragraph, as if forgetting his own euphoria, Zweig's conviction has started to slip. 'We are only sorry,' he continues, that 'you do not feel that so vital, dynamic and revolutionary a principle as yours, once launched upon the world, will continue to be effective, until it has finally overcome all the blunt resistance the world can offer.'[9] For Zweig, in the 1930s, the world is the patient. Resistance is blindness. It is the strongest weapon or bluntest instrument the mind has at its disposal against the painful, hidden, knowledge of the unconscious. But in Zweig's reading, resistance stretches its meaning into the farthest reaches of public, political life. Freud is a revolutionary and it is the world that is resisting, although psychoanalysis will be victorious in the end. Without so much as a blush of theoretical embarrassment, he fearlessly lays the terms of the private clinical psychoanalytic encounter across the world of nations. By 1934, in a subsequent letter, he is even more emboldened. 'Freud and Tyranny (capital T) together – impossible', he declares: 'Either one follows your profound teachings and doctrines, controls one's emotions, adapts them to serve as positive forces in the world, and then one must fight for the liberation of man and the dethronement of national states [. . .] or one must impose upon mankind as ideal for the future his gradual suppression in a fascist system.'[10] The choice is clear – psychoanalysis, or fascism.

Freud and Zweig's correspondence opens in 1927, when Zweig writes to Freud requesting permission to dedicate his book on anti-Semitism to him. His debt to Freud, he writes, is threefold – for reintroducing the 'psyche into psychology', for the 'obeisance' that anti-Semitism owes to Freud, for the 'restoration' of Zweig's 'whole personality' (there is, and will be, no qualification – this is the utmost devotion).[11] But note how even here, in this first humble approach to a figure who unmistakably bears all the features of the master, Zweig can effortlessly fold his own personal debt to psychoanalysis into the world of politics. On the subject of anti-Semitism the world 'owes obeisance to Freud'. Zweig's acute personal debt is that of the world. By the time the correspondence ends, it is clear that the world's debt has not been, and will not be, paid, not in their lifetime at least. Zweig's last letter to Freud is dated 9 September 1939, the day of the outbreak of the Second World War.

Zweig's equivocations have the strongest resonance for today: which Freud should we believe, or with which of Freud's two moods, as laid out by Zweig in the 1930s, should we concur? Freud confident of the final victory of his science, or Freud watching darkness descend over Europe? Should we today read Freud's words of despair as 'passing gloom' or indeed as the profoundest and still relevant 'Freudian judgement'? After all the legacy of the 1930s is still with us – we are no closer, we might say, to Zweig's confidently proclaimed 'liberation of man and the dethronement of national states'. Anti-Semitism, which provides the opening occasion for their correspondence, still forms part of the fabric of Europe; except that today, as the story of the Marrano descendants suggests, it is linked, in complex and multidetermined ways, to the Jews' entry into the world of nations, one of the most immediate legacies of the crisis Freud and Zweig were witness to in their times. How those links should be thought about, whether there is any connection between a rise in European anti-Semitism and the actions of the state of Israel has become one of the most contested issues of our time. Few would dispute, however, that the 1948 creation of Israel was decisively affected, if not decided, by the Nazi genocide. In November 1938, shortly after fleeing Nazi Austria for London, Freud declines to contribute to a special issue of *Time and Tide* on anti-Semitism on the grounds that he has been too personally implicated, and that the task should fall to non-Jewish people. At the end of his letter to the editor, he asks somewhat disin-genuously: 'Ought this present persecution not rather give rise to a wave of sympathy in this country?'[12]

Of all people Freud should know that hate most often does not give rise to love, but to more hatred. 'Our hate', writes Joan Rivière in 1937, 'is distributed more freely than our love.'[13] Hatred propagates, feeds on itself. None of this has gone away. In *I Have Heard the Mermaids Singing*, part two of psychoanalyst Christopher Bollas's extraordinary novella trilogy on the life and thoughts of an analyst, a group of characters sit in a café in Hampstead in London (unmistakably Giraffe on Rosslyn Hill) and muse about the world post the 'Catastrophe', as 9/11 is termed. They are discussing an essay by analyst Rosalind Ryce and musing on her thoughts: 'she would state that the unconscious reason why people go to war with one another – like Super-power's beating up of other countries, or Israel's military domination of the Palestinians – is that hate is pleasure'.[14] 'The pleasure of hating others', comments the analyst on whom the book turns, 'exceeds the national interest in befriending the world.'[15] Hatred is one of the psyche's most satisfying emotions. In the face of such hatred, Zweig moves to Palestine in 1933, Freud finally and reluctantly as an exile to London at the very last moment in 1938. From Vienna to Haifa, they offer one version – from the heart of the battle as one might say – of what psychoanalysis can tell us about the fate of nations in the modern world.

Zweig's confident assertion that psychoanalysis will finally overcome 'all the blunt resistance that the world has to offer' is worth pausing at. In the most common political vocabulary, resistance is tied to liberation, it represents the break in the system where injustice gives way to freedom. You resist tyranny, you resist oppression, you resist occupation. More important, perhaps, you resist 'resistance' being described as anything else (for example in post-war Iraq, you resist struggle against US occupation being described as nothing more than foreign-backed opposition to new democratic freedom). The conference at the London School of Economics which provided the original occasion for this essay was entitled: 'Flesh and

Blood: Psychoanalysis, Politics, Resistance'. 'Resistance' came at the end, after politics, one step away from psychoanalysis, declaring its progressive allegiance – as if to suggest that the link between psychoanalysis and resistance, if you are thinking politically that is, might be remote or precarious to say the least. What would it have looked like if 'resistance' had appeared midway or caught between the two? It is, I would suggest, the most troubled term in the triptych – hence the title of this essay and book. If in political vocabularies, resistance is the passage to freedom, for psychoanalysis, it is repetition, blockage, blind obeisance to crushing internal constraint. For Zweig, only the overcoming of resistance in this psychoanalytic sense will allow the world to be saved. The aim of psychoanalysis, he states firmly in another letter, is to release energy into the world 'against the forces of reaction'. Instead of festering inside the mind, or being dissipated in writing – he is a writer so this is harsh self-condemnation – such forces 'should express themselves in real life, there creating order, establishing connections, overcoming inhibitions, making decisions, surmounting re-sistances'.[16] In this, the private and public aims concur. It is of his resistances that Zweig most urgently desires to be cured: 'Things are going marvellously well', he writes in a letter addressed to 'Dear and revered Mr Freud' in 1932, 'as far as resistance and resolution are concerned.'[17] ('Warmest greetings and best wishes for the overcoming of your resistances', Freud ends a letter of 1934.)[18] In this vocabulary, then, resistance is not the action of the freedom fighter, the struggle against tyranny, the first stirring of the oppressed; it is the mind at war with itself, blocking the path to its own freedom and, with it, its ability to make the world a better, less tyrannical, place.

For these two Jewish writers, charting the inexorable rise of fascism in their time, tyranny (or un-freedom) and resistance therefore go hand-in-hand. They are brothers-in-arms. Fascism is a form of resistance, a carapace against what the mind should, ideally, be able to do with itself. Something shuts down, closes cruelly into its allotted and unmovable place. The 'vicious mean world', Zweig writes in 1934, is grown as 'rigid as a machine'.[19] 'Is not the frightful struggle you have been waging for about forty years (or more?) against the fallacies, taboos, and repressions of our contemporaries', he writes to Freud in 1932, 'comparable with the one the prophets waged against the recalcitrant nation of their day?'[20] It is the task of the psychoanalytic prophet to rail against the nation.

In the letters that pass between Freud and Zweig, psychoanalysis therefore appears, perhaps more boldly and prophetically than anywhere else, as a critique of national self-enchantment. Nationalism is the supreme form of resistance to the pain of psychoanalytic insight, because it allows a people to believe absolutely in love of itself (national passion would then be one of the chief means of at once denying and performing the pleasures of hatred). Zweig writes as a German and a Jew. As a German, he cannot bear 'to see this nation carrying around with it a false, trashy, vain image of its great and frightful achievements and suffering'; as a Jew, he defends himself against the offshoot of such vain, trashy self-love in anti-Semitism.[21] Unlike Freud, Zweig will move to Palestine – indeed that move forms as much the backdrop or core of their correspondence as the rise of fascism. But although Zweig makes the move to Palestine, he cannot bear it. He cannot make the transition from the violent abuse and disabuse of national identity in Europe to renewed national passion which will be the story of so many Jews in Palestine. Zweig's disillusionment with the 'flight-flight' into 'Rousseauist' or 'Imperialist' Zionism, as he terms it, is total: 'I have established quite calmly', he writes to Freud in 1935, 'that I do not belong here.'[22] 'All our reasons for coming here were mistaken.'[23] Against the whole drift of the Jewish people who migrate massively from Europe to Palestine immediately after the war, Zweig leaves Palestine for Germany at the invitation of the GDR government in 1948 on the eve of the establishment of the state of Israel. Already in 1934, Zweig had been doubly disaffected – caring no longer for Germany, 'the land of my fathers', unenthusiastic about living in Palestine with the Jews.[24] 'Such a passion', Freud writes in response, 'is not for the likes of us.'[25] Freud welcomes the fact that Zweig is 'cured' of his 'unhappy love' for his 'so-called Fatherland'.[26]

If we return to Freud's famous letter on Zweig's return to Palestine, quoted above, we then find that it is heavily qualified: 'our forebears lived there for perhaps half or perhaps a whole millennium', he writes but then adds in parenthesis '(but this too is just a perhaps)'. He continues: 'and it is impossible to say what heritage from this land we have taken over into our blood and nerves', and then qualifies again in parenthesis: '(as is mistakenly said)'.[27] With these two rarely quoted asides, Freud dismantles the twin pillars of the Jewish claim to Palestine. Perhaps we lived there, perhaps not; it is a mistake to claim that the land flows in our blood. As far as nationhood is concerned, flesh and blood – or in Freud's formula 'blood and nerves' – is a suspect form of belonging.

It is of course a strikingly modern critique. As Neal Ascherson pointed out in an article which appeared in the London *Observer* on the sixtieth anniversary of Hitler's defeat in April 2005, it seemed perfectly acceptable to Churchill, for example, that millions of people should be shunted around the world – roughly ten to twelve million by the time the war was over – in the search for purity of the nations. Like so many of his contemporaries, 'he believed that a nation state should be racially homogeneous to be secure and healthy'.[28]

Freud is often branded a conservative politically for his suspicions about Communism, his views of women, and the often autocratic nature of his procedures (one might wonder what is left). It is nonetheless crucial that for nationalism in its most venerated form he had neither time nor space. It was Dostoyevsky's great failure, he writes in his essay 'Dostoyevsky and Parricide', that he landed 'in the retrograde position of submission to both temporal and spiritual authority', blindly in thrall to the Tsar, the God of the Christians, and to 'a narrow Russian nationalism', a position which, he comments dryly, 'lesser minds have reached with smaller effort'.[29] Dostoyevsky, he pronounces, with an uncharacteristic finality of judgement, 'did not achieve freedom', he became a 'reactionary'.[30] None of this of course detracts from Dostoyevsky's achievement as a writer, but it too implies, as Zweig suggests, that energy 'dissipated' into writing can leave the subject powerless as a political agent, vulnerable to the false promises of autocracy. In this analysis, nationalism is resistance at large. Like submission to the Tsar and to God, it requires a drastic narrowing of internal horizons.

Although, as we shall see, the formula is finally too blithe, Zweig is right to start at least from the premise that psychoanalysis pitches itself against tyranny inside and outside the mind. More than once, Freud himself runs a line straight from one to the other. It is because we are creatures of the unconscious that we try to exert false authority over ourselves. Autocracy is in itself a form of resistance, a way of staving off internal panic. The news that reaches our consciousness, he writes in 'A Difficulty in the Path of Psychoanalysis' of 1917, is deceptive and not to be relied upon, but we submit all the more willingly to its dictates. We do not want to hear the internally unsettling news that might come from anywhere else. We are never more ruthless than when we are trying to block out parts of our own mind. 'You behave like an absolute ruler who is content with information supplied him by his highest officials', Freud addresses a fictive audience, 'and never goes among the people to hear their voice.'[31] Like Tony Blair, for example, who regularly boasted of being the listening Prime Minister, notably in the 2004 election campaign, but who never allowed the people – a million on the streets against the Iraq war – to affect him. Blair, we could say, wanted the form, without the potentially self-decaying stress, of democracy. Beware of the political leader who will not listen – or who boasts of listening, or appears to be listening, but hears nothing. You can be sure that he is spending a huge amount of energy, energy that could fruitfully be used otherwise, in warding off unconscious, internally dissident, messages from himself.

To the question, Why did Blair so unequivocally offer his support to George Bush? David Clark, Labour government adviser before he became one of Blair's strongest critics, has suggested that many of Blair's policies and most of his mistakes, notably on Iraq, could be explained by weakness of will, that he is 'mesmerised' by power. According to this argument it was not the boldness or courage of his convictions that led Blair to war, but the 'calculation that, whatever the risks, it would ultimately prove to be *the line of least resistance*'.[32] Here resistance is associated with weakness, the easy option, choosing a path that may seem unlikely, difficult, or even self-defeating but which, in this case because of a counter-pull, the pull of power in Clark's analysis, is in fact the easiest, if not the only, path to take. Freud uses the same phrase when he is trying to explain the choice of hysterical symptom at the very beginning of his work, when he suggests that an unconscious thought, struggling to evade the censor and achieve expression, will follow the easiest path it can take, and attach itself to a pre-existing bodily complaint. Anna O suffered from tetanus in one arm. As she watched over her dying father, prey to contrary passions of grief and revolt, she tried to stretch it out to ward off a hallucinated snake, only to find that her arm had gone to sleep. From that point on, the tetanus pain would be provoked by the sight of any snake-like object. The arm was the part of the body most amenable to her inner distress. The discharge of affect, Freud writes, follows 'the path of least resistance'.[33] Something has been prepared in advance and the unconscious seizes on it to make its presence felt. In these early thoughts then, resistance drops its guard at the slightest provocation. Resistance, as in Clark's analysis of Blair, is weak and willing. Like Dostoyevsky, in thrall to God and Tsar, Blair submits to Superpower and goes where he is led.

But while this analysis may seem supremely tempting, it will not take us far enough. It makes life, just as it made the process of analysis, too easy. Freud does not stay here for long. Even while he is offering this view of resistance as gentle, yielding, temporary obduracy – something that silently makes way for the unconscious – his thoughts on the matter are starting to follow a very different drift. Resistance hardens. Slowly but surely, it takes up its full meaning as struggle against the unconscious, and from there, as canny, resourceful and above all stubborn refusal to cooperate. Freud has to abandon his early hypnotic procedure, because it conceals the resistance; it does not do away with it but merely evades it 'and therefore yields only incomplete information and transitory therapeutic success'.[34] By bringing the unconscious so effortlessly to the surface, hypnosis leaves the patient, when they return to their normal state, more or less exactly as they were before. From this point on, as much as resistance of the conscious to the unconscious, resistance means resistance to the psychoanalytic treatment. 'The task [of analysis]', Freud writes in 1907, 'consists of making the unconscious accessible to consciousness, which is done by overcoming the resistances.'[35] Without resistance, no analysis. There can be no access to the unconscious, hence no analytic treatment, without a fight.

Once Freud makes this move, once resistance becomes the core of psychoanalysis, everything gets far more difficult. So much so that the difficulty of resistance will in some sense dominate the rest of Freud's work and life. And once this happens, then Zweig's blithe conviction that psychoanalysis can defeat resistance, in the mind and in the world of nations, will become harder to sustain. In today's political climate, with no sign of diminution in national passion and its dangers, I believe that we have to understand why. Zweig's starting exhilaration – that the world's resistance to unfreedom will be undone – has not been borne out by events (it was not borne out by the events that immediately followed). We need to follow the path leading Freud to redress his own optimism in the way that so dismayed Zweig in 1933. For Zweig, as we have seen, Freud was a prophet, and a prophet's vision is rarely actualised in the real world. *Prophets Outcast* is the title of an anthology edited by Adam Shatz of *The Nation* that includes all the dissident Jewish voices, past and present, in Palestine.[36] Calling Freud a prophet, Zweig may have been closer to the truth than he would have liked, at least consciously, to think. But it is not only Freud's writing that issues a caution to the belief that psychoanalysis will finally triumph, sway the world and dethrone the nations. Zweig's own fiction offers no less a challenge, and nowhere more clearly than in the extraordinary, but little known, novel – the offspring in many ways of his correspondence with Freud – which he writes from the heart of Palestine.

When Zweig returns from his first visit to Palestine in 1932, he plunges into a depression. 'I am deep in my work', he writes, 'and equally deep in depression.'[37] Physically exhausted by his journey, dispirited by the terrible political situation in Berlin, it is nonetheless to his work that Zweig ascribes the greater part of his despair. Zweig is writing a short novel about the Dutch-Jewish writer Jacob Israel de Haan, who was murdered in Jerusalem in 1924. 'The figure of this Orthodox Jew who "reviled God in Jerusalem" in clandestine poems and who had a clandestine love-affair with an Arab boy – this important and complex character', he writes to Freud, 'gripped my imagination while the blood was still not dry in the whole affair.'[38] The trip to Palestine brought the 'old plan' to life again and he sketched away at the novel while in the country itself, making a plan he describes as useful and 'indeed fascinating'.[39]

But the plan falls apart when Zweig discovers a 'flaw at the most vital spot': de Haan, it turns out, was not murdered by Arabs at all, as he had believed for seven years, but by a political opponent, a radical Zionist

'known to many people and still living in the country today'.[40] De Haan had
started out an active Zionist – indeed as a lawyer he had defended Ze'ev
Jabotinsky, the subject of Chapter 4, who was the founder of Revisionist
Zionism, when he was arrested by the British in 1920. But he slowly lost
faith and turned against the Zionists in Palestine. A member of the
Orthodox movement Agudath, he made himself hated when he headed
a delegation to the press baron Lord Northcliffe to protest at the tyranny of
official Zionism in 1922. Although Zweig does not name him, it is now
believed that Yitzhak Ben-Zvi, a member of the highest council of the
socialist Zionist Haganah who would become the second President of Israel,
was involved in contracting the murder of de Haan. He was killed by a
chalutz, a Jewish emigrant to Palestine who worked as a pioneer in the early
settlements, 'because his hatred of political Jewry had turned him into a
traitor and informer'.[41]

At first Zweig receives this discovery as a 'frightful blow', but then he
realises that this fact was 'far better than the old': 'it compelled me to see
many things accurately without pro-Jewish prejudice and to examine the
political murder of one Jew by another exactly as though it were a political
murder in Germany'.[42] It compelled him, he continues, 'to tread the path of
political disillusionment yet further, as far as necessary, or possible – further
than was good for me'.[43] What Zweig has discovered – and in this he is way
ahead of his time – is that Jewish nationalism is not, cannot by very dint of
being nationalism be, innocent. Because of the opposition from the
indigenous peoples which it was bound to encounter (as Jabotinsky
acknowledged), but also because it enlists and requires such passionate
identification, Zionism cannot help, although it will go to great lengths to
this day to repress this internal knowledge, but be a violent – that is,
internally, as well as externally, violent – affair. The discovery is a blow to
Zweig, yet it is – he writes to Freud – precisely through the 'collapse' of his
original plan that his novel, which 'condemns nationalism and political
murder even among Jews', finds its 'true dimension'.[44]

Zweig could of course have dropped the novel when he realised his
mistake. He could have chosen not to offend Jewish sensibilities by probing
this case too deeply. Instead, rather like his hero whom he names de Vriendt
– the novel is called *De Vriendt Goes Home* – he chooses to pursue his path to
its painful, violent, end, and thereby to court the wrath of the Zionists
among whom he is living in Palestine. Disillusioned with Jewish nationalism, announcing that disillusionment to the world by writing the novel,
Zweig, we could say, boldly repeats de Haan's original offence. For this he
too, like de Haan although not so dramatically, will be ostracised: 'I am a Jew
– heavens, yes,' he writes in 1936, 'but am I really of the same nationality as

these people who have ignored me ever since *De Vriendt* came out?'[45] (in his correspondence with Freud he admits to the profoundest, most troubling, identification with his character).

But it is not just in its critique of nationalism that Zweig's novel offers a type of Freudian text for our times. It is as if the first shock to his system, the fatal flaw in his original plan, leaves Zweig free to demolish, not just one, but all false gods. There is no boundary – of religious, national, sexual identity – that de Vriendt does not cross. Zionism is, in his view, a mistake. The hubris of man usurps the role of God (this was the classic critique of Zionism by one section of Orthodox Jews). De Vriendt dreams of the 'fall of Zionism' and, in what is surely a deliberate parody of Theodor Herzl's largely failed diplomatic initiatives, he has fantasies of a recruiting campaign across Eastern Europe ending with a congress in Vienna where 'the claim of the Zionists to stand as representatives of the Jewish people would be explicitly denied'.[46] And although he is Orthodox, the fiercest critic of Zionist secularism, he pens blasphemous poems, discovered by his horrified religious supporters after his death, which have this to say about God:

> Prophets and saviours – we await them still;
> With earthquake, famine, strife, we fight in vain;
> There is no work to make us men again;
> Thou gav'st us but the arts to hate and kill.
> [. . .]
> Wool and wadding and wax have stoppered Thine ears,
> Thy hands are too smooth to help, like the smooth skin of fish;
> Thou art far above our labours and troubles and tears;
> As a God for the white man Thou art all that the white man could wish[47]

This God – blind, privileged, white – could have been lifted straight out of Freud's onslaught against the delusions of religious faith, *The Future of an Illusion*, where he refers, not favourably, to 'our present-day white Christian culture' (and indeed probably was) (or perhaps Tariq Ali's *Clash of Fundamentalisms*). Finally – adding insult to injury we might say – if homosexuality is de Vriendt's guilty secret, the curse of a capricious God, it is also ecstatic release into freedom, the repository of his utopian dreams, the place he goes in pursuit of a better world. By roughly half a century Zweig anticipates the idea advanced by psychoanalytic critic Leo Bersani, that homosexual passion provides the only possibility of a narcissistically shattering but utopian liberation from the constraints of the ego, the over-controlling and pro-prietorial self: 'It was a terrible and shattering experience [. . .] That is his deep impulse: to fling away the twisted self, to be rid of the false fortuitous embodiment, and set its atoms free for fresh embodiment under a more fortunate star, in a better hour.'[48]

Pushing his novel much further than he needed to go (and too far, as he himself says, for his own good), Zweig has created a true Freudian anti-hero. As an anti-Zionist and friend to the Arabs, he betrays the Jews; as a homosexual, he betrays the Arabs (his lover's brother also wants to kill him); he betrays the religion of his fathers as a reviler of the faith. Zweig, we could say, leaves no stone unturned. For this he suffers terribly, not just as one of the *Verlatene* or the forsaken, as de Haan became known, but in his own mind (it is, he writes to Freud, a 'kind of self-analysis').[49] Reading the correspondence it feels that he would not have been able to write this novel, which he eagerly and anxiously sends to Freud on the eve of publication, if the founding spirit of psychoanalysis had not presided over its conception, if he had not been able to guarantee its safe passage into Freud's hands. 'Now it really is out; you have it in your hands,' Zweig writes to Freud after a halt in the publication due to misprints, 'and you will feel how much it owes to you.'[50]

One could read the message of this novel quite simply as the one Edward Said lifted out of Freud's last work on Moses in his 2001 talk 'Freud and the Non-European': in order to save the new nation from too rigid and self-regarding an identity, to modulate the certainties of Zionism and open it up both from without and within, in order to stop the tragedy that will unfold in Palestine, Zionism needs Freud.[51] Or to put it in the rather different words of de Vriendt: to confuse 'the Lord's people of Israel with modern Nationalism [. . .]' means paralysis and weakness at the heart'.[52] The new nation will not be able to tolerate the vision of this sexually complex, sceptical, blaspheming Jew. Zweig kills off his own prophet. In this rendering, Jewish nationalism entails violence, not only against the Arabs, but also by Jew against Jew. This does not involve denying Arab violence against the Jews in Palestine (as the novel's portrayal of the Arab riots of 1929 makes clear). But in the spirit of psychoanalysis, which sees moments of failing or slippage as the path to unconscious truth, it is the basic flaw, the collapse of the original plan, that gives to this novel its true dimension. Deftly Zweig shifts the dramatic centre from the curse of homosexuality to the curse of nationhood. Note that in this he also anticipates the development of psychoanalytic studies which has likewise shifted from the politics of sexuality to the politics of nation states over the past decade. Once Zweig makes his discovery that de Haan was murdered by Zionists, then he can write the story of his disillusionment with nationalism into the body – across the flesh and blood – of the nation-in-waiting. Near the end of the novel, an old Jew lies dying in a remote village where de Vriendt's assassin finds

himself as he flees the arm of the law. To save the old man's life, he offers his
blood, but the dying man will not take it. There will be no redemption for
this crime.

Although Zweig – and indeed Freud in his essay on Dostoyevsky – suggests
that writing can dissipate the energies needed to transform the world, and, in
the latter case, make the writer prey to autocracy, love of God and Tsar, in
this novel Zweig has suggested a rather different role and destiny for fiction.
And that is, that literature can give a public shape and audience to realities
which the dominant view of the world – what de Vriendt terms despairingly
'the spirit of the time' – needs terribly to include in its vision, but which it
cannot tolerate or bear to see.[53] For this relationship between fiction and the
unconscious, Zweig offers one of the most graphic metaphors, seized from
his own flesh and blood. He suffers from a visual complaint that will
eventually blind him. 'Through the gap in the retina', he writes to Freud of
hallucinations provoked by his disorder, 'one could see deep into the
unconscious.'[54] 'My right eye', he continues, 'is playing a trick on me
[. . .] in the act of seeing a small bubble is produced in the retina, as a camera,
so that in the centre of my field of vision I see a dim round gluten, which is
more or less opaque, surrounded by a dark ring.'[55] Within this frame,
grimacing faces have started to appear, day and night 'literally at every
moment, both when my eyes are closed and when they are open'.[56]
Changing more or less with the rhythm of his pulse beats, these faces
are first unmistakably Jewish, then recumbent men, dying and decomposing,
until they mutate into death's heads and often too 'something like the
portraits of intellectuals wearing the clothes of remote centuries, complete
with skull-cap and pointed beard' (on one solitary occasion he sees a
decomposing female face).[57] Offering these images to Freud – a trick 'I
cannot conceal from you as a psychologist' – Zweig shows the darkness of
his mind peopled by Jewish faces in decay (the faces he had lovingly charted
in his 1920 *The Face of Eastern European Jewry*).[58] Was he anticipating horror,
reaching back to his forefathers, or simply registering in the depths of his
unconscious a vision of mortality as the ever-present underside (or pulse
beat) of nations?

By the time Zweig writes this in 1930, Freud knows that access to the
unconscious is far harder than he had originally envisaged. The unconscious
does not take the path of least resistance, to use that early phrase; it chooses
the path where resistance most strenuously does its work. By the end of his
life Freud will talk, not of resistance *to* the unconscious, but resistance *of* the
unconscious, as if the unconscious had become active in refusing knowledge
of itself.[59] The mind, like the world of the 1930s and I would say today, is a

frightening and fortified place. Zweig's final disillusion with Zionism comes when he joins a demonstration with left-wing workers only to have them 'keep up the nationalistic fiction that they did not understand me when I spoke German'.[60] They had his speech translated into Hebrew 'as though', he continues wryly, 'all 2500 of them did not speak Yiddish at home'.[61] 'And', he continues, 'all this took place with the left-wing Paole Zion [the Zionist Socialists], who are attacked by the other "righter" Social Democrats as being international.' It is the last nail in the coffin, the moment that precipitates his decision to leave: 'So we are slowly thinking of leaving but it will take some time.'[62] Zionism in 1935 shuts out the clamour of the world, represses its own international dimension, silences the voices or languages it does not want to hear.

As Edward Said pointed out in his talk on Freud's *Moses*, the international does not just include Europe, but needs to expand still further to include the Egyptian component of Israel's own past. 'The misunderstanding of Egyptian pre-history in Israel's religious development', Freud writes to Zweig in 1935, 'is just as great in Auerbach as in the Biblical tradition. Even their famous historical and literary sense can only be an Egyptian legacy'[63] (a quote which confirms Said's reading). 'Europe', as Zweig writes to Freud in 1938, 'is now such a small place.'[64]

At the beginning of this essay, we saw Zweig battling to retain his faith in the future of psychoanalysis in the face of Freud's despair. It would seem, then, that this was no 'passing gloom' on Freud's part, but the profoundest confrontation of psychoanalysis with the outside world, a world it is so often – and so wrongly – seen to ignore. Nor does it seem to be a coincidence that Freud's and Zweig's dismay about the world of nations, together with Freud's despondency about the future of his science, intensify when Freud realises the increasing difficulty of psychoanalysis in the consulting room. As soon as Freud defines the task of psychoanalysis as the struggle against resistance, he recognises the new challenge that faces him. We aim, he writes in 1907, to arrive 'at the distorted material from the distortions'.[65] But inevitably, he acknowledges, with reference to his magisterial failure in the case of Dora, 'a portion of the factors that are encountered under the form of resistance remains unknown'.[66] As with mourning, as with femininity, both of which he famously describes as a great 'riddle', as indeed with the unconscious itself, Freud has to allow that there are limits to psychoanalytic knowing, places where it cannot, finally, go. 'It is not so easy', he writes in the same year, 'to play upon the instrument of the mind.'[67] Shakespeare gives him his cue. Rosencrantz and Guildenstern are set upon by Hamlet to solve the riddle of his despair, but when Hamlet invites them to play the fiddle, they refuse even when he begs them and tells them it is as easy as lying. Hamlet's response, which Freud quotes, is scathing: 'You would pluck out the heart of my mystery [. . .] '*Sblood, do you think I am easier to be played upon than a pipe?*'[68] Although Freud is mocking those who claim they can cure neurosis without submitting to the rules of his craft, the one to whom he is issuing the caution is, surely, himself.

So what is the last resistance? Appropriately perhaps, we reach it, as Freud did, only at last. In 1926, in an addendum to *Inhibitions, Symptoms and Anxiety*, Freud lists no fewer than five types of resistance (resistance has multiplied). Three stem from the ego: repression, transference and the gain from illness. The fourth is the resistance of the unconscious itself. But the fifth arises from the superego – 'the last to be discovered', (hence my title), 'also the most obscure though not always the least powerful one'.[69] Last but not least, as one might say (Derrida referred to himself as 'le dernier des juifs' which can translate as 'the last of the Jews' but also as 'last but not least' or 'last and least', depending on your ideological inflection). Crucially, this is not the force that Freud describes as resisting recovery because it clings to the advantages of being ill – like the neglected, exploited and subjugated wife whose illness subordinates her inconsiderate husband to her power.[70] Sadly, this is not a force that calculates so wisely, so cleverly, so well. The force of this fifth and last resistance is far more deadly, because it arises out of the pleasure the mind takes in thwarting itself. 'It seems to originate', Freud explains, 'from the sense of guilt or the need for punishment and it opposes every move towards success, including, therefore, the patient's own recovery through analysis.'[71] There is almost a tautology here. Resistance arises from resistance. There is, Freud writes, 'a resistance to the uncovering of resistances'.[72] By the time he gets to his famous late essay of 1937, 'Analysis Terminable and Interminable', this force appears as more or less insurmountable: 'No stronger impression arises from the resistances during the work of analysis than of there being a force which is defending itself by every possible means against recovery and which is absolutely resolved to hold on to illness and suffering.'[73] We are dealing, he writes, with 'ultimate things'.[74] 'We must bow to the superiority of the forces against which we see our efforts come to nothing.'[75]

Freud is talking about the superego – the exacting, ruthless and punishing instance of the mind through which the law exerts its pressure on the psyche. In the correspondence with Zweig, it is also shadowed, as for example in this quote, cited earlier, when Zweig was in euphoric mood: 'Either one follows your profound teachings and doctrines, controls one's emotions, adapts them to serve as positive forces in the world, and then one must fight for the liberation of man and the dethronement of national states, or one must

impose upon mankind . . . his gradual suppression in a fascist system.' In fact
the full quote reads: 'one must fight for the liberation of man and the
dethronement of national states which are only substitutes for the Father-
Moloch. Or one must *perpetuate this Father-Moloch and* impose upon mankind
as ideal for the future his gradual suppression in a fascist system.'[76] Zweig's
optimism, his yearning and willed conviction that psychoanalysis will
triumph and dethrone the nations depends therefore on toppling the
instance of the law inside the mind. There will be no more burnt offerings,
no false idols. Children will no longer be sacrificed to assuage the wrath of
the gods.

Despite the passion between Freud and Zweig, or perhaps as intrinsic to
that passion, this forms the basis of the most profound difference between
them, which is finally far more than a difference of mood. In Zweig's
vocabulary, you adapt, you control. By a flick of the analytic switch, as it
were, you turn emotions into a positive force in the world. By 1937, Freud is
somewhere quite else. If the superego is the seat of the last resistance, it is
because it is the place of tyranny inside the mind. Perversely it draws its
power from the unconscious energies it is trying to tame (hence for Slavoj
Žižek, after Lacan, the irreducible obscenity of the law). It is overwhel-
mingly powerful. 'There is often no counteracting force of a similar order of
strength,' Freud had already written in 1923 in *The Ego and the Id*, 'which the
treatment can oppose to it' (unless the analyst plays the part of 'prophet,
saviour, redeemer' to which all the rules of analysis are opposed).[77] It is also,
for Freud, tied irrevocably to the death drive, the instance of violence inside
the psyche which, in the second half of his life – the half dominated by war –
led him to revise his theory of mental life. We are not, as he puts it in his
1937 essay, 'exclusively governed by the desire for pleasure'.[78] There is a
pleasure in subjugation; there is a pleasure – hence the last resistance – in
pain. Idealisation of self and nation is a way of submitting to a voice that will
never be satisfied. You may be able to soften the commands of the superego;
indeed this will come to be defined as one of the most crucial aims of
analysis. But you cannot overthrow it. Zweig's language of control – 'either
one controls one's emotions' – repeats the edicts of the voice it is trying most
earnestly to assuage. You are never more vulnerable to autocracy than when
you think you have dispensed with the law. Faced with this resistance,
Freud's language darkens, takes on the colours of the crisis that has by now
almost reached his door: 'we are reminded that analysis can only draw upon
definite and limited amounts of energy which have to be measured against
the hostile forces. And it seems as if victory is in fact as a rule on the side of
the big battalions.'[79] (This is the year before the *Anschluss* when the Nazis
will invade Austria and Freud leaves for England.)

'Analysis Terminable and Interminable' is famous, or rather notorious, for Freud's conclusion that the bedrock of the psyche is the man's fear of passivity, the woman's wish for a penis. Rereading it for today, this does not seem to be the most crucial, or 'ultimate' thing (times, or perhaps I, have changed). Or rather, although it is indeed where Freud ends, this is an instance where, as in most nineteenth-century novels, the so-called final moment or ending feels a bit like an attempt to tidy up, bring things to a finale that is trumped, or at least seriously confused, or challenged, by what has come before. What stands out in this essay is the force of resistance as a general principle, resistance as the canny, ever resourceful activity of the human mind. In the face of this resistance, Freud becomes not just speculative, as Derrida so convincingly showed him to be on the concept of the death drive, not quite or only defeated, but something more like cautious, humble almost (not his dominant characteristic). The whole field of enquiry, he writes, 'is still bewilderingly strange and insufficiently explored'.[80] A year later he will describe his own Moses project as built on feet of clay. But here he goes further, as his endeavour seems to be coming apart, almost literally, in his hands. Resistance is everywhere, spreading into places he can no longer specify. Either, he writes, the libido is too adhesive, in which case the analyst feels like a sculptor working in hard stone as opposed to soft clay; or it is too mobile, dissolving, washing away the imprint of analysis as if it had never been: 'we have an impression, not of having worked in clay, but of having written on water'.[81] In his famous essay on 'The Mystic Writing Pad', Freud had used as his analogy of the mind the child's game, where first you write, then you erase what you have written by lifting the top sheet leaving a clean page with the trace, or memory of what you have written underneath (he was trying to explain how the mind is fresh to receive impressions from the outside world while retaining the traces of the unconscious).[82] Now, however, Freud is writing on water. There is no more precarious inscription than this. Psychoanalysis will continue to do its work but without illusions. It would be the direst form of pretension to claim, in 1937, but not only in 1937, that psychoanalysis could permanently dispose of the perils of the world or of the mind.

In fact Zweig, in other moments (other moods), is only too aware of the limits of analysis. He knows only too well that the mind only wants to pursue its own path. Writing De Vriendt is a terrible experience for him that brings his own repressed homosexuality to light: 'I was both, the Arab (semitic) boy and the impious-Orthodox lover and writer.'[83] But the knowledge, as he puts it, is 'to no avail'. It simply plunges him into depression. Controlling one's emotions is no solace: 'The liberated instinct wants to live its life right through emotionally, in phantasy, in the flesh and blood of the mind.'[84] 'Flesh and blood' points to the wily, recalcitrant force of the unconscious, as much as it does to the compelling, reluctant, intimacies of kinship and of war. The last resistance is in the flesh and blood of the mind.

For all that, Zweig's political analysis of his and Freud's moment was astute, and still relevant for our times. This passage could be read as a diagnosis of Zionism today:

> Fear of death and of spirits have made religions what they are, the 'salvation of the soul' has swallowed up the salvation of the living human being and has handed over the state to the armed forces, so that the custodians of the states and their inhabitants are today, as in the time of Saul, on the one hand priests and on the other soldiers, and our age which is so technically terrifyingly armed compels our thoroughly uncivilised fellow men to dwell in greater fear than our forebears did, but with the same basic emotions.[85]

To evoke once more the Marrano descendants, carrying history in their 'flesh and blood', who are trying to return to the Jewish religion of their forebears: they want to claim an allegiance unbound to orthodoxy, not as conversion, but one that can still perhaps bear the traces of their peculiar story – an affinity, not an identity in the custodianship of armed forces and of priests.

Nothing in this essay finally detracts from the necessity or indeed possibility of resistance in its more familiar political guise. Since the time of Freud's and Zweig's correspondence, resistance has mutated, shifted its location and shape, alighting in places and forms that neither of them could have anticipated. 'After about 10pm', writes Rachel Corrie in *My Name Is Rachel Corrie*, staged at the Royal Court in 2005, 'it is very difficult to move because the Israeli army treats anyone in the streets as resistance and shoots at them. So clearly we are too few.' (The play was cancelled on the eve of its performance on 22 March at the Theatre Workshop in New York and then staged at the Minetta Lane Theatre in November 2006.)[86] Indeed, Palestinian resistance to Israel's occupation of the West Bank and Gaza, one of the longest-running occupations of our time, could fairly claim the title 'the last resistance' for itself. We would then be talking of resistance not as obduracy, but as challenge, like psychoanalysis one might say, to the powers that be, even while it has been the immense difficulty of such a challenge that has been the subject here. It is also a premise of psychoanalysis that the symptom is economically inefficient, too demanding; the carapace – the wall – will break. In his book *On the Border*, which describes a life of dissident activism in Israel, Michael Warschawski defines as his overriding aim: 'To resist by all means any attempts to close up the cracks in the wall.' But he too does not underestimate the difficulty: 'we are talking about fighting for a redefinition of who we are'.[87]

Or to return to the heart of the history taking shape here: Resistance in one of its most famous incarnations – the very emblem of the word for many – as Resistance to Nazism itself (which Freud did not live to see, but which will be central to the life and work of Marcel Liebman, the subject of Chapter 12 in this book). 'This word', Derrida writes in his meditation on resistance to, and within, psychoanalysis, 'which first resonated in my desire and imagination as the most beautiful word in the politics and history of this country [. . .] charged with all the pathos of my nostalgia, as if what I would have wanted not to miss at any cost would have been to blow up trains, tanks and headquarters between 1940 and 1945.'[88] 'Why', he asks 'has this word come to draw to itself, like a lover, so many other significations, virtues, semantic and disseminal opportunities?'[89]

The point of this first essay has been to issue a caution. Psychoanalysis remains for me the most powerful reading of the role of human subjects in the formation of states and nations, subjects as driven by their unconscious, subjects in thrall to identities that will not save them and that will readily destroy the world. I also believe that it offers a counter-vision of identity as precarious, troubled, uneasy, which needs to be invoked time and time again against the false certainties of our times. But it is precisely *analysis*, and we should not ask too much of it. If we do, we risk, like Zweig does at moments, asking it to play the part of redeemer, prophet, saviour, which is, as Freud pointed out, to go against the spirit not to say the therapeutic rules of psychoanalysis itself. If psychoanalysis is persuasive, it is because – as Freud came more and more to acknowledge – far from diminishing, it has the profoundest respect for the forces it is up against.

Near the end of his life, when he is suffering from the throat cancer that will finally kill him, Freud offers to read his last great work, *Moses the Man*[90] to Zweig who, although not yet blind, already then in 1935 can barely read: 'I picture myself reading it aloud to you when you come to Vienna,' Freud writes, 'despite my defective speech.'[91] 'When can I read it to you?' he writes again the following month (it is his hardest work, written across the passage into exile, and will take another two years for Freud to complete).[92] 'I am writing by lamplight,' Zweig writes to Freud in 1937, 'when I should not really do this.'[93] It is one of the most moving moments or strains of their correspondence: the two men reaching out to each other through their physical failing. Perhaps this tentative encounter can serve as a graphic image for what might be involved – as the world darkened around them – in trying to make the unconscious speak. The point of this first essay has been simply to suggest that we should not underestimate the difficulty in the times ahead.

*Opening address, London School of Economics, 'Flesh and Blood: Psychoanalysis, Politics, Resistance', May 2005.

Notes

1 'Dialogue Jacques Derrida – Hélène Cixous', *Magazine Littéraire*, 5 February 2002.
2 Kobi Ben-Simhon, 'The Long Road Home', *Ha'aretz*, 24 March 2005.
3 Ibid.
4 *The Letters of Sigmund Freud and Arnold Zweig*, ed. Ernst L. Freud, trans. Elaine and William Robson-Scott (New York, New York University Press 1970), 8 May 1932, p. 40.
5 Neri Livneh, 'How 90 Peruvians became the latest Jewish settlers', *Guardian*, 7 August 2002; Chris McGreal, 'Gaza's settlers dig in their heels', *Guardian*, 4 February 2004.
6 'Dialogue Jacques Derrida – Hélène Cixous'.
7 *Letters*, 21 August 1930, p. 9.
8 Ibid., 8 September 1930, p. 10.
9 Ibid.
10 Ibid., 10 February 1934, p. 62.
11 Ibid., 18 March 1927, p. 1.
12 Sigmund Freud, 'Anti-Semitism in England,' 1938, *The Standard Edition of the Complete Psychological Works*, 24 vols (London, Hogarth 1953–73), vol. 23, p. 30.
13 Joan Rivière, 'Hate, Greed and Aggression', in *Love, Hate and Reparation – Two Lectures by Melanie Klein and Joan Rivière*, Psychoanalytic Epitomes, vol. 2, (London, Hogarth 1977), p. 16.
14 Christopher Bollas, *I Have Heard the Mermaids Singing* (London, Free Association Books 2005), p. 146.
15 Ibid., p. 148.
16 *Letters*, 16 November 1932, p. 47.
17 Ibid., 8 January 1932, p. 33.
18 Ibid., 6 November 1934, p. 97.
19 Ibid., 10 February 1934, p. 64.
20 Ibid., 29 May 1932, p. 43.
21 Ibid.
22 Ibid., 2 December 1930, p. 23; Arnold Zweig, *De Vriendt Goes Home*, trans. Eric Sutton (New York, Viking 1932), p. 54; *Letters*, 1 September 1935, p. 108.
23 *Letters*, 1 September 1935, p. 109.
24 Ibid., 21 January 1934, p. 57.
25 Ibid., 28 January 1934, p. 59.

26 Ibid.
27 Ibid., 8 May 1932, p. 40, my emphasis.
28 Neal Ascherson, 'Free to live again', *Observer*, 17 April 2005.
29 Freud, 'Dostoyevsky and Parricide', 1928 (1927), *Standard Edition*, vol. 21, p. 177.
30 Ibid., p. 187.
31 Freud, 'A Difficulty in the Path of Psycho-Analysis', 1917, *Standard Edition*, vol. 17, p. 143.
32 David Clark, 'A weak man who bends to power, not political vision', *Guardian*, 29 March 2005, my emphasis.
33 Sigmund Freud and Josef Breuer, *Studies on Hysteria*, 1893-95, *Standard Edition*, vol. 2, p. 208.
34 Freud, 'Freud's Psycho-Analytic Procedure', 1904 (1903), *Standard Edition*, vol. 7, p. 252.
35 Ibid., p. 253.
36 Adam Shatz, ed., *Prophets Outcast – A Century of Dissident Jewish Writing about Zionism and Israel* (New York, Nation Books 2004).
37 *Letters*, 29 May 1932, p. 41.
38 Ibid.
39 Ibid., 29 May 1932, p. 42.
40 Ibid.
41 Ibid., 1 May 1932, p. 38.
42 Ibid., 29 May 1932, p. 42.
43 Ibid.
44 Ibid., 16 November 1932, p. 45, 30 November 1932, p. 50.
45 Ibid., 15 February 1936, p. 121.
46 Zweig, *De Vriendt*, p. 53.
47 Ibid., p. 300, p. 79.
48 Ibid., pp. 112-14.
49 *Letters*, 8 September 1930, p. 12.
50 Ibid., 29 November 1932, p. 45.
51 Edward Said, *Freud and the Non-European* (London, Verso, with the London Freud Museum, 2003).
52 Zweig, *De Vriendt*, p. 44.
53 Ibid.
54 *Letters*, 10 September 1930, p. 14.
55 Ibid., 8 September 1930, p. 10.
56 Ibid., p. 11.
57 Ibid.
58 Ibid., p. 10, Arnold Zweig, *The Face of East European Jewry*, 1920, ed. and trans. Noah Isenberg (Berkeley, University of California Press 2004).
59 Freud, *Inhibitions, Symptoms and Anxiety*, 1926, *Standard Edition*, vol. 20, p. 160.
60 *Letters*, 1 September 1935, p. 109.
61 Ibid.
62 Ibid.
63 Ibid., 15 March 1935, p. 105.
64 Ibid., 18 June 1938, p. 161.

65 Freud, 'Freud's Psycho-Analytic Procedure', p. 252.
66 Freud, *Fragment of an Analysis of a Case of Hysteria*, 1905 (1901), *Standard Edition*, vol. 7, p. 109.
67 Freud, 'On Psycho-Therapy', 1905 (1904), *Standard Edition*, vol. 7, p. 262.
68 Ibid.
69 Freud, *Inhibitions*, p. 160.
70 Freud, *Fragment*, p. 44.
71 Freud, *Inhibitions*, p. 160.
72 Freud, 'Analysis Terminable and Interminable', 1937, *Standard Edition*, vol. 23, p. 239.
73 Ibid., p. 242.
74 Ibid.
75 Ibid., p. 243.
76 *Letters*, 10 February 1934, p. 62, my emphasis.
77 Freud, *The Ego and the Id*, 1923, *Standard Edition*, vol. 19, p. 50 n.
78 Freud, 'Analysis Terminable and Interminable', p. 243.
79 Ibid., p. 240.
80 Ibid., p. 241.
81 Ibid.
82 Freud, 'Note upon the "Mystic Writing-Pad"', 1925 (1924), *Standard Edition*, vol. 19.
83 *Letters*, 29 May 1932, p. 42.
84 Ibid.
85 Ibid., 16 November 1932, p. 46.
86 *My Name Is Rachel Corrie*, taken from the writings of Rachel Corrie, eds Alan Rickman and Katharine Viner (London, Royal Court 2005), p. 34.
87 Michel Warschawski, *On the Border*, trans. Levi Laub (Boston, South End Press 2005), p. 205, p. 212.
88 Derrida, *Résistances de la psychanalyse* (Paris, Galilée 1996), p. 14.
89 Ibid., p. 14.
90 Freud's original title for the work known in English as *Moses and Monotheism, Standard Edition* (1938), retranslated as *Moses the Man and Monotheistic Religion* by Jim Underwood (London, Penguin 2006).
91 *Letters*, 2 May 1935, p. 106.
92 Ibid., 13 June 1935, p. 107.
93 Ibid., 10 August 1937, p. 146.

2

Displacement in Zion*

I seek to protect my nation by keeping it from false limits [. . .] I shall
never agree that in this matter it is possible to justify injustice by pleading
values and destinies.

Martin Buber, 'Politics and Morality', 1945

A person gets 'displacement' as he gets asthma, and there is no cure for
either.

Maroud Barghouti, *I Saw Ramallah*, 2004

One news item taken from the stream of disturbing news that pours daily
out of Israel–Palestine, has particular resonance for thinking about displacement in modern times. It is the story of Maayan Yaday and her husband
hauling their packing cases into their new home in the tiny settlement of
Nezer Hazani just as Ariel Sharon was making his announcement of 2004
that he was planning to make Gaza 'Jew-free'. Five years before, Maadan
Yaday had been Croatian and a Catholic, but with a fervour made all the
more intense by Sharon's 'betrayal', she insisted that this was her land – Israel
and not Palestine: 'Now I am a Jew,' she stated, 'I understand that this is our
land.' What is so striking about this story is not, however, the somewhat
surreal nature of that claim, but the misplaced energy with which she
defended it. It was precisely *because* she had been Croatian and a Catholic
that she understood the danger besetting the Jewish people, with whom her
identification was now total. 'In Croatia', she explained, 'we gave up one
piece of land, then they wanted another piece of land.' For 'they', read
Muslims. From Croatia to Palestine, history was not so much repeating, as
simply reproducing itself: 'The Muslims don't want to stop. They want our
souls and they want our blood.'[1]

Although Maayan Yaday had met her Israeli husband when she was
working as a cocktail waitress on a cruise ship, she could still be categorised –

and most certainly she sees herself – as a displaced person. 'I was seven years in that war in Croatia [. . .] But people here will not give up like the Croatians and just leave.' She sees herself, that is, as someone who has been forced, under pressure of intolerable political circumstances, to leave her home. That she so fully enters into a religious and historical identification with the land of her exile may, at first glance, seem to make her untypical. After all, one of the main, explicit or implicit, reproaches against refugees, asylum seekers and indeed most immigrants is that they are not, ethnically and culturally, one of us, that they do not *fit in*. But Maayan Yaday is not alone, I would like to suggest, in her ability – we might call it a need – to transfer one unbearable historical identity into another. Remember that to choose to live in an Israeli settlement is to choose to place yourself more or less directly in a line of fire (it is also a fact that, from the 1930s, emigration to Israel has increased whenever the conflict has intensified).

In December 2003, Daniel Ben-Simon of *Ha'aretz* wrote a long feature on the rise of anti-Semitism in France and the breakdown of relations between Muslims and Jews. One schoolgirl in a Jewish high school located in a suburb of Seine-Saint-Denis stated 'Because of the anti-Semitism, I feel I will always remain a Jew in the eyes of others so I want them to know I am proud to be a Jew and proud of Israel.' This is of course a very different case. This French schoolgirl is turning to her Jewish identity as a legitimate response to hatred. Unlike Maayan Yaday, she is, it can be argued, making a claim on her own past. There is nonetheless an irony here, as the week before Ben-Simon had written an equally long feature on the increasingly isolated Muslim community of France (reading them one after the other, very naively I wanted all the people from each article to sit in a room with each other). But this young girl is not pondering what might be wrong with her own country. She is also, like although unlike Maadan Yaday, internally if not literally, on the move. Fear generates an identification – with somewhere else. It travels. And, in doing so, it becomes its own fortress. She wants 'them' to know that she is 'proud of Israel'. [2]

How much does this young French woman know about the nation of Israel? Does she know what the state is perpetrating against the Palestinians in the name of the Jewish people as she speaks? Does she know that 'ethnic transfer' is something now being openly discussed? Today there is a greater displacement and dispossession of Palestinians inside and out of the Territories than at any time in Israel–Palestine since 1948. According to David Grossman, writing in 2003, the country is 'more militant, nationalist and racist than ever before'. [3] At a meeting on anti-Semitism in London in February 2004, Varda Shiffer, former chairperson of the Israeli Section of Amnesty International, observed that there is – there can be – no discussion of racism in Israel. Since racism equals anti-Semitism, it is impossible for a racist to be a Jew.[4] This is not a new phenomenon. Writing in the 1980s Shulamith Hareven noted that Rabbi Haim Druckman, at the time a member of Knesset, had objected to the passage of a law against incitement to racism on the grounds that only Jews could be its victims.[5]

I would hazard the guess that the schoolgirl in France knows about the suicide bombings. But there was no allusion whatsoever to the conflict in her interview with Ben-Simon. She was simply proud of Israel. It is not for me to judge her; indeed I have every sympathy with her predicament. French anti-Semitism is real. Between 2002 and 2004, which saw a rise in anti-Semitic incidents, 2500 French Jews emigrated to Israel, double the preceding annual rate. My sense is that, should she follow them, her pride in Israel, born on French soil out of fear and hatred, would, like a tiny cherished crystal in the soul, become her claim. And her view of the Palestinians would blend and blur with the colours of the Muslims of France.[6]

These two stories take us to the heart of the matter. In the analysis of the migration and displacement of peoples, the normal reference is to the physical movement of bodies across boundaries. In a paradox that may well be a defining feature of our age, these boundaries have become at once increasingly mobile or porous (more and more people on the move as an effect of globalisation), and increasingly entrenched (more restrictions and policing of borders). To leap for a moment to a very different historical legacy – when Gillian Slovo spoke at the unveiling of the plaque to Ruth First and Joe Slovo in Camden in 2003, she simply contrasted the welcome with which her parents had been greeted in Britain as political exiles in the 1960s with Britain's policy on asylum seekers today. But in discussion of this dilemma of our times, not enough attention is paid to the accompanying mobility and immobility of the mind. What happens to a mind on the move? There is a common truism of what goes by the name of postmodern theory that because people today are caught in so many histories and places, likewise identities, miming the uncertainties of nations, are dissolving and unravelling themselves. Both Maayan Yaday, and the French schoolgirl, suggest that this is not the case. There is a baggage of the mind. When you move across a national boundary, you are just as likely to carry your enemies with you. Nothing, as psychoanalysis will testify, is ever simply left behind. We need to understand the peculiar relationship between the shifting sands of migration and the fortress of the soul. Whenever a door in the world is opened, a closet of the heart can just as equally well close (the open door is of course at best a mixed blessing for anyone who feels they have been pushed). In a world of teeming diasporas, how, or perhaps we should be asking *why*, do identities – against the surface drift, as it were – so fiercely entrench themselves?

To answer, or rather ask, this question, we need Freud. When I first saw the title for the series of Amnesty lectures of which this essay was originally part – 'Displacement, Asylum, Migration' – my attention was drawn to the term 'displacement', as it was to 'resistance' in the London School of Economics conference title, 'Politics, Psychoanalyis, Resistance', which provides the opening chapter of this book. Once again the word – 'displacement' – although it was not, I suspect, intended psychoanalytically by the organisers, but geographically and politically, is a key psychoanalytic term. Interestingly for the purposes of this discussion, when it first appears early in the work of Freud, it signals the mobility – not to say agility – of mental life. The mind has a remarkable capacity to move its psychic energies from one quantity to another: 'in mental functions something is to be distinguished,' writes Freud, in 1894, 'which is capable of increase, diminution, displacement and discharge'[7] (note just how early, three years before *Studies on Hysteria* and close to a decade before he started writing *The Interpretation of Dreams*). At this point in his thinking, Freud seems genuinely taken unawares – pleasantly surprised might be going too far – by the movements that the mind is capable of. It is the basic discovery of psychoanalysis that the mind cannot be held to one place. None of us are ever simply the child of the place where we are meant to be. Displacement gives, if you like, a more fluid, creative, dynamic component to the idea of the unconscious which famously de-centres man from his own mental self-possession (it is probably purely a matter of personal preference which idea – the splitting of the mind, or the perpetual motion of the mind – you find most disorienting).

But as the idea of displacement progresses in Freud's thinking, it starts to change its hue. Battens down as it were. It comes more and more to mean substitution. There is something you cannot bear to think about or remember, so you think about, or remember, something else. A young man recalls, with disarming and enchanting vividness, a lyrical moment from his childhood with a young girl in a bright yellow dress in a field. He does not want to remember that the visit to his young cousin was precipitated by the failure of his father's business.[8] I wake from a dream in terror at a burning house, because I do not want to notice the infant, ignored in the general conflagration, who has been abandoned by her mother in a nearby street in a pram. All this is unconscious – which is why it works so well. We are the past masters at getting rid of something un-masterable so that we can panic at the threat, which then becomes as inflexible as our own violent response to it, of something else. From displacement to projection is a single step. Although I have come halfway round the world, in flight from a country where I could never have even set eyes on you, yet you are the one – now, today – who will be answerable for my fear. Whole histories can hang on this turn. From the very beginning, the story of the founding of Israel is full of moments of just such historical displacement. For the early Jewish settlers in Palestine, in flight from the Russian pogroms at the end of the nineteenth century, the barely armed Arab marauders took on the features of mass city rioters buttressed, if not incited, by the full apparatus of the state.[9] When you move from one nation to another, whatever you find before your eyes, what, or rather who, do you see?

But if Israel–Palestine has a particular resonance in this context, it is because of the immense complexity with which it surrounds the issue not only of displacement but that of rights. Two displaced peoples, the Jewish people and the Palestinians, forced to leave their land – at least 700,000 in the case of the second in 1948, so that the first people can have a home (one displacement leads to another). Two peoples claiming the right to national self-determination, each one supporting that right with another one – the right of return – which definitively pulls the ground from under their antagonist's claim, saps the very foundations on which the first claim rests. The law of return stipulates that any Jew, but only any Jew, throughout the world, including one who was only a matter of months ago a Croatian and a Catholic, has the right to settle in Israel. The right of return of the Palestinians demands that the Palestinians have the right to re-enter a land in which the majority of citizens believes that to allow this would demographically, as well as politically, destroy the nature of the state (although, according to a recent calculation, only 2 per cent of Israelis live on refugee land).[10] Add to this the fact that, although the clash is between two peoples, the right to the land is justified on radically discrepant grounds or histories – one biblical, going back 2000 years, one based up to 1948 on a far more recently lived connection between the native and her soil. In fact even that is a simplification – for the earliest Jewish settlers in Palestine, the right to a state would emerge as much out of the up-building of the land as out of the mists of time. 'It was the service to the soil', Chaim Weizmann, first President of Israel, wrote, 'which determined the right in our favour.'[11]

'I belong here.' The statement is almost impossible to contest – grammatically it consists of a shifter ('I'), a performative ('belong') and an indexical sign ('here'). It depends for its truth on the moment of utterance, even if it claims an eternity of time. This is my land because this is where I see myself. Now and for ever. We have entered the region of the heart. Between two claims for national self-determination there cannot in fact be any arbitration at law. This is Yeshayahu Leibowitz, the Israeli philosopher and dissident, in his 1976 article, 'Rights, Law and Reality':

> Fortunate is the people whose conception of its tie to its country is recognised by others, for should this connection be contested, no legal argument could establish it [. . .] Considerations of historical 'justice' are irrelevant. The conflict is not one of imaginary 'rights'. Nor is it a clash between 'Justice and Justice' – since the legal (or moral) category of justice does not apply.[12]

What, we might ask, does it in fact mean to say that nationhood is a 'right'? Bhikhu Parekh has argued that some of the most important exchanges and responsibilities between individual subjects – of loving and caring for example – cannot fall under the mantle of rights or only do so at the gravest cost.[13] He is talking about individuals and the clash between the concept of rights and another very different vision of ethical or virtuous life. The problem posed by Israel–Palestine is different. This is a situation where the idea of rights can be seen tearing itself apart from the outside and from within. Nationhood is not a right, it is a claim; agonistic, most likely to destroy another. Self-determination is a myth, because as a right it depends on the other's recognition. The worst delusion of all perhaps is that of national selfhood. Not just because no nation in the twenty-first century, nor indeed the twentieth, can be anything other than an in-mixing of peoples and hence selves (Israel is in full panicked confrontation with that reality as I speak). But because the idea of self-sufficiency, in the world of nations, is a complete myth. This is just one of the very many ironies of Israel's original constitution as a nation state. 'Paradoxical as it may sound,' Hannah Arendt wrote in her 1944 essay 'Zionism Reconsidered', 'it was precisely because of this nationalist misconception of the inherent independence of a nation that the Zionists ended up making the Jewish national independence entirely dependent on the material interests of another nation.' Theodor Herzl, author of *Der Judenstaat*, the founder of political Zionism, 'did not realise', she wrote, 'that the country he dreamt of did not exist, that there was no place on earth where a people could live like the organic national body he had in mind and that the real historical development of a nation does not take place inside the closed walls of a biological entity'. 'As for nationalism,' she remarked, 'it never was more evil or more fiercely defended than since it became apparent that this once great and revolutionary principle of the national organisation of peoples could no longer either guarantee true sovereignty of people within or establish a just relationship among different peoples beyond the national borders.'[14] Arendt's point is simple – the more the nation state affirms itself as a biological, self-sufficient entity, the less it will be able to save the people it was created to protect.

To recap: no national 'right', as in organic and pregiven. No self-determination, as in self-sufficiency, of nations. To which we can add – circling back to the topic of this essay – no singular selfhood. Rights, as John Rawls has stressed, although without drawing the implications for his own theory, relies on a fully rational, monochrome, conception of the person. I must know who I am when I claim them. But if the mind is not its own place? If my claim delves into the depths of my own history, trawling through my dreams and nightmares, to create its own law? The image we have of displaced persons tends to be cast in terms of endurance, survival, the fierce adherence of all human creatures to their own life. It bears no investigation of inner worlds. I suggest instead we see peoples on the move at least partly as sleepwalkers, trundling through each other's dark night.

Three writers can help us to explore this question. Most honestly, I simply love all three. Freud is one – Shulamith Hareven, the Israeli writer, and W.G. Sebald, the German émigré, are the other two. Two of them are Jewish and all of them move dramatically across national boundaries in the course of their lives: Freud from Vienna to England, Sebald from Germany also to England, Hareven from Poland to Palestine.[15] Each of them are, although in radically different ways, the harshest of self-diagnosticians, my answers of sorts to Maayan Yaday and the schoolgirl from Saint-Denis. All three are storytellers, master craftsmen who allow us to glimpse the past as it ferments inside the mind.

When Freud applied the term 'displacement' to the internal migrations of the psyche, he could hardly have expected that by the end of his life it would, in the forced exile of peoples, so hideously concretise itself. He himself would become an exile, leaving Austria as late as he could in the summer of 1938. Even after the *Anschluss*, he had been reluctant to depart. He was of course a privileged refugee (according to rumour President Roosevelt interceded with the Nazi authorities on his behalf), an elite among elites – unlike his sisters who were left behind. 'Practically everybody who in world opinion stood for what was currently called German culture prior to 1933', wrote American journalist Dorothy Thompson, in her 1938 *Refugees – Anarchy or Organisation?*, 'is already a refugee.'[16]

In December 1938, barely six months after going into exile and less than a year before he died, in a little commented but highly significant moment, Freud wrote recommending Thompson's book to his friend and benefactress, Princess Marie Bonaparte, who had played such a crucial role in getting him, and his library, safely out of Austria.[17] This is worth noting in itself. It's not quite the kind of book one would expect Freud to read, nor was Thompson, one might say, Freud's kind of woman (she had written a scathing review of *The Ego and the Id* in 1924 – clearly he bore no grudges). Thompson was an extraordinary pioneering political journalist. The director of publicity for the New York Woman Suffrage Campaign, chief of the Central European News Service before becoming a freelance writer, she achieved notoriety when she succeeded in 1932 in securing an interview with Hitler. Her greatest claim to fame would be her activities on behalf of refugees: 'the dispossessed racial and political minorities' of Europe, nine million of them, according to the blurb of her book: 'There will be more of them tomorrow and even more of them the day after' – four million who had been compelled under political pressure to leave their homes since the end of the First World War – 'the most pressing of humanity's many problems'.[18] Freud is one of millions. In this almost dying gesture, Freud universalises his predicament, finds himself making common cause with the refugee.

'As I write this', Thompson begins, 'the news from Europe is distressing in the extreme.'[19] Her book is a plea for an internationally financed pro-gramme for mass settlement – a political solution to what she insists is a political problem (her activities on this score are considered to have been influential in the formation of Roosevelt's Advisory Committee on Re-fugees). 'Horrified humanitarianism', she insists, is not enough.[20] Although her book is dated (how could it not be?), both her plea for international accountability and her indictment of the Great Powers for betraying the Armenians and the Assyrians have much to tell or remind us of today. The Jews are of course central to her analysis. Prior to 1933, fewer than two thousand German Jews had emigrated to Palestine. After the Nuremberg laws, 118,000 fled, of whom about a third would choose to settle in Palestine.[21]

Reluctant to countenance the grimmest outcome of Nazi persecution, Thompson wants the Nazis to be used. Her model for raising finance is the settlement of German Jews in Palestine made possible by means of a trade-and-transfer agreement between the Nazi government and the Ha'avara company in Palestine, an organisation for the transfer out of the country of the capital of German-Jewish emigrants. Those only 'theoretically interested in the refugee problem', as she puts it, can be left to work out what was uppermost in the minds of the Nazis: 'whether their interest was primarily in increasing their exports, or primarily in getting rid of their Jews'.[22] Hannah Arendt was scathing, accusing the Zionist Organization of doing 'business with Hitler', and in the process showing that their sole interest was in the

Yishuv[23]. Thompson is not naive. She knows the deal is sinister. She wants the Jews out of Germany at any cost. Without sentimentality or under-statement, Thompson charts the journey – political, geographic, financial – that takes the Jewish people out of the heart of a persecutory Europe and into Palestine.

Thompson believes in the Jewish 'up-building' of Palestine. In tones unmistakably resonant of mid-century Zionism, she sees Palestine as redemptive for the Jews: 'There the sons and daughters of the persecuted Eastern European Jews grow up to be healthy creatures who do not bear the stigma of their Jewishness any more, but feel themselves to be happy and healthy human beings.'[24] In a much-commented moment in *Der Judenstaat*, Herzl had argued that a state for the Jews would be 'a rampart of Europe against Asia, an outpost of civilisation as opposed to barbarism'.[25] Thompson also believes in a form of 'enlightened twentieth-century imperialism' – her phrase – 'a really grandiose scheme for developing backward territories with displaced Europeans'.[26] But there is a limit to such benign imperialism and that limit is Palestine. Contrary to Herzl, for Thompson European grandi-osity does not finally fulfil itself, but rather crashes, in the Middle East. Arab resistance to the Jewish presence has made the dream of mass emigration impossible. There can therefore – 'at least for the moment', she writes – be no solution to the problem of Jewish refugees. Many Jews already in Palestine or wanting to emigrate may be 'prepared to fight and die for a country which they consider their homeland' (as Herzl put it: 'only the desperate make good conquerors').[27] But 'unless the difficulties between Arabs and Jews can be cleared up and a reconciliation effected', Palestine must, she writes, be considered a 'danger spot for the Jews'. 'All hopes of anything like mass emigration to Palestine have to be buried.'[28]

Ideals can place you in danger. Palestine is no solution for the Jews. The Jews will not be safe – and in this history surely bears her out – in Palestine. In a classic psychoanalytic move, which I am sure was not her intention, Thompson suggests that flight, fortification – your best protection – can turn out to be the worst defence. She is a pragmatist, but running under the surface of her analysis is the warning that I like to think was the one Freud was communicating to Marie Bonaparte. In a gesture of glorious and truly creative heroism, escaping the horrors of Europe, the Jews are in danger of transporting their own legacy of displacement, directly and perilously, onto the soil of Palestine. In his extraordinary story, 'The Story of Hirbet Hiz'ah', S. Yizhar, one of Israel's most important post-war writers, offers just such an analysis of the displacement of one history of suffering directly onto another. Watching the forced evacuation of Palestinian villagers from the village of Hirbet Hiz'ah during the 1948 War of Israeli Independence (termed the *nakba* or 'catastrophe' by the Palestinians), a young Israeli soldier suddenly sees the exile (*Galut*) of his own people unfolding before his eyes: 'Something suddenly became clear to me in a flash. At once I saw everything in a new, a clearer light – Galut. This is Galut. Galut is like this. This is what Galut looks like.'[29]

In 1930, Freud had written what has become a famous letter to Dr Chaim Koffler of the Jewish Agency who had written to him and other prominent European Jews asking them to criticise British policy in Palestine. In response to the Arab riots of that year, Britain was restricting Jewish access to the Western Wall in Jerusalem and Jewish immigration:

> I cannot do what you wish. I am unable to overcome my aversion to burdening the public with my name and even the present critical time doesn't seem to me to warrant it. Whoever wants to influence the masses must give them something rousing and inflammatory and my sober judgement of Zionism does not permit this. I certainly sympathise with its goals, am proud of our University in Jerusalem and am delighted with our settlement's prosperity. But on the other hand, I do not think that Palestine could ever become a Jewish state, nor that the Christian and Islamic worlds would ever be prepared to have their holy places under Jewish care. It would have seemed more sensible to me to establish a Jewish homeland on a less historically burdened land. But I know that such a rational viewpoint would never have gained the enthusiasm of the masses and the financial support of the wealthy. I concede with sorrow that the baseless fanaticism of our people is in part to be blamed for the awakening of Arab distrust. I can raise no sympathy at all for the misdirected piety which transforms a piece of an Herodian wall into a national relic, thus offending the feelings of the natives. Now judge for yourself whether I, with such a critical point of view, am the right person to come forward as the solace of a people deluded by an unjustified hope.[30]

This is a harsh judgement. The Jewish people are deluded and their hope is unjustified. If Freud was wrong about the hope – there would be a Jewish state in Palestine – he may nonetheless have been right about the element of willed delusion involved ('It is the Zionists' good fortune that we are considered mad,' wrote Chaim Weizmann, 'if we were normal, we would not think of going to Palestine, but stay put, like all normal people.')[31] Freud's strongest criticism – 'I can raise no sympathy at all' – is directed at the 'misdirected piety' – or 'baseless fanaticism' – which 'transforms a piece of an Herodian wall into a national relic'. It is reserved, that is, for the process

whereby a people historically and symbolically burden the land as the
foundation of their claim upon it. Above all the danger resides in that
moment or process of substitution. I do not see the people of Palestine; I see
the land aglow with my own destiny (Raja Shehadeh, the Palestinian lawyer
and human rights activist, calls this 'pornography of the land').[32]

Israel Zangwill's formula for Zionism is well known: 'A land without a
people for a people without a land.' In fact the Arab people were not
invisible as the most cursory perusal of the literature of early Zionism makes
clear. To this brute fact, Freud is adding something else. What allows you to
ignore the people before your eyes is the force of piety: magical – or as Freud
terms it 'omnipotent' – thought. 'I know that such a rational viewpoint
would never have gained the enthusiasm of the masses and the financial
support of the wealthy.' What Freud will not join in, or put his name to, is
mass identification. He will neither rouse nor inflame. He wants nothing to
do with national identity raised to a pitch. Freud's caution stems from his
distrust of the group mind. As we shall see later, it is clear from his letters and
writings on mass psychology – the focus of Chapter 3 – that his distrust first
arises from being the target of mass hatred as a Jew. As a Jew he dreads the
mob, as a Jew he pulls back from national passion (the Zionist move from
such dread to such passion is not one he is willing to make). But unlike most
of the leaders of the world today, Freud can praise the resilience and
endeavour, not to say the survival, of his people, without having to exempt
them from baseness.

In this letter, Freud makes the most careful and resonant distinction
between two ways of being in the world, indeed between two forms of
Zionism, one could also say. One which, living in the real world, quietly and
soberly works to achieve its ends (the University of Jerusalem, the prosperity
of the settlements, by which he means the agricultural work of Jewish
immigrants); the other which, recognising no obstacles, ruthlessly sweeps
across the earth and its people. 'It will be Jewish' – Weizmann again –
'whether the Arabs want it or not'; 'There is no power on earth that can stop
the Jews from getting to Palestine.'[33] Or in the words of David Ben-Gurion
in 1948 (responding to the US proposal to establish international trusteeship
over Palestine): 'We are masters of our own fate. We have laid the
foundations for the establishment of the Jewish state and we will establish
it.'[34]

'In sympathy with the goals' of Zionism, as Freud makes a point of stating
in his letter, he places himself firmly in the rank of those who believed that
Jews should travel to Palestine, and make it their home, but on condition of
not usurping the land and rights of the Arab people. No one who agitates
today for a more open policy on asylum and immigration can possibly

oppose these early migrations of the Jews, who from 1933 were fleeing Nazi Germany for their lives. In 1935, Freud wrote to L. Jaffe of the Keren Ha-Yesod, the World Zionist Organisation's funding body, praising his foundation as a 'great and blessed instrument' and a 'sign of our invincible will to survive'.[35] Once again, therefore, the problem is not the movement of bodies, but thought fastening on and seizing its ground (the survival of one people at the cost of another). Migration, therefore, but no national relics. No magical thinking. On the eve of the genocide in Europe, in a gesture which is counterintuitive to say the least, Freud warns the Jewish people, struggling to survive as a people, not to fall prey to the omnipotence of their dreams.

Shulamith Hareven was one of Thompson's refugees. Little known outside Israel, she is one of the country's most revered writers. Born in Poland in 1930, she escaped the Nazis with her family and moved to British-ruled Mandatory Palestine, where, as a member of the Haganah, she participated in the creation of the state (she served as a medic at the front during the 1948 war). She was also a founder of Galutz, the Israeli military radio station, and worked with Jewish immigrants from Arab countries as an officer in the Israeli Defense Force. Hareven was born as Freud's life, together with the life of the Jews in Europe, is entering its last phase. Fleeing Europe for the *Yishuv*, she is witness to the two key events of Jewish history – the Shoah and the birth of Israel – which Freud would not live to see. But if her story embodies that of the new nation, her own voice is rarely in tune with the refrain of the state. She went on to be a journalist and writer – the first woman to be made a member of the Academy of Hebrew Language – a peace activist, founder of Peace Now in 1978, and one of the most outspoken critics of the Israeli government (in 1995, the French magazine *L'Express* nominated her as one of the hundred women who 'move the world'). Hareven defined herself as an outsider. Her desert trilogy, *Thirst*, centres on the lives of a miracle-hater, Eshkar, who only partially enters the spirit of the Hebrews as they journey through the desert out of Egypt, a prophet, Hivai, who has lost the art of prophecy and leaves his people for a thicket in the rift of the Jordan, and a young man named as Salu, but with enough allusions to conjure up Isaac, who cannot find his place because he is the child of a father who had sought to kill him.[36] There is no triumphalism in these stories. When Hareven returns to the primordial displacement of her people, she charts their history at a critical, loving, distance.

Wary, like Freud, of collective identification, Hareven repeats – now with the benefit of hindsight – his fears for the Jewish people in Palestine. Her strongest reproach to the nation is the price the individual has paid for such a powerful, and powerfully enforced, collective dream. 'A constant process is at work', she writes in her 1988 article, 'Israel: The First Forty Years', 'that relentlessly represses the individual's needs and feelings [. . .] Its roots are to be found in the generation of the founding fathers, who determined the patterns of life here for many decades, perhaps having no other choice at the time.'[37] 'The price was prodigious', she continues, 'even at the time: the early years of Zionist settlement in Palestine are replete with stories of suicide, collapse, bodily and mental anguish; the sound of weeping at night is an almost permanent counterpoint to the refrain of pioneering Zionism.'[38] This is not common talk. Hareven is recording the mostly unheard protests, the night-time anguish, of a displaced people whose pain was meant to be effortlessly transmuted into the vocabulary of the pioneers. 'We will bring them here', Golda Meir announced, 'and turn them into human beings.'[39]

As psychoanalysis would attest, such silence becomes its own legacy. Hardness towards the individual – 'not only an ethos, but almost a religion' – required of the individual 'absolute silence regarding his own hardships', an ethos into which Holocaust survivors would also be 'ensnared'.[40] Sole witnesses to the event which many see as providing the ultimate rationale for the new state, for a long time they said nothing. If Freud did not live to see the Holocaust, nor did he witness – although this much he could surely have predicted – that in the short span between its horrors and the creation of Israel, the tragedy of the European Jews would not just be lived, but repressed. For Hareven, Israel has never fully reckoned with the consequences of being a nation solely of immigrants – the first generation to grow up in the country was a generation without grandparents – 'a society of persons who had undergone dreadful experiences, but were silent'.[41]

For the state to flourish, identification with the new ethos was to be absolute. Or in the words of the teacher in her 1980 short story, 'The Witness', as he exhorts the young boy, Shlomek, who has fled war-torn Poland for Palestine: 'You know the expression: "Be part of the group or die?"'[42] 'My role as an educator', he comments later, 'was to build a new generation, proud and magnanimous and cruel' – he is citing Jabotinsky, founder of the ultra-nationalist youth movement, Betar (to whom I return in Chapter 4).[43]

'The Witness' is perhaps Hareven's most famous story. It is written in the first-person voice of the young Israeli whose task it is to absorb Shlomek into the new nation. The tale is not presented as autobiography, although it is the only non-autobiographical piece Hareven chose to include in her autobiographical compilation, *Yamim Rabim*, or *Many Days*, of 2002, which was the last of her writings published during her life (she died in 2003). But just how closely, and critically, it brushes against her own history can be

measured by the fact that the teacher, also born in Poland (a fact he prefers
not to recall) came, like Hareven, to Israel at the age of eleven; and by its
ironic, almost scathing representation of the young boys in the class who are
being proudly groomed for recruitment by the Haganah, of which Hareven
herself had been a member. When one such, Boaz, is on the verge of being
defeated in a brawl with Shlomek, the teacher intervenes on his side: 'I was
sure that in the coming year when the officers of the Haganah arrived to
look their age group over, Boaz would be chosen as commander material
[. . .] I could not allow his leadership to be undermined.'[44]

But if this story has become celebrated, it is for the way it documents the
silencing by the *Yishuv* of what was happening to the Jews of Europe. Idith
Zertal has done most to chart the ambivalence – to put it mildly – with
which Israel treated the survivors arriving on its shores (they were routinely
referred to as 'dust' and 'soap' – this last a triple allusion to Nazi soap, the
pallor of their skin compared with the native-born Sabras, and to someone
pliable and easily moulded into shape).[45] 'Look, when I came to Israel this
was an ideological, elitist society', Aharon Appelfeld comments in a recent
interview. 'Anyone who came from the camps was considered a person with
emotional and physical defects.'[46] When the Minister of Education and
Culture, Ben-Zion Dinur, submitted to the Knesset for its first reading the
Holocaust and Heroism Remembrance Law – Yad Vashem, 1953 – whose
purpose was to establish a memorial for each and every Jew slain, the one
category not mentioned was the survivors, the only living people with a true
memory of the event (what could also not be mentioned were the
'collaborator' trials being held at the same time in the Israeli courts which,
as Zertal points out, have never been incorporated into Holocaust memory).

Through the voice of a narrator whose utter shallowness is displayed on
every page, Hareven's story allows us to enter this experience from the side
of the victim (although as we shall see, the status of 'victim' is the last one
Hareven feels should be claimed by Israel). No less important, it goes back in
time to that moment, decisive as she believes for the new nation, when the
full extent of the horrors was not yet known. Shlomek is a survivor from the
beginning, not the end of the war, who has witnessed the massacre of his
whole family by the Nazis (hence the title of the story) – his father was
hanged by the Nazis on Passover, his mother and two brothers killed in the
forest when they ventured out in search of bread. No one at the school
believes him. They treat him as a fantasist and liar. In the eyes of the
burgeoning nation, he is no more or less than a displaced person needing to
be assimilated into his new place: 'Soon you'll look like everyone else and
talk like everyone else, and no one will be able to tell that you weren't born
here.'[47] Shlomek is therefore both witness and messenger. He talks. In this

alone Hareven rewrites, in something like an act of grace, the silence of her generation, gives them back their voice.

Faced with this willed blindness, Shlomek takes to scribbling in Polish, at night, the details of the murders. His frantic nocturnal jottings, accompanied by daytime silence, become the only way he can continue to testify. The climax of the story comes when a leader of the *Yishuv* arrives from the Jewish Agency 'in a burst of glory' to address the school.[48] After a speech detailing the gravity of the war but with 'prophecies of consolation', Shlomek rises to his feet, to the consternation of the gathering, and delivers his deathly message: 'Comrade Benio, I have a question to ask you. There is evidence that the Germans intend exterminating all the Jews of Europe living under their rule. Have the national institutions any knowledge of this, and if so, what do they propose to do about it?'[49] It is the question of the wise fool. It is the truth (more than once the narrator has told Shlomek that the absolute truth was not the most important thing). Comrade Benio believes the claims to be exaggerated: 'But, I tell you comrades, that even if this grave news, or even part of it, proves to be true [. . .] even then we will not be able to do anything.'[50] 'Our first duty, our sacred, duty is to the remnants of our people gathered here: we have no greater duty than our duty to the great pioneering venture of building Eretz Israel.'[51] Shlomek flees the school that night – 'without a coat, in his sandals and short trousers' – making his way past Arab villages to the High Commissioner to whom he delivers his eyewitness report to events that the whole world, including the *Yishuv*, will finally be forced to recognise. 'Why couldn't he have waited', the teacher declaims, 'why did he run away in the night as if his conscience wasn't clean?'[52]What he doesn't ask is what difference it would have made, given that the new nation has so fully, as Comrade Benio attests, exonerated itself from any responsibility for the Jews of Europe. Hareven has written the supreme story of displacement – not in Freud's early sense of free mobility in the mind, but in his later sense of something that blocks its own pathway as it moves, shedding the debris of pain as it distils itself into its stubborn, bright, new constellation.

It has become a truism to say that the Holocaust is exploited by the state of Israel to deflect criticism of its own policies. In her obituary for Gideon Hausner, Attorney General at the time of the Eichmann trial, Hareven contrasts his humility in the face of the Shoah with the politicians 'who take the name of the Holocaust in vain [. . .] the arrogant hacks who were not there but who have no qualms about manipulating the Holocaust, using it as a political ploy or as an excuse to turn others into victims' (her description of the 'Shoaologists' and 'Shoah Business' who 'milk it for all its worth' makes Norman Finkelstein seem tame in comparison).[53] It is because she has so vividly charted the resistance to suffering in the founding of the state that Hareven's critique of the political use of the Holocaust in Israel today acquires such moral authority. In order to become itself, the nation stifled pain ('perhaps having no other choice at the time').[54] But suffering is not the same thing as victimhood. If, as she suggests, the nation has always been ashamed of the first, it has embraced the second as a new, fortified, identity that licenses its own violence against the Palestinians ('an excuse to turn others into victims'). 'If my only identity is that of the victim, the world's deterministic and doomed victim, I may (or so it seems) commit any atrocity.'[55] Why, she asks with reference to Hausner, has 'the principle of statehood embodied in trial, as opposed to the ghetto mindset behind revenge [. . .] never been taught in our schools'?[56] Every schoolchild knows 'the desperate acts of our history by rote. In how many Israeli schools are court rulings taught?'[57]

'It is as if all of Zionism', she writes in her 1986 essay 'Identity: Victim', 'is dependent on our not knowing and not wanting to know.'[58] Now it is the mundane quality of normal life in Israel that is being repressed. All that can be seen is 'the eternal victim, alone in the world, who sits upright on his throne with his eyes closed, smothering all other peoples (especially the Arabs), and is always, always right, right with the cold, blind righteousness of the victim above whose head flutters the banner, "Vengeance is mine!" '[59] In fact in the thirty-four years between the Declaration of Independence and the first Lebanese War, there were only five weeks of all-out war involving the bulk of the IDF; and, according to an IDF spokesman, in the years preceding the war, terrorism had in fact been in decline (thirty-seven casualties in three years, and in the year prior to the war, one). In the process, as Hareven sees it, Israel not only licenses aggression towards the Palestinians, it is also wreaking destruction upon itself: 'The upshot, then, of presenting things as though Israel faced a threat to its existence, the danger of a holocaust, is that by our own talk and with our own hands we generate situations in which dozens or hundreds of times as many of our people fall as are killed in all the acts of terrorism combined, and without an iota of justification.'[60] Israelis are left no chance of identity 'except to be either murderers, the murdered, or both'.[61] What, she laments, has any of this to do with Judaism?[62] If only Israelis could, instead, see themselves as the inheritors of a people with a four-thousand-year history of responsibility, conscience and appeals for social order and justice, then: 'even if, often in history I have been the victim of others, I will never oppress those weaker than myself and never abuse my power to exile them'.[63]

In the history of the nation, the Holocaust has therefore been called on not once, but twice to conceal the truth. First the vulnerability of persons (only the collective exists), then the power of the new state. To the concept of displacement, Hareven therefore adds a new twist. To make what may seem a strange analogy, Roland Barthes once analysed the way fashion pulls clothes so far from their functional purpose that the reason we wear them can suddenly return as the surprising, bright idea of a new season: as in 'it will be a long, warm winter this season' to advertise coats (as if the idea that coats were intended to keep you warm could be a glamorous afterthought). This apparently trivial example can serve to make a difficult, even deadly serious, point. Speaking of something can be, paradoxical as it may sound, a way of not speaking about something. It can be a means to ensure that the true unbearable felt humiliation of a catastrophe as it might impact on a nation, not as rationale or apology for state power, but as memory, is still being repressed. Perhaps this is the most disturbing meaning of displacement – when a traumatic history is loudly invoked, with devastating political consequences, almost as a smokescreen for itself.

None of this is to suggest – as should not need stressing – that the Holocaust is not a real traumatic memory for the Jewish people. Nor that a nation does not have a right to legitimate self-defence. But the tragedy of Europe did not simply pass into the nation's mind and it is not simply, as in innocently, being invoked today. Israeli soldiers are regularly sent on visits to Auschwitz in order to strengthen their resolve. Responding in July 2003 to questions about the killing of Palestinian children by the Israeli army (in the conflict at that time, one in five dead Palestinians was a child), the commander in Gaza starts by taking responsibility: 'Every name of a child here, it makes me feel bad because it's the fault of my soldiers', but by the end of the conversation he has – in the words of the interviewer – returned to being 'combative', invoking the Holocaust as his rationale: 'I remember the Holocaust. We have a choice, to fight the terrorists or to face being consumed by the flames again.'[64] There are suicide bombings on the part of the Palestinians in which Israeli children have died; they have rightly been described as unacceptable crimes. But the flames on the streets of Jerusalem and Tel Aviv are not the flames of the Holocaust (any more than the Muslims of Croatia are the same as the Arabs of Palestine). Nor can the building of the wall, targeted assassinations, the destruction of the entire infrastructure of Palestinian life and the daily humiliation of the people be justified as a legitimate security response. Something is in excess. For psychoanalysis, something arises in excess when there is something else you cannot bear to think about. What would the situation in Israel–Palestine look like if the commander in Gaza deduced from his 'memory' of the Holocaust, for example, a shared vulnerability of peoples? What kind of a nation would Israel become if the state ceased to promote omnipotence as the answer to historical pain? To recall Hareven: 'Even if often in history I have been the victim of others, I will never oppress those weaker than myself and never abuse my power to exile them.'

To conclude, briefly, with W.G. Sebald, who in his life and writing brings the art of displacement, in all its ambiguities and multivalence, to the rarest pitch. Many readers have found themselves asking if the story of his 2001 novel, *Austerlitz*, of the young Jewish boy sent to England in 1939 on a Kindertransport, is his own. It isn't of course. Sebald is not Jewish. But in this book, and to some degree in *The Emigrants*, Sebald throws himself into the mind of German-Jewish suffering with such understated, desolate intensity that critics are inclined to cry either miracle or theft. Sebald is himself an emigrant. He left Germany for England in 1966. Alongside his passion for the earth and contours of the land of his new home, he writes stories of persons lifted out of a past that neither he nor they have left behind. It is as if moving out of Germany enjoined on him the task of a very peculiar form of remembrance – something a million miles from being a claim on the past. This is history not as fragment – that would be too easy, too bland; it is memory numbed by the sheer effort of resisting and retrieving itself. Sebald puts himself in the other's place – through Austerlitz he imagines himself as a Jew. As with *The Natural History of Destruction*, which goes into the archives to call up the mostly forgotten and silenced story of the destruction of German cities in the last year of the war, Sebald – not unlike Hareven but from the other side of her story – delves into shame, tells the narrative of his nation in reverse.

Austerlitz speaks to an unnamed narrator whom he meets at stations and in hotels, often by chance although every encounter also feels like a summons. Austerlitz has chosen this narrator as the vehicle for his own memory of a story he has been in flight from all his life. 'The past', in the words of Daniel Ben-Simon, 'is ahead of us.'[65] The nation's future – I understand him as saying – depends on what we will allow, or can bear, the past to be. Sebald writes in the future perfect tense that Jacques Lacan terms the tense of analytic time: not the past of what I once was and am no more (repression), nor what I have been in what I am still (repetition), but what '*I will have been for what I am in the "process of becoming"*'.[66] This makes nationhood, like memory, endless. Neither redemptive nor retributive, it is not something that can be taken out, brushed down and used. It is not enough to wear the banner of the dead and claim to speak in their name. If we do not want to disappoint them, as Elizabeth Bowen once put it, we must go further. Perhaps we have to go out and meet them (she was also writing about the legacy of the Second World War).[67] This is from near the

end of the book when Austerlitz is trying to remember his father who
disappeared shortly after saving his child:

> I felt, as I was saying, said Austerlitz, as if my father were still in Paris and
> just waiting, so to speak, for a good opportunity to reveal himself. Such
> ideas infallibly come to me in places which have more of the past about
> them than the present [. . .] It seems to me then as if all moments of our
> life occupy the same space, as if future events already existed and were
> only waiting for us to find our way to them at last [. . .] And might it not
> be, continued Austerlitz, that we also have appointments to keep in the
> past, in what has gone before and is for the most part extinguished, and
> must go there in search of places and people who have some connection
> with us on the far side of time, so to speak.[68]

'As I was saying, said Austerlitz', 'And might it not be, continued Austerlitz';
'so to speak.' Memory is as hesitant as it is imperative. In the most intimate
details of his grammar, Sebald at once bids memory come, and slows it
down.

This dull, cruel, urgent pacing of memory is crucial. Sebald seems to be
saying two things that go to the heart of this essay. There is no limit to the
potential for identification – this is displacement in Freud's earliest creative
sense. In Sebald's mind any German can become a Jew, and perhaps must
try. But all identities are dangerous unless they are given up, qualified – here
the syntax of Austerlitz is the key – at the very moment that they are
claimed. Otherwise they will become a fortress, the grounds for a new and
killing form of certainty. And no end of dreadful deeds will be enacted in
their name.

To conclude, then, with fortresses. Not least because the security fence in
Israel, ruled illegal by the International Court of Justice, was before the court
and had been condemned by Amnesty International, sponsors of the lecture
that provided the original occasion for this essay, in the week when the
lecture was delivered. But if it seems appropriate to end with fortresses, it is
also because in a way this essay has been about nothing else: fortresses on the
ground and in the head. Austerlitz is an architectural historian – he is a
lecturer at a London institute of art history – long before he goes in search of
his own past. He is obsessed with buildings of war and conquest. Before he
gets to the concentration camp in which his parents most likely perished, he
tells us, through the meticulous analysis of ramparts and weaponry down the
ages, that power is all the more futile the more it tries to entrench itself
behind a wall of self-defence. A wall is a false memory – destructive of others
and asking to be destroyed. It is also a form of displacement (perhaps the

sheerest of them all), since it sidelines, or rather endlessly moves elsewhere, what then becomes – automatically and *because he has built it* – the defendant's most vulnerable point. This is, as I see it, also Freud's and Hareven's insight. In this passage Austerlitz is commenting on the star-shaped fortresses of Coevorden, Neuf-Brisach and Saarlouis:

> It had been forgotten that the largest fortifications will naturally attract the largest enemy forces, and that the more you entrench yourself the more you must remain on the defensive, so that in the end you might find yourself in a place fortified in every possible way, watching helplessly, while the enemy troops, moving on to their own choice of terrain elsewhere, simply ignored their adversaries' fortresses, which had become positive arsenals of weaponry, bristling with cannons and overcrowded with men. The frequent result, said Austerlitz, of resorting to measures of fortification marked in general by a tendency towards paranoid elaboration was that you drew attention to your weakest point, practically inviting the enemy to attack it.[69]

And again, on Antwerp in the nineteenth century: 'Although the whole insanity of fortification and siegecraft was clearly revealed in the taking of Antwerp, said Austerlitz, the only conclusion anyone drew from it, incredibly, was that the defences surrounding the city must be built even more strongly than before.'[70] Such defences are living on borrowed time. 'It is often, says Austerlitz, our mightiest projects that most obviously betray the degree of our insecurity.'[71] What all my three writers seem to me to be saying is that we need a non-defensive form of memory if the world is to be a fairer, not to say safer, place.

One final anecdote, taken from Sara Roy's presentation at the event organised in November 2003 in tribute to Edward Said who had died in September. These are the opening lines:

> Not too long ago, two reporters for the Israeli newspaper, *Yediot Ahronot*, were given the opportunity to purchase 100 olive trees. These trees, they discovered, were uprooted from Palestinian lands razed by Israel for the building of the new 'security' wall or separation barrier in the West Bank. Among these gnarled trees, some of which have found new homes in Israeli parks and private residences, was a 600-year-old olive tree selling for $5500 at an Israeli nursery.[72]

Some forms of displacement are simply a crime.

*Revised version of a lecture first delivered as Oxford Amnesty Lecture, 12th series, 5 February 2004; published in Kate E. Tunstall, ed., *Displacement, Asylum, Migration* (Oxford, Oxford University Press 2006).

Notes

1 Chris McGreal, 'Gaza's settlers dig in their heels', *Guardian*, 4 February 2004.
2 Daniel Ben-Simon, 'Monsieur, this is not the true France', *Ha'aretz*, 26 December 2003.
3 David Grossman, 'Two Years of Intifada', *Death as a Way of Life – Despatches from Jerusalem*, (New York, Farrar, Straus, Giroux 2003), p. 177.
4 She was speaking at a meeting of the Jewish Forum for Justice and Human Rights, 9 February 2004.
5 Shulamith Hareven, 'Identity: Victim', 1986, *The Vocabulary of Peace: Life, Culture and Politics in the Middle East*, (San Francisco, Mercury 1995), p. 149.
6 While writing this essay I read in *Ha'aretz* a feature on the settlers of Gush Katif in Gaza, which includes the following comment from Laurence Baziz, a former Parisian who has lived in the settlement for eighteen years: 'They [the settlers] are very attracted by the soul, the ideological theme [. . .] There is a rise of Islamic influence in France. The French themselves don't like outsiders; there are a great many French people who feel the takeover of Islam. I illuminate that point'. *Ha'aretz*, 20 February 2004.
7 Sigmund Freud, 'The Neuro-Psychoses of Defence', 1894, *The Standard Edition of the Complete Psychological Works*, 24 vols (London, Hogarth 1953–73), vol. 3.
8 Freud, 'Screen Memories', 1899, *Standard Edition*, vol. 3.
9 Tom Segev discusses the extent to which later Arab attacks were seen as pogroms in *One Palestine Complete – Jews and Arabs under the British Mandate* (London, Abacus 2000), pp. 137-8, pp. 180-1, pp. 324-5.
10 According to Daud Abdullah of the Palestinian Return Centre, 2 per cent of Israelis live on refugee land, 62 per cent of all refugees came from rural areas in Mandate Palestine, most of which villages are still vacant; over 75 per cent of Israelis live in 15 per cent of Israel's area. Letter to the *Guardian*, 9 January 2004.
11 Chaim Weizmann, 'Awaiting the Shaw Report', Paper 116, *Letters and Papers*, ed. Barnett Litvinoff (New Brunswick, NJ, Transaction Books 1983) vol. 1, set B p. 591.
12 Yeshayahu Leibowitz, 'Right, Law and Reality', 1976, in *Judaism, Human Values and the Jewish State*, ed. Eliezer Goldman (Cambridge, MA, Harvard University Press 1992), pp. 230-31.
13 Bhikhu Parekh, 'Finding a Proper Place for Human Rights,' *Displacement, Asylum, Migration*.
14 Hannah Arendt, 'Zionism Reconsidered', 1944, 'The Jewish State Fifty Years After – Where Have Herzl's Politics Led?', 1946, both in *The Jew as Pariah*, ed. Ron Feldman (New York, Grove Press 1978), p. 156, p. 172, p. 141.
15 In the original version of this essay, the second writer was David Grossman. In order to avoid repetition of the essay on Grossman, Chapter 5 in this

collection, I have replaced him with Hareven, a felicitous opportunity as I see it, since she is a writer I have only started to read recently, and whom I admire enormously.

16 Dorothy Thompson, *Refugees – Anarchy or Organisation* (New York, Random House 1938), p. 45. See also Edward Timms and Naomi Segal, eds., *Freud in Exile – Psychoanalysis and its Vicissitudes*, (New Haven, Yale University Press, 1988).

17 Ernest Jones, *Sigmund Freud – Life and Work*, vol. 3, *The Last Phase: 1919-1939* (London, Hogarth 1980), p. 254.

18 Thompson, *Refugees*, p. 5.

19 Ibid., p. 3.

20 Ibid., p. 6.

21 See David Goldberg, *The Divided Self – Israel and the Jewish Psyche Today* (London, Tauris 2006), pp. 117-18.

22 Thompson, *Refugees*, p. 107.

23 Arendt, 'Zionism Reconsidered', p. 139.

24 Thompson, *Refugees*, p. 78.

25 Theodor Herzl, *The Jewish State*, 1896, 2nd edn (Central Office of the Zionist Organisation, London 1934), p. 29.

26 Thompson, *Refugees*, pp. 102-3.

27 Herzl, *The Jewish State*, p. 70.

28 Thompson, *Refugees*, pp. 78-9.

29 S. Yizhar, 'The Story of Hirbet Hiz'ah', 1957, trans. from the Hebrew Harold Levy, *Caravan*, A Jewish Quarterly Omnibus, ed. Jacob Sonntag (Yoseloff 1962).

30 Sigmund Freud, *Freudiana – From the Collections of the Jewish National and University Library* (Jerusalem, 1973), cited by Yosef Hayim Yerushalmi, *Freud's Moses – Judaism Terminable and Interminable* (New Haven, Yale University Press 1991), p. 13.

31 Weizmann, 'Zionism Needs a Living Context', 1914, in Arthur Hertzberg, *The Zionist Idea*, (Philadelphia and Jerusalem, Jewish Publication Society, 1977), p. 575.

32 Raja Shehadeh, *The Third Way – A Journal of Life in the West Bank* (London, British Zionist Federation, 1919), pp. 87-9.

33 Weizmann, 'Awaiting the Shaw Report', p. 598; *Zionist Policy – An Address*, British Zionist Federation 1919, p. 10.

34 David Ben-Gurion, *Israel – A Personal History*, trans. Nechemia Myers and Uzy Nystear (New York, Funk and Wagnalls 1971).

35 *Freudiana*, cited by Yerushalmi, *Freud's Moses*, p. 13.

36 Shulamith Hareven, *The Desert Trilogy*, 1988, 1990, 1996, trans. from the Hebrew by Hillel Halkin, (San Francisco, Mercury (1996).

37 Hareven, 'Israel: The First Forty Years', 1988, in *The Vocabulary of Peace*, p. 109.

38 Ibid.

39 Cited in Hareven, 'Israel: The First Forty Years', p. 101.

40 Ibid., pp. 110-11.

41 Ibid., p. 111.

42 Hareven, 'The Witness', 1980, trans. Dalya Bilu, in *Stories from Women Writers of Israel – An Anthology* (New Delhi, Star 1995), p. 78.

43 Ibid., p. 82.
44 Ibid., p. 81.
45 Idith Zertal, *Israel's Holocaust and the Politics of Nationhood* (Cambridge, Cambridge University Press 2005), and *From Catastrophe to Power – Holocaust Survivors and the Emergence of Israel* (Berkeley, University Of California Press 1998).
46 Dror Mishani, 'The Two Continua of Over There', *Ha'aretz*, 22 September 2006, p. 2.
47 Hareven, 'The Witness', p. 73.
48 Ibid., p. 90.
49 Ibid., p. 91, p. 92.
50 Ibid., p. 94.
51 Ibid.
52 Ibid., p. 98.
53 Hareven, 'The Man Who Descended into Inferno', 1990, in *The Vocabulary of Peace*, p. 142.
54 Hareven, 'Israel: The First Forty Years', p. 109.
55 Hareven, 'Identity: Victim', p. 152.
56 Hareven, 'The Man Who Descended into Inferno', p. 141.
57 Ibid.
58 Hareven, 'Identity: Victim', p. 151.
59 Ibid.
60 Hareven, 'Israel: The First Forty Years', p. 96.
61 Ibid., p. 116.
62 Ibid.
63 Hareven, 'Identity: Victim', pp. 152-3.
64 Chris McGreal,'I can't imagine anyone who considers himself a human can do this,' *Guardian*, 28 July 2003.
65 He was speaking at the Second Pan-European Conference, held in Canisy, February 2003.
66 Jacques Lacan, 'The Function and Field of Speech and Language in Psychoanalysis', 1953, *Écrits* trans. Alan Sheridan (London, Tavistock 1977), p. 86, my emphasis.
67 Elizabeth Bowen, *The Heat of the Day*, 1948, (Harmondsworth, Penguin 1962), pp. 91-2.
68 W.G. Sebald, *Austerlitz*, (London, Hamish Hamilton 2001), pp. 359-60.
69 Ibid., pp. 19-20.
70 Ibid., p. 21.
71 Ibid., pp.16-17.
72 Sara Roy, 'The Legacy of Edward Said'. Symposium organised by the *London Review of Books*, School of Oriental and African Studies, London University, 28 November 2003. Thanks to Sara Roy for sending me the piece. See also Adam Philps, 'Palestinian Olive Trees Sold to Rich Israelis', *Palestinian Monitor*, 28 November 2002.

3

Mass Psychology*

It is a commonplace assumption that psychoanalysis only deals with individuals. More, or worse – loyal to its origins in the social milieu and mind of its founder, Sigmund Freud – the only individuals it deals with are an unrepresentative minority of the respectable, bourgeois and well-to-do. And yet, as Freud points out in the opening paragraph of *Mass Psychology and the Analysis of the 'I'*, without the presence of others, there can be no mental life. 'On close examination,' he writes, 'the antithesis between individual or mass psychology, which at first glance may seem to us very important, loses a great deal of its sharpness.'[1] We only exist through the others who make up the storehouse of the mind: models in our first tentative steps towards identity, objects of our desires, helpers and foes. The mind is a palimpsest in which the traces of these figures will jostle and rearrange themselves for evermore. From the very earliest moment of our lives – since without the rudiments of contact, the infant will not survive – we are 'peopled' by others. Our 'psyche' is a social space.

With one, short, exception, all the texts discussed in this essay were written after the First World War, while the last one, *Moses the Man and Monotheistic Religion*, was composed while the clouds of the Second were gathering across Europe. In fact, you could argue that the whole of Freud's writing life was shadowed by the catastrophe biding its time, waiting in the wings, which will finally come to its cruel fruition with the outbreak of hostilities in September 1939, barely two weeks before he died. In 1897, two years after the first German publication of *Studies on Hysteria,* the Emperor of Austria, Franz Josef, reluctantly confirmed the anti-Semite Karl Lueger as mayor of Vienna (he had refused to do so no less than four times).[2] From that point on, no Jew in Austria could ignore the fact that the collective, or mass, identity of Europe was moving against the emancipatory tide. Enlightenment, the belief that a cool-headed reason could rule the world, was a dream; while the despised and dreaded unreason of the night

would soon be marching on the streets. In a way this should have been no
surprise to Freud. Such inversions were the hallmark of his craft. Nonetheless there are moments where Freud appears to be struggling to catch up
with his own insights. From *Mass Psychology* to *Moses the Man*, his last major
work, all Freud's writings on collective life share a question. What drives
people to hatred? Even in their dealings with those to whom they are closest,
Freud muses, people seem to display a 'readiness to hate', something
'elemental' whose roots are 'unknown'.[3] As if Freud had made two utterly
interdependent discoveries that also threaten to cancel or wipe each other
out, taking the whole world with them. No man is an island: you are the
others who you are. But the mind is also its own worst enemy; and there is
no link between individuals, no collective identity, which does not lead to
war.

In 1914, Freud had set out the basic terms of what has come to be known
as his second 'topography'. A previous distinction between love and hunger,
the drives of desire and those of self-preservation, between the other and the
'I', breaks down when he alights upon the problem of narcissism, the
subject's erotically charged relationship to her- or himself. If you can be your
own object, the neat line between impulses directed towards the self and
those tending towards the other starts to blur. But it is no coincidence that
this discovery of subjects hoist on their own self-regard should bring him up
so sharply against the question of how we connect to the others around us.
How indeed? No longer is it the case that what we most yearn for in others is
the satisfaction of our drives; what we are no less in search of, and
passionately require, is to be recognised, acknowledged, seen. Freud is
often wrongly taken to be interested only in the sexual drives (or, for the
truly reductive version, only in 'sex'), but that is half the story. If we need
others, it is not so much to satisfy as *to fashion* ourselves. And in this struggle
to conjure, and hold fast to our identities, there is no limit to what we are
capable of. From the outset, identification is ruthless; we devour the others
we wish to be: 'Identification [. . .] behaves like a product of the first *oral*
stage of libido organisation in which the coveted, treasured object was
incorporated by eating and was annihilated as such in the process.'[4] Over-
turning his model of the mind in the face of war, Freud thus arrives at the
problem of collective life. But he does so on the back of an analysis that has
made such life, in anything other than a deadly form, all but impossible.

What is a mass? At first glance, Freud's answer to this question would
seem to be contemptuous. ' "The people" ', he writes to his fiancée, Martha
Bernays, in August 1883, 'judge, think, hope and work in a manner utterly
different from ourselves' (if the scare quotes indicate a caution about his own
category, they also suggest his distaste). In a letter to her sister two years

before he had described them as a 'different species', 'uncanny', knowing the meaning of neither 'fear nor shame'. And yet even here there is a subtext. Anti-Semitism gives a different historical substance and context to what might otherwise appear as no more than a familiar and conservative revulsion against the mob. As a Jew, Freud knows what it is like to be the target of collective hate. In an altercation about an open window during a train journey to Leipzig in the same year, someone in the background shouts out: 'He's a dirty Jew!' 'With this,' he writes to Martha in December, 'the whole situation took on a different colour [. . .] Even a year ago I would have been speechless with agitation, but now I am different. I was not in the least frightened of that mob.' They were just a group of travellers sharing a train compartment. But, under the pressure of race hatred, the voice of one turns into a 'mob'.[5]

Even when Freud's remarks cannot be softened by such historical allusions, his revulsion seems to be at odds with a far more compassionate, politically nuanced, critique. As he continues his letter of August, it becomes clear that the 'people' are 'utterly different', not due to some inherent failing in their nature, but because they are so beset. The 'poor people', who become just '*the poor*', are 'too helpless, too exposed, to behave like us'; in their 'lack of moderation' they are compensating for being 'a helpless target for all the taxes, epidemics, sicknesses, and evils of social institutions'. By 1921, when *Mass Psychology* appears, the 'people' have become the 'masses'. Certainly the shift of vocabulary might suggest that any traces of empathy have been lost. The masses are gullible, suggestible, out of touch with reality, blind. Although Freud rejects Gustave Le Bon's idea of a specific herd-instinct, he accepts most of his characterisation of a mass as at once all-powerful and a mere straw swaying in the wind. Gathered-together individuals become both too heavy (the mass comes into being as *critical mass*) and too light; threatening – 'ready, in its awareness of its own strength, to be dragged into all sorts of atrocities such as might be expected only from an absolute, irresponsible power'– and prone: 'It wants to be dominated and suppressed and to fear its master.'[6] Freud acknowledges that masses are capable of 'great feats of renunciation in the service of an ideal';[7] they can rise as well as sink. But, whether lofty or base, people *en masse* are only inspired to an *extreme*. Averse to innovation, conservative; always – since time immemorial – the same.

Above all, the mass, lacking all inhibition, exposes the unconscious of us all: 'the unconscious foundation that is the same for everyone is exposed'.[8] Like the pervert and the hysteric, the mass, from which the bourgeoisie no less fiercely like to distinguish themselves, is showing us something that we all need to see (the mass is also contagious, which means that none of us is immune). Ugly, the mass lifts the veil of the night, releasing humans from cultural constraint – in the mass, man is allowed to do what no individual would dare. At moments, it is as if the mass *becomes* the unconscious – without logic, knowing 'neither doubt nor uncertainty', living a type of collective dream. Freud may be repelled; he may be frightened (despite the bravura of his letter to his fiancée in 1883). But he has also made man in the mass the repository of a universal truth: that human subjects suffer under the weight of repressive cultural imperatives that force them against their nature. By the time he writes *The Future of an Illusion* in 1927, that early insight into the poor as the bearers of the worst 'evils' of social institutions has become even more political and precise:

> If a culture has not got beyond the point where the satisfaction of some participants requires the oppression of others, maybe the majority (and this is the case with all contemporary cultures), then, understandably, the oppressed will develop a deep hostility towards a culture that their labour makes possible but in whose commodities they have too small a share.

'It goes without saying', he concludes, 'that a culture that fails to satisfy so many participants, driving them to rebellion, has no chance of lasting for any length of time, nor does it deserve one.'[9]

Although Freud calls his text 'Mass Psychology' (from the German '*die Massen*'), the core of his work centres on two great social institutions, the army and the church, and two intensely intimate conditions – being in love and hypnosis, in which, to use his own formula, we are dealing with 'if the expression will be permitted' a 'mass of two'.[10] Faced with such moments of awkwardness, most translations prior to Jim Underwood's for the new Penguin Freud, notably Strachey's *Standard Edition*, have chosen to translate 'mass' as 'group', giving us a 'group of two members', which no doubt causes less of a conceptual stir. But it is not for nothing that Freud, having first charted his path through the most threatening aspect of behaviour in the mass, lands us in the middle of two of society's most prized and refined collectivities, and at least one of its most cherished states of mind. In our normal run of thinking, there are 'groups' and there are 'masses' – the first of which it is assumed, unlike the second, always keeps its head in bad times. In fact we could say that it is the role of church and army, great policing institutions both, to channel the one into the other, to offer – against any menace in the wider world – the sanctuary of the group. In an ideal world, so this logic might go, there would be no masses, which however fiercely bound together, always seem unruly, as if threatening something loose. Freud's view is more radical, cutting through such precious distinctions. For all their gravitas and grace, church and army, in their very ability to generate unquestioning, sacred, loyalty, are microcosms of what they most fear. They seed what they are meant to contain.

It is central to Freud's thinking on this topic that what binds people together, for better and worse, is their commitment to an internal ideal. Because we are narcissists, we will only relinquish, or even circumscribe, our self-devotion for something or someone that we can put in the same place. Something that makes us feel good about ourselves. Something that tells us, even if we are a multitude, that somewhere, somehow we are also the only one. And that whatever we do – and this is the killer, so to speak – we are a cut and thrust above the rest. To be part of a group is to push everything hated to the outside (which is why for Freud, along with the more mundane, territorial reasons, nations go to war). Freud's originality however is to add to this insight the idea that rivalrous hostility towards the other is integral to the very formation of the group. I will suspend my hatred of the other, and bind my fate with his, if you – mentor, leader, father, God – recognise *me*. Clearly there is something amiss. How can rivalry be redeemed by the clamour for such exclusive attention? In one of his most trenchant, and clinically deceptive, formulas, Freud states: *'a primary mass is a number of individuals who have set one and the same object in the place of their ''I''-ideal and who have consequently identified with one another in terms of their ''I''.'*[11] That is what it means to become as 'one'. I will identify with you, but only on condition that the ideal you take for your own has become my internal psychic property. The group is an orchestrated flight into inner superiority, which everyone is then presumed to share. In a paradox Freud never succeeds in unravelling, hostility is suspended by narcissistic acclaim. But what this means is that when men – since it is most often men – band together to go to war, another state of war, barely refined, is most likely to be going with them.[12]

Two things, Freud insists, distinguish his account from the previous literature on which he so copiously draws (only Chapter 1 of *The Interpretation of Dreams* can rival *Mass Psychology* for the lengths to which he goes to incorporate other theories on his topic): love relationships: 'Let us remember that the existing literature makes no mention of them'; and the tie to the leader: 'For reasons that are as yet unclear, we should like to attach particular value to a distinction that the existing literature tends to underrate, namely that between leaderless masses and masses with leaders'; again, only a few pages later: 'we would already venture to level a mild reproach against the authors of the existing literature for having done less than justice to the importance of the leader as regards the psychology of the mass'; and even more forcefully towards the end: 'the nature of the mass is incomprehensible if we ignore the leader'.[13] 'The essence of a mass', Freud writes, 'consists in the libidinal attachments present within it.'[14] Love, then, and devotion to the leader are what binds. If the mass is held together by some force, 'to what force could such an achievement be better ascribed than to eros, which holds the whole world together?'[15]

Leaving aside for a moment the fact that the world does not obviously 'hold together', as Freud of course knows well, it is worth pausing here, and asking what Freud means by love. For psychoanalysis, as he explains, 'love' has a very wide range. It includes 'self-love, parental and infant love, friendship, general love of humanity, and even dedication to concrete objects as well as to abstract ideas'.[16] To deny the libidinal component of these attachments is only for the 'feeble-hearted'.[17] So, Freud concludes, 'we shall try adopting the premise that love relationships (to use an inert expression: emotional ties) also form part of the essence of the mass mind'.[18] It is on this basis that Freud takes us into the analysis of church and army. Love, it turns out, follows the path of identification when the loved object, requiring like a leader total surrender, *usurps* the place of the 'I' (all roads, it seems, lead back to the 'I'). So what are these love relationships or emotional ties which bind subjects *en masse*? They are precisely the experience of *being loved*; or to put it in more clichéd terms, not what I give to you, but what you give, or do for, me. To ignore the role of the leader, Freud writes, is not just a theoretical shortcoming but a practical risk. Under cover of a leader's love or benevolent knowing, even the world at its most perilous feels safe. Thus, he argues, it was not the realities of the battlefield, but ill-treatment by their superiors, that caused the breakdown of Prussian soldiers during the Great War.

And yet Freud is aware that this love of the leader is a precarious gift. Barely concealed behind any leader is the father who was hated as much as he was revered. In *Mass Psychology*, Freud slowly moves back to the theory first advanced in *Totem and Taboo* of 1913: that society originally came into being on the back of a primordial crime. The brothers banded together to murder the father who controlled all the women of the tribe. Once the deed was done, only guilt, plus the dawning recognition of the danger each brother now represented to the other, caused them to bind together and lay down their arms. Whether you accept the historical account or not – and there are no historical grounds to do so – Freud's myth, as always, is eloquent. Trying to explain how love averts hatred, his intellectual trajectory here, the very movement of his text and of his argument, takes a strikingly different path (regressive as he would say of the mass mind), as slowly but surely, he moves away from mutuality to murder. How solid can any group identification possibly be if the leader we love and who loves us all as equals is also, deep in the unconscious, the tyrant who must be killed? It would seem that the mass is only held together, like those first brothers, because it is aghast at its own history, its own actual and potential deeds. A mass freezes into place at its own dread. At the heart of Freud's analysis of the mass entity is a self-cancelling proposition. We love the other most, or need most to be loved by the other, when – from that other and from ourselves – we have most to fear. It is a 'miracle', Freud writes, that the individual is willing to 'surrender his "I"-ideal, exchanging it for the mass ideal embodied in the leader'.[19] A miracle like love, one might say; or like the belief that love conquers all.

It is almost too easy to see in Freud's portrait of the leader the outlines of his own personal drama as the founder of psychoanalysis. More simply, to see him as issuing a demand: Love me. Ever since the split with Jung in 1914, the year after he wrote *Totem and Taboo*, Freud had reason to fear that the love his followers bore him was laced with a hostility that could threaten his movement. What if his group, instead of being a free association of like-minded individuals, were one of those 'artificial masses', like church and army, in need of 'a certain external compulsion [. . .] to prevent them from falling apart'?[20] The only thing preventing a mass from behaving like an 'ill-mannered child', 'impassioned, unsupervised savage', or worse, like a 'pack of wild animals' is the agreed conditions laid down for it to function.[21] When Freud draws on W. McDougall's *The Group Mind* to lay out these requirements – a measure of continuity, a specific conception of the group's 'nature, function, attainments and aspirations', contact with related but differing collective entities, traditions, customs and institutions particularly such as bear on the relationship of its members with one another, a careful grading and differentiation of functions – it reads at least partly as a countdown against bedlam, his own wish to bind the chaos he might himself have unleashed.[22] As if he were describing a model for a psychoanalytic institution that would be a cross between a secret society and a bureaucratic machine. In *Mass Psychology*, we can see Freud already struggling with a dilemma that psychoanalysis as an institution has not solved to this day, even while it is the one institution that recognised that dilemma as foundational to what any subject, any institution, might be. How to aim for perfected organised continuity given the cruel ambivalence lurking within our most cherished forms of allegiance?

In his 1907 paper 'Compulsive Actions and Religious Practices', Freud suggests that religious ceremony shares its nature with compulsive or obsessional neurosis, in which subjects ritually perform actions designed to ward off the intolerable burden of a guilt-ridden mind. Condemned to the endless repetition of meaningless gestures, lacking the symbolic weight of the sacred, the compulsive neurotic, with his 'half-funny', 'half-sad' distortion of a private religion, is a clown.[23] Or perhaps a parodist, who mocks the petty rituals that in the modern day and age are thrusting the deeper content and meaning of religious faith to one side (one objection of enlightenment, Haskalah Jewry to the Orthodox in Freud's time was that they were burying the spirit of Judaism under a tide of observational constraints).[24] If religion apes neurosis, being part of a religious collective also assuages the mind. 'Even one who does not regret the disappearance of religious illusions in today's cultural climate', Freud concludes Mass Psychology, 'will concede that, while they still held sway, they afforded those in thrall to them their strongest protection against the threat of neurosis.'[25] Mass formation, and none so powerfully as religious mass formation, is therefore one of the most effective systems a culture creates to keep its subjects sane. It does this by deluding them with the false consolations of belief; but above all by allowing them to repeat, in the daily actions required of them as testament to that belief, the behaviour of a subject who knows he has a great deal to atone for. It keeps them sane but only by mimicking, and thence preserving, the very form of neurotic obsession. 'One might venture to construe' neurosis as 'individual religiousness', Freud writes in the 1907 paper, and religion as a 'universal compulsive neurosis'.[26] The neurotic – this is from the last pages of Mass Psychology – creates his own 'fantasy world, religion and system of delusion', but in so doing he is merely 'echoing the institutions of humanity in a distorted form'.[27] Once again, man's most revered institutions hold at the heart of their being the forms of disturbance from which they are intended to protect mankind.

In the move from Mass Psychology to The Future of an Illusion and Moses the Man, the question of faith gradually usurps that of mass formation only to rejoin, slowly but surely, the man in the crowd. To the end of his life, Freud was convinced that his view of faith as deluded, worse as a reaction formation akin to a neurotic disorder, was the view that set him most at odds with the surrounding culture. Translations prior to that of Jim Underwood have lost the link between religion as compulsion (as in Zwangsneurose) and Freud's later death drive or repetition compulsion (Wiederholungszwang), a link that drives religious sensibility firmly towards the demonic. Less repellent than sexuality, less radically disorienting than the idea of the unconscious, such a vision of religious belief nonetheless threatened to breach the most strongly fortified symbolic ramparts of civilised man. Even when he was writing Moses the Man across the Anschluss of Austria and his exile to London in 1938, Freud persisted in thinking that his critique of religion placed him at risk. He was a target of persecution first as disbeliever, only then as Jew: 'I should now be persecuted not only for the way I think but on account of my "race".'[28] 'The only person this publication may harm', he writes at a particularly defensive moment in *The Future of an Illusion*, 'is myself.'[29]

In many ways, Freud's critique of religion, laid out most ruthlessly in *The Future of an Illusion*, appears as something of a footnote to his view of the mass. After all, in *Mass Psychology*, the masses discard reality in favour of 'affectively charged wishful feelings'; they never 'thirst after truth'; they 'demand *illusions*'.[30] Although *The Future of an Illusion* is also the text in which Freud most loudly acknowledges their oppression, from its opening section, the masses appear as the concentrate of their worst attributes (lethargic, unreasonable, unpersuadable, incapable of restraint). For anyone wanting to limit the damage, Freud's response to the acrimony unleashed by *The Future of an Illusion* in *Civilization and its Discontents* two years later only makes matters worse. 'The whole thing is so patently infantile, so incongruous with reality, that to one whose attitude to humanity is friendly, it is painful to think that the great majority of mortals will never be able to rise above this view of life.'[31] This does not sound friendly. Galled, humiliated ('it is even more humiliating . . .') – Freud loses patience like an irascible father trying to correct the homework of his child. Unless they happen to be the child whose tale he recounts in *The Future of an Illusion*, precociously distinguished by his love of 'objectivity', who, when told that a fairy story was not true – a story to which other children had been listening 'with rapt attention' – 'assumed a scornful expression and withdrew'.[32] Who, we might ask, is most to be pitied in this story – the boy trapped in his deadening 'matter-of-factness', or the other children, whose reverie he will presumably have torn apart with his contempt? For Freud, engaging with the opponent he conjures for the sake of argument throughout *The Future of an Illusion*, this anecdote is meant to be decisive. Like the child, humanity will stop believing when it grows up: 'a turning away from religion must be expected to occur with the fateful inexorability of a growth process' (note how that 'fateful' places our cool emancipation from faith in the lap of the gods).[33] Nothing in the twenty-first century to date suggests this is the case.

The Future of an Illusion is a diatribe. In many ways it is also, I would suggest, Freud's most un-Freudian text, and one which will return to haunt him in the final years of his life. Religion infantilises the people, consoles them for the inconsolable, suppresses their wholly legitimate and unanswerable fears. The world is brutish and nature does not care. When we most think to have controlled her, she strikes ('coldly, cruelly, without a qualm').[34] The elements mock our restraint, the earth heaves and splits open, waters drown, storms blow everything away. This is Freud in

imitation of Lear. Add the contingency of human diseases, the random
inevitability of our own deaths, and we have every reason to despair: 'there
remains an uncomfortable suspicion that the bewilderment and helplessness
of the human race is beyond remedy'.[35] To add insult to injury, we heap
suffering upon each other: 'passions rage in the elements as they do in the
human heart'.[36] Enter religion, which tells us that none of this – in the final,
cosmic, order of things – matters. We are protected by a benevolent God
who redeems our helplessness even when we are unaware (although
believing in Him of course helps). Most simply, we are watched over.
Someone is looking. The values of our ideals are, Freud repeats here from
Mass Psychology, narcissistic in nature. Even more than our saviour, God is
our spectator. The citizens of America, which proclaims itself 'God's own
country', share with the Jewish people, although Freud coyly does not name
them here, the belief that God has made their nation his own: 'and for one of
the forms in which humans worship the deity that is indeed true'.[37] How
deep must be the narcissistic wound of humanity, if the only way to redeem
it is to feel yourself swelling to the measure of the heavens?

The Future of an Illusion offers Freud's most passionate defence of the order
of reason. There is, he insists, no 'higher authority'.[38] Vernunft in German,
which means reason or even more prosaically 'good, common, sense', has
none of the ambiguous flexibility of Geistigkeit, central to Moses the Man,
which hovers between 'intellectuality', but with none of the negative
connotations of aridity attaching to it in the English, and 'spirituality', as
an internal quality with no specifically religious meaning (a term therefore
eloquently suspended between heart and brain). 'Reason', on the other
hand, brooks no argument (as in 'it stands to reason'). Freud is pitting
'reason' against 'illusion', pitting, at its crudest, the educated elite against the
mass – a 'split', as his opponent in the text argues, between the 'philosophical
thinker' and the 'uneducated mass'.[39] Once again Freud's view of the people
en masse is uncharitable. As Freud describes them, the arguments for religious
belief are self-defeating, 'oddly out of harmony with one another': our
forefathers believed them; we possess proof from distant times; no justification of belief is permitted or required.[40] But, according to Freud's own
analysis, this is the logic of the unconscious or what he defines in a famous
passage in The Interpretation of Dreams as 'kettle logic', the logic of a man
defending himself against his neighbour's charge that he has returned his
kettle in a damaged state: I never borrowed it; it doesn't have a hole; the
hole was there when you lent it to me. Freud therefore knows that the
illogic of this form of reasoning is a sign that a particularly deep vein of
psychic investment (Besetzung) has been tapped. Strachey translated Besetzung as cathexis, the Latin inappropriate, the technicality off-putting for a

term meant to indicate our most heartfelt and obdurate attachment both to others and to parts of ourselves. Underwood's more recent version offers instead 'charging', as in an electrical current, which is far closer to the urgency of Freud. Of all people, Freud should know better than to think that you can walk into this part of the mind and try to *reason with it*. No one enters here without being burnt.

Freud allows his fictional opponent to articulate many of these criticisms (this is the only text, apart from his 1926 *The Question of Lay Analysis*, in which Freud personifies one half of the argument he is almost always having with himself). But he does so only the more stubbornly to argue him to the ground. Freud believes not only that religious belief is deluded and infantile, but also that it deprives human subjects of freedom (it is the ultimate form of surrender). Because religion ultimately fails to console humans for death, so it shifts increasingly and inexorably into the domain of human affairs, arrogating to itself the ethical life, whose precepts are meant to keep subjects in their place. It is therefore a way of subduing their legitimate internal revolt against the constraints and injustices of culture, on which Freud, as we will see in Chapter 8, was so articulate from the time of the First World War. At moments, Freud's defence of his position reads like Bertolt Brecht's Galileo whose discoveries, as the Church well knew, were a threat as much to secular as religious authority. 'Truth', states Galileo in Brecht's play, 'is the child of time, not of authority'; 'I believe in the gentle power of reason, of common sense over men'.[41] Compare Freud: 'the voice of the intellect is a low one, yet it does not cease until it has gained a hearing'[42] (Freud compared himself directly with Copernicus, as well as with Darwin, for dethroning man from the centre of all things).

What Freud desires most fervently in this work is that man should generate his ethical precepts out of himself, that he should 'leave God out of it entirely', and 'frankly concede the purely human origin of all cultural institutions and rules'.[43] He does not therefore want the constraint of culture abolished. Unlike some of his later followers, such as Herbert Marcuse and Wilhelm Reich, he was no libertarian; indeed he believed that religion was failing to make man moral, was not taming the 'anti-social drives' *enough*. If man knew himself to be the source of his own authority, he would not seek to overturn the precepts of culture; he would try to *improve* them. Presumably – if we recall Freud's statement that a culture based on flagrant inequality does not deserve to survive – he would make them more just. Freud's biographer Ernest Jones is convinced that Freud's positive interest in religion, which the reader would be forgiven for not picking up here, stemmed not from theological concerns but from 'the ethical teach-ing', particularly 'on the theme of justice'.[44] 'By withdrawing his expectations from the Beyond and concentrating all the forces thus released on earthly existence', Freud concludes near the end of his text, 'he will doubtless manage to make life bearable for all and ensure that culture quite ceases to oppress.'[45] In this he anticipates many of today's critics of fundamentalism. A secular polity would make the world a better place.

And yet there remains something unpersuasive about this text. By the time Freud wrote it, he had become convinced that religion preserved deep inside its unconscious archive a forgotten or repressed historical truth. God is the direct descendant of the primal father; that is why, in our petitions to the deity, our dreadful helplessness is our strongest suit. By reiterating here his belief in a primary parricide at the origins of all culture, Freud is allowing therefore that religion is a form of reminiscence, and that this historical reality is what endows it with much of its powers. And yet he sweeps past this recognition with remarkable haste. Not to say panic. Of course 'acknowledging the historical value of certain religious teachings increases our respect for them', but that, he insists, in no way invalidates the desire to do away with them. 'Quite the contrary!' It is 'thanks to these historic residues' that the analogy between religion and neurosis can be made; as with the neurotic patient it is time to replace repression with 'ratiocination'. In any case, 'we need make no apology' for departing from 'historical truth' in providing a rational motivation for culture as this truth is so distorted as to be unrecognised by the mass of humanity.[46] This is indeed kettle logic and to see it you do not have to accept Freud's view of primary murder at the origins of mankind: there is a truth in religion; it is so distorted the masses cannot see it anyway; reason is more important than historical truth.

As with *Mass Psychology*, it is as if murder returns to haunt the barely acquired, fragile, rational civility of the tribe. Freud does not know where to put this murder, because he loves his new theory and in *Moses the Man* he will place it at the very core of the Jewish tradition and faith; indeed murder will become what most intensely ties the Jewish people to their law. The question, as Freud knows only too well, is not whether religion is true but why it has the power to bind its adherents (a fact to which he will ascribe the Jew's ability to survive). What matters, we might say, is not reason and reality, but – to refer again to *Mass Psychology* – the force of human identifications, whether lethal or redemptive (indeed often both). Or, going back to the very beginning of Freud's work, people – and the force of this later writing is to show how that includes 'peoples' – invent themselves out of their memories; what counts is not the accuracy, but the productivity, not the strictness, but the movement, of the meanings we make. Near the end of *The Future of an Illusion*, Freud agrees that reason can do nothing when religion proclaims a 'superior spiritual essence whose properties are indeterminable and whose purposes are unknowable'.[47] The German here is 'geistigen Wesens'; a term untranslatable into English as we have already seen, meaning spirituality or intellectuality or both. In the end, Freud leaves us with the glowing residue of his own conviction – something that cannot be fully determined, grasped or known (like the unconscious we might say). What if religion were determined by tradition, memory, murderousness, by indefinable qualities of being and of the mind? What if – as one of the twentieth century's most famous godless Jews was perhaps best placed to discover[48] – this, or at least some of this, is what it means to belong?

On 6 May 1926, an address by Freud was read to the Vienna lodge of B'nai Brith (Sons of the Covenant), an order representing Jewish cultural, intellectual and charitable interests originally founded in the United States, to which Freud, outcast as he had felt himself to be in the beginning, had addressed many of his early papers. 'Whenever I felt an inclination to national enthusiasm,' he states, 'I strove to suppress it as being harmful and wrong, alarmed by the warning examples of the peoples among whom we Jews had lived.' 'But', he continues, 'plenty of other things remained over to make the attraction of Jews and Jewry irresistible – many obscure emotional forces all the more powerful the less they could be expressed in words, as well as a clear consciousness of an inner identity, the intimate familiarity of the same psychic construction' ('die Heimlichkeit der gleichen seelischen Kon-struction', translated by Reik as 'the secrets of the same inner construction').[49] This identity, which Freud here as elsewhere scrupulously detaches from national passion, was not simple; and, even though he will refer to it on occasion as an essence, in many ways as we shall see it was not 'clear'. It was after all the whole burden of his 1919 paper on the uncanny – 'Das Unheimliche' – that what is heimlich or 'homely/familiar', the term he uses here, is intimately, not to say eerily, related to its opposite. Nonetheless, what Freud is describing is undoubtedly a sense of belonging. Crucially, that sense stems from those same dark, obscure 'emotional forces' ('all the more powerful the less they could be expressed in words') that Freud will turn on so ruthlessly in The Future of an Illusion the following year.

In 'A Religious Experience', written in the same year as The Future of an Illusion, Freud tells the story of a young American physician who first discards all religious belief and then is promptly reconverted by an inner command, after witnessing the corpse of an old woman laid out on the dissecting table. Freud, in one of his most reductive moments, traces the conversion to deferred obedience to the man's Christian father, against whom the young man, appalled by the sight of the 'sweet-faced old woman' (for which read the mother), had momentarily but violently rebelled. And yet he knows that the very simplicity of his own analysis – 'so simple, so

transparent' – deceives: 'One cannot avoid asking whether [. . .] anything at
all has been gained as regards the psychology of religious conversion.'[50]
What, to repeat his own question in *The Future of an Illusion*, are the obscure
emotional forces – 'whose properties are undeterminable and whose
purposes are unknowable' – on which religious affiliation relies?[51] Or in
the words of *Moses the Man*: 'From what springs do some ideas, particularly
religious ideas, draw the strength to subjugate individuals and nations
alike?'[52] In the final years of his life, under the threat of impending exile,
Moses the Man erupts as the unfinished business of *The Future of an Illusion*, as
the return of its repressed. 'We find to our surprise', Freud writes in the first
Viennese foreword to the last essay of *Moses* (the second was written in
England), 'that progress has forged an alliance with barbarism.'[53] Freud
knew he had not answered the question of his earlier work; something, in
his words, 'remained over'. But it was another ten years, in the last major
work of his life, before he offered his final unexpected reply.

If *Moses the Man* returns Freud to the question of religion, it also returns him
to that of mass psychology. The Jewish people become the testing ground of
how viable it is to insert the notion of the unconscious into collective life.
Much will hang on this, but if anything Freud is now more cautious: 'It was
not easy, I admit, bringing the concept of the unconscious into mass
psychology'; and increasingly unsure as he proceeds: 'We do not find it
easy to transfer the concepts of individual psychology to mass psychology.'[54]
By 1938, this 'mass' has become as much a national, as a religious, entity; at
issue now is the strength of religion to subjugate 'individuals *and nations*
alike'.[55] Religion, Freud more or less states, forges nations. Nationhood is,
or can be, a religious passion. Freud may have wanted to believe that
religious beliefs would go away; but instead he seems to be issuing a rather
different warning – against the power of national identities, as everything in
more recent times confirms, to endow themselves with the aura of the
sacred.

Faced with the rise of Nazism and the growing prospect of invasion and
exile – although until February 1938 he persisted in thinking that the
Anschluss could be averted – Freud found himself up against nationalism in
two of its most radically disconcerting shapes. Both can be felt pressing on his
study of Moses. On the one hand, a ruthless and expansive German
nationalism, its masses in thrall to their leader (Nazism as hypnotic collectivity in its purest most deadly guise); on the other, the nationalism of a
dispossessed people, arising at least partly in response to the excesses of the
first, but whose history and inner identity offers – or at least this is Freud's
hope and claim here – the possibility of another, more nuanced, form of

belonging. Freud does not mention Hitler in this work; he could hardly do so of course as long as he remained in Austria where the bulk of the work was written. But it is, surely, impossible not to see the German leader, traced in a type of grotesque reflection, behind the man held – as Freud puts it in his opening lines – to be the 'greatest son' of the Jewish people. Remember too that Freud up to now has offered no portrait of the leader; in *Mass Psychology*, there was no sign of the figure on whom, as he repeatedly insisted, his whole analysis relied.

In his address to B'nai Brith, Freud spoke of 'national enthusiasm' as 'being harmful and wrong, alarmed by the warning examples of the peoples among whom we Jews had lived'. Jewish national belonging must be different. In his famous letter of 1930, after the Arab riots in Palestine, he refused an appeal from Dr Chaim Koffler of the Jewish Agency to add his voice to those of prominent European intellectuals calling for a reversal of British policy on access to the Wailing Wall and on Jewish immigration to Palestine. Writing to Ferenczi in 1922, Freud had spoken of 'strange secret yearnings in me – perhaps from my ancestral heritage – for the East and the Mediterranean'; but these yearnings aroused his own suspicion, and when Arnold Zweig returned from a visit to Palestine in 1932, he described it as this 'tragically mad land' that has 'never produced anything but religions, sacred frenzies, presumptuous attempts to overcome the outer world of appearance by the inner world of wishful thinking'.[56] (Both the letter to Koffler and the exchange with Zweig are discussed at length in Chapters 1 and 2 of this collection.)

Yet despite this anxious recognition and recoil (in which we can recognize a barely concealed orientalist revulsion towards the East), in his letter to the Jewish Agency, Freud does not rule out the creation of 'a Jewish homeland'. By 1935, he describes the World Zionist Organisation as 'a great and blessed' instrument in its endeavour 'to establish a new home in the ancient land of our fathers'.[57] By then what is at issue for Freud, and not only for Freud, is 'our invincible will to survive'.[58] In *Moses the Man*, Freud attempts the almost impossible task of squaring the circle of this tragic historical moment. Can there be a form of survival for a people that does not fatally – fatally, that is, for itself and for the others against whom it stakes its claim to existence – entrench and sanctify itself? Freud does not seem to believe for a minute, as he does for religious faith, that 'national enthusiasm' can be reasoned away. What is the likely fate of a longing that you can only, in his words, 'suppress'?

It may seem odd to suggest that the thesis of *Moses the Man and Monotheistic Religion* is simple; after all the book is, as Yosef Yerushalmi describes it in his magisterial reading – *Freud's Moses – Judaism Terminable and Interminable* –

possibly the most opaque of Freud's works.[59] It was published piecemeal and with anxiety, the first two parts in *Imago*, the third with two 'mutually contradictory' prefaces – the first of which stating that it will never be published – while the complete text was not published until after he died.[60] The work is repetitive and uneven, bearing all the signs of a hesitation only partly explicable by the length of time it took him to write it and the unique historical conditions under which it was composed ('internal misgivings coupled with external constraints').[61] Freud was never at ease with it: 'I miss the sense of oneness and solidarity that ought to exist between the author and his book'; he could see how it might appear as 'a cast-iron figure resting on feet of clay'; or 'a dancer balanced on the tip of a single toe.'[62] To read Freud's *Moses*, writes Lydia Flem, 'is to read Freud writing *Moses*'.[63] It is in *Moses the Man* that Freud famously describes historical writing, on which he is himself at least partly engaged here, as a corrupt and murderous craft: 'The corruption of a text is not unlike a murder. The problem lies not in doing the deed but in removing the traces.'[64] By the time Freud arrived in England, the work was haunting him 'like an unlaid ghost'.[65] Accompanying him on his last journey, *Moses the Man* is, we could say, Freud's phantom limb (the hysteric of his earliest work returns at the end of his life). In the words of Russian Formalist Viktor Shklovsky, this is writing as '*attenuated tortuous speech*', whose point, as he puts it in words remarkably resonant of psychoanalysis, is to 'examine the object, *to dismember it*, to represent it not only as they [the artists] saw it, *but as they knew it*.'[66]

And yet, despite this oddness ('unorthodoxy' or 'eccentricity' in the words of Strachey), it is one of Freud's most fiercely determined texts. Freud believes that Moses was an Egyptian, a prince, priest, or high official belonging to the ancient monotheistic cult of Aton that was swept away with the death of its founder, the Pharaoh Amenthopis or Akhenaten, in 1358 BC. Whereupon, Moses seized a semitic tribe, slaves of Egypt, as his people and led them to freedom in Canaan on condition that they adopt the religion to which his own people had proved so pitifully inadequate. The people rebel against Moses and murder him (not this time because he owned all the women, but because of the dreadful severity of his law). From that point onwards, monotheism and the crime fade in the life of the nation until, generations later, they meet up with a second Moses, son of the Midianite priest Jethro, who belongs to the cult of the volcanic god Yahweh, to which – in an act of partial historical remembrance and atonement – the religion of the first tribe is slowly but surely assimilated.

Freud takes his thesis of the murder of the first Moses from a then famous work by Sellin published in 1922 (when Freud was told that he had later recanted, he famously replied that Sellin was mistaken and should have stuck to his original idea). He takes the account of the second Midianite priest from the historian Eduard Meyer, and several of his contemporaries who argued that the Jewish tribes 'from which the people of Israel eventually emerged' took on a new religion at a certain point in time, not at Sinai, as the Bible has it, but in the locality of Meribah-Kadesh in a stretch of country south of Palestine.[67] Freud's crucial move – in a theoretical gesture that mimes the story he tells – is to *merge* them. Barely concealed behind the unity of the Jewish people, inside its most intimate, *heimlich*, 'inner identity' is an uncanny, *unheimlich*, doubling (for Freud doubling is one of the most effective vehicles of the uncanny). Nothing simply belongs. Once again the issue is not the – much contested and indeed dubious – accuracy of his narrative, but its effects. Like a compulsion, Freud's account and his history repeat themselves: 'constant repetitions and recapitulations' to use Strachey's terms.[68] What does it mean to insist, as Freud does here, that a people were founded, their divine election established, not in one unanswerable moment of recognition between the people and their God, not once, but twice? Freud was not alone in pointing to this duality in Jewish history, but he adds and embroiders, making it the driving force of the people. *Moses the Man* – the original title only recently restored in Underwood's translation – is therefore something of a misnomer. What type of historical novel was Freud envisaging that cuts its hero into two?

> Putting our conclusion in the shortest possible form of words, to the familiar dualisms of that history (*two* peoples coming together to form the nation, *two* kingdoms into which that nation divides, *two* names for god in the source writings of the Bible) we add two new ones: *two* religious inaugurations, the first forced out by the second but later emerging behind it and coming victoriously to the fore, *two* religious inaugurators, both of whom went by the same name Moses.[69]

It is, as Freud was only too aware, an embarrassment of riches that is also the cruellest act of dispossession.[70] Imagine a child from a broken home with a father and a stepfather, stating in all innocence, as pure matter of fact: 'I do not have one' (meaning 'I do not have *one* father, but *two*'). Freud is sowing dissension in the tribe. He does not want his people unified. Or if he does, he wants them unified differently. Not singular, created once in an act of divinely sanctioned recognition, which henceforth will brook no argument, but torn internally by the fragments of a complex, multiple past.

Above all, he wants the Jewish people, and through them all people, to imagine the unimaginable – to contemplate the possibility that the most binding social ties are forged through an act of violence. 'All these distinctions', Freud writes, 'are inevitable consequences of the first, namely that one component of the people had been through what has to be defined as a traumatic experience that the other had been spared.'[71] Trauma therefore first splits, and then forms, *fuses* the group. What binds people to their leader is that they killed him, although remembering the deed takes time. When Yerushalmi criticises Freud for suggesting that the Jews repressed this memory, given that 'the most singular aspect of Jewish tradition [is] its almost maddening refusal to conceal the misdeeds of the Jews', he is however missing the psychoanalytic point.[72] It is the characteristic of any compulsion (*Zwang*) that you endlessly berate yourself, that you atone, with unflagging and elaborate ceremonial, for everything apart from the one thing you most fear you might have done. For Freud, the subsequent emergence of Christianity, in which the son lays down his life for humanity, should be read as the next verse of this epic of denial and atonement (it must have been a dead father if only the death of a son can redeem it; and if a voluntary death is the penance, then murder must have been the original crime).

But if this narrative has a logic, one which we by no means have to accept at every turn, Freud's boldest move is to place at the heart of the group what it would most like to dispose of. The original, lost, faith returns to the group, slowly and tentatively, after a first ruthless rejection. Only after the encounter with the second Midianite priest does monotheism become the defining feature of religious belief. Right at the heart of the best, most fervently held conviction, Freud places doubt (we believe because we are not sure). Right at the centre of group adherence, he places killing. In 'The Disillusionment of the War', as we will see in Chapter 8, he had stated that we had not 'sunk so low as we had feared' because we had 'never risen as high as we believed'.[73] Now he spells it out. We are all killers or capable of being so, if only unconsciously. This is not however the soft insight that it might first appear to be, as in: we are all murderers at heart. By binding this insight into group life, Freud drives a stake through collective self-idealisa-tion. As if he were asking nations to consider a very different, less glorious, form of reckoning with themselves. To be a member of a group is to be a partner in crime. You are guilty by association.

As the new millennium already bears witness, war is almost invariably justified in terms of an outside danger or threat: the other is the aggressor; it is only in order to survive that you kill. Freud offers a counter-history. He takes slaying, at which subjects *en masse* excel, and hands it back to the people. Even the most innocent of people (and for Freud there are no pure innocents), believe somewhere that they are also culprits. What effect might it have on modern-day rhetoric against terrorism, or on its accompanying refrain of good versus evil, if it were acknowledged that what binds a people together, what drives a nation self-righteously across the globe, are the unspoken crimes and failings of its own past?

Moses's Egyptian provenance is central to this narrative, not just because it announces and crowns the losses and dislocations to come (in the opening line Freud acknowledges that he is denying robbing, depriving the Jewish people of their founder, or, as he puts it, 'their greatest son' – the German *abzusprechen* means more literally to 'take back the saying of').[74] But because, as Edward Said stresses in his vital rereading of the work for Israel–Palestine at the present time, it inscribes the Jewish people in a non-European heritage, 'carefully opening out Jewish identity toward its non-Jewish background' (while also attesting, as Egyptologist Jan Assman puts it in his 1997 study, *Moses the Egyptian*, to the fundamental importance of Egypt in the history of mankind).[75] This is a plea for a model for nationhood that would not just accept the other in its midst, nor just see itself *as other*, but that grants to that selfsame other, against which national and political identities define themselves, a founding, generic status at the origins of the group. Freud knows that this is a form of sacrilege as well as a huge risk, and not just to himself. After all, it was he who insisted in *Mass Psychology* that panic or breakdown in the mass is the result of loss of belief in the leader, not of legitimate fear even in the face of real danger. At the very moment when the Jewish people have most reason to fear, when they are faced with the rise of a leader who will set as his aim the destruction of the mass of European Jews, Freud removes their most ardently possessed figurehead at a stroke. Why, if not, surely, to suggest that it is time for groups to look for less rigid, potentially abject, forms of psychic and spiritual cohesion?

In fact it is possible to read *Moses the Man* as a critique of monotheism *tout court*. The gift that Moses bestows on his people is one that cannot be borne. This monotheism is 'rigid', intolerant, expansive and imperialist.[76] Claiming universality, it demands – in a gesture that has nothing to do with a critique of national identity – that 'godhood give up its national confines'.[77] As it gained in strength under Amenhotep, it achieved 'ever-greater clarity, consistency, brusqueness'.[78] The father-god it introduces is 'boundlessly dominant', 'jealous, strict and inexorable'.[79] In a word, monotheism is awful (US policy of 'shock and awe' in the 2003 invasion of Iraq could be said to take its cue from just such monolithic forms of psychic coercion). Monotheism ushers religious intolerance into the world. For Assman, it is a counter-theology because it renders idolatrous ancient polytheisms whose principle characteristic was that of being infinitely *translatable* into each other. Prior to monotheism, peoples worshipped different gods, but no one contested the existence of foreign gods or the legitimacy of foreign forms of worship. When monotheism cries false to strange gods, it shuts itself off and, with it, a whole galaxy of potential connections: 'False gods cannot be translated.'[80]

This was, as Assman calls it, the 'Mosaic distinction', and 'the most outspoken destroyer of the Mosaic distinction was a Jew: Sigmund Freud.'[81] In the long tradition that made Moses Egyptian, either historically (Manetho, Strabo, Toland) or in affinity, initiated into 'hieroglyphic wisdom and mysteries' (Spencer, Warburton, Reinhard and Schiller), it is always the rigid difference between monotheism and a more copious religious profusion that is stressed.[82] Jews were hated. Freud's stated objective in his work was, not as might have been expected, to understand anti-Semitism in the mind of the hater, but 'how the Jew came to attract this undying hatred'.[83] By making Moses an Egyptian, Freud liberates his people from the beginnings of their own theocracy. The founding moment of an oppressive law and intolerant faith fall outside Jewish jurisdiction. 'Who', Freud asks in a footnote, 'prompted the Jewish writer Heinrich Heine in the nineteenth century to complain about his religion as "the plague we dragged along with us from the Nile Valley, the unhealthy ancient Egyptian faith"?'[84] Judaism, to use the expression of Martin Buber in his essay 'The Two Centres of the Jewish Soul', 'itself is not of the Law'.[85] Freud is releasing Judaism from its own obduracy, its rigid orthodox strain. It is then perfectly possible to move from here back into the mystical counter-tradition inside Judaism itself. Writing to Jung in 1909, after a numerological discussion of the number 62, Freud states: 'Here is another instance of the specifically Jewish character of my mysticism.'[86] Kabbalah shares with psychoanalysis its belief in hermeneutics and the infinite permutations of words (Freud discusses the plurality of God's name in *Moses*). It also always contained an anarchic streak. Like the sixteenth-century mystical messiah Shabtai Svi, Freud can be seen as an iconoclast, leading his followers and his people, against the Law, into apostasy and freedom. (And in the *Zohar*, major document of the kabbalistic tradition, Moses is an Egyptian.)[87]

The Law will not strike. Thus Freud reads Michelangelo's 'wonderful', 'inscrutable' statue of Moses in San Pietro in Vincoli in Rome, as the prophet frozen in the moment before he breaks the tablets, restraining his anger, reining back his wrath as he descends from Mount Sinai to the spectacle of his backsliding people. He reads him, that is, as curtailing, even if only for a moment, the punishing component of his own God-given Law. There is no higher 'mental achievement', Freud concludes, than such restraint (we can feel the strength of Freud's own efforts to control himself in the face of his increasingly dissident followers). Freud visited the statue, which must have played its part in his later study, whenever he was in Rome as a type of pilgrimage, creeping out of the 'half-gloom' to 'support the angry scorn of the hero's glance', 'as though I myself belonged to the mob upon whom his eye is turned'. He is therefore Moses *and* the people (split in two like the history of the Jews that he will much later recount). But it is surely noteworthy that the only moment in all his writing when Freud identifies himself with the mob, he does so as *idolater*.[88]

If this were all, then *Moses the Man* might become prime evidence in the case for Freud's rejection of his own Jewish legacy (the book was criticised by some as anti-Semitic). As critics like Marthe Robert who take this line have pointed out, Freud did on occasion refer to his Jewishness as the bearer of hereditary illness, or 'taint'.[89] But, if we read through the text again, it seems that Freud is far more equivocal than this. Monotheism, together with the violence of its earliest history, is not just 'ruthless', 'intolerant', 'inexorable'; it is also the foundation of ethical life. If anything Freud makes even stronger in this last work the tie between guilt and justice: 'the act of patricide with which social order, the moral law, and religion had first come into being'.[90] Or in the words of Bluma Goldstein: 'violent acts can serve as a source not only of spirituality and intellectual achievement, but also of ethical codes for a just and virtuous life'.[91] As we have seen, in Freud's account, the Jewish people become so forcefully a group because of the murder that first bound them together. Only an unconscious identification of this depth and virulence will work. Because they are always unconsciously atoning, so they are always watching and being watched to make sure that the treatment they mete out to others is fair. Freud famously claims in *The Future of an Illusion* that justice arises out of envy: if I cannot be privileged, no one must.

But if the Jews are a just people, it is also because the Egyptian Moses gave to them a god 'as all-loving as he was all-powerful', who 'held out for men, as their highest goal, a life lived in righteousness and truth'. [92] (Akhenaten described himself in his inscriptions as 'living in *ma'at*' – 'truth, righteousness').[93] 'Is it not about time', asks the author of the article on anti-Semitism that Freud cites in his short piece, 'A Comment on Anti-Semitism' of 1938, 'we stopped tossing [the Jews] favours when they have a right to justice?' [94]

It does not matter, therefore, that the first Moses was slain; what was finest in his tradition survived and slowly but surely it usurped the law of the volcanic Yahweh who might appear, according to the more obvious sequence of events, to have replaced it. Amenhotep had been a pacifist. According to tradition, he rejected 'in his ethics all hatred and all acts of violence', sublimating all aggression, in the words of Freud's contemporary, psychoanalyst Karl Abraham, to an 'unusually far-reaching degree', allowing his religion to languish because, out of touch with reality, he lived in the peaceful idyll of his own dreams (Abraham was one of Freud's inner circle but the article is strangely not referred to by Freud).[95] Yahweh was, on the other hand, a conqueror, 'violent and bloodthirsty'.[96] 'For a people on the point of taking violent possession of fresh places to settle,' Freud writes, 'the god Yahweh was undoubtedly more suitable.'

Now we can perhaps see more clearly the advantages, as well as the fully political import, of having two Moses. Not just to disrupt the crushing monolith of national identity, but also so that Judaism, saved from its most exacting features (and one might add any conquering ambitions), can still be the fount of wisdom in the world. 'No one doubts', Freud states near the beginning of the final essay, that 'it was only the idea of this other god that enabled the people of Israel to survive all the blows of fate and has kept it alive to this day.'[97] Freud, we could say, takes the Jewish people's greatest son away with one hand, and gives him back with the other. The people, or rather the best of the people, survive. Freud's saga is a political narrative for our times. The Jewish people had two possible paths that they could take, and their history – in ways borne out so dramatically today – would be the struggle between them. In Freud's narrative, justice, not settlement, ethics not land, enables the Jewish people to survive. But he hardly could have anticipated that this split between his two figures of Moses, between conquering settlement and a people living in justice, would have such an afterlife, that, ten years after he wrote his work, it would become the most disturbing and intractable legacy to the Jewish people of the founding, in 1948 of the Israeli nation state. On 19 March 2004, Rabbis for Human Rights took out a full-page advertisement in Ha'aretz to express their support for their colleague Rabbi Arik Ascherman, on trial in Jerusalem for trying to prevent the demolition of two Palestinian homes: 'Zion will only be redeemed through justice and those who return to her through acts of righteousness.'[98] The first Moses, writes Freud, 'held out for men, as their highest goal, a life lived in righteousness and truth'.[99]

In Moses the Man, therefore, the question of faith is slowly but surely displaced by that of tradition: 'in what form is effective tradition present in the life of peoples'?[100] (This is Yerushalmi's basic argument.) The point, then, is no longer to dissipate faith with a blast of reason, but to understand, even respect, the unconscious transmission of mass or group. To understand why people, from generation to generation – with no solid ground and in the teeth of the most historically unsympathetic conditions – hold on (the ties of the mass have shifted into the descent of a people). Individual and collective join at the seam of historical identities transmitted over time – the analogy between the two, Freud insists here, is 'complete'.[101] If not Judaism as Law, then Jewishness as tenuous but tenacious remembrance, in the unconscious memory traces of the people, passes down through the ages. Freud never stopped believing in the inheritance of acquired characteristics even when science had moved on to genetics, even while he acknowledges here that biology has rejected this belief. It is, we could say, through Jewishness or *for Jewishness* that Freud's Lamarckianism also survives – in his discussion of *Moses*, Ernest Jones describes it as the 'weakest link'. Something is passed down even if we do not know how. As Freud wrote to Arnold Zweig: 'our forebears lived there [. . .] it is impossible to say what heritage from this land we have taken over into our blood and nerves'.[102] However much you try to destroy the law of the father, you are obedient to him at least in the unconscious interstices of inherited memory and time. For ever. Pushing it, you could argue that the very concept of 'deferred obedience', not to mention the primal murder of the father and indeed the whole Oedipal structure – all reiterated here – are intended to secure this legacy, this recognition of something all-enduring inside the mind, which was as violently repudiated as it was clung to by Freud. After all, his myth of Oedipus simply states that man kills his father and then must identify with the father he kills (the dead father enters the soul).

Turning to the future, we could say that the question of his Jewish identity propels Freud towards the idea of 'transgenerational haunting', a concept forged by Hungarian émigré analysts Maria Torok and Nicolas Abraham, significantly in the aftermath of this historical moment, as they tried to understand the silent persistence of the Holocaust in the minds of second-generation Jews. A child can be the bearer of the unspoken and often unspeakable legacy of her or his parents (the legacy passes in the unconscious not in the bloodstream).[103] You do not need Lamarck to believe that the sins and suffering of the fathers are visited on the sons. 'The deeper motives for hatred of the Jews', Freud writes, 'are rooted in the remote past. They operate out of the unconscious of nations.'[104]

What cannot be known or spoken now becomes key. In 1930, in the preface to the Hebrew edition of *Totem and Taboo*, Freud made this, his perhaps most famous statement about his Jewish identity:

> No reader of [the Hebrew version of this book] will find it easy to put himself in the emotional position of an author who is ignorant of the language of holy writ, who is completely estranged from the religion of his fathers – as well as from every other religion – and who cannot take a share in nationalist ideals, but who has never repudiated his people, who feels that he is in his essential nature a Jew and who has no desire to alter that

nature. If the question were put to him: 'Since you have abandoned all these common characteristics of your countrymen, what is there left to you that is Jewish?' he would reply: 'A great deal and probably its very essence.'[105]

No faith, no language, no nationhood – as Said stresses, Freud defines himself here as Isaac Deutscher's non-Jewish Jew; but for all that, or even *because of that*, he is Jewish in essence.

In the third and final essay, written across the passage into exile, things take a new turn. It is in this essay that Freud argues that the Jewish people are the bearers, and originators, of *Geistigkeit*, an intangible quality that, as we have already seen, represents the best of intellectuality (without the aridity), the best of spirituality (without religious constraint). Unquestionably an advance or progress – *Fortschritt*, the *fort* is the mark of the irrevocable, as in 'from this time on' or 'no turning back' – *Geistigkeit* stands for that moment when man's beliefs achieved a level of abstraction without which there would never have been ethics, justice, truth. It rides the distinction between paternity and maternity, the one a logical inference, the other an unavoidable empirical fact (motherhood is something affirmed by the evidence of the senses). The supreme achievement is to worship a god 'one cannot see'.[106] *Geistigkeit* leads humans to acknowledge 'spiritual powers' which, although they cannot be grasped by the senses, manifest 'undoubted even super-powerful effects'.[107] Freud writes this without so much as a backward glance to *The Future of an Illusion* in which, as we saw, any such powers were deeply suspect (although the question of emotional forces of 'indeterminable properties' and 'unknowable purposes' was already there).

Now to define a force as intangible or unknowable is to accord it the highest praise: ask Freud what was left to him that is Jewish and he would reply: 'A great deal and probably its very essence', although he continues, 'he could not now express that essence clearly in words'. 'We are as a group a mystery', Wulf Sachs, Lithuanian Jew and first practising psychoanalyst in South Africa, writes to Freud from Johannesburg on 1 August 1939 in response to reading *Moses the Man*, 'to ourselves and others.'[108] In the middle of writing the work, Freud writes to his sister-in-law Barbara Low on the death of psychoanalyst David Eder: 'We were both Jews and knew of each other that we carried this miraculous thing in common, which – inaccessible to any analysis so far – makes the Jew.'[109] *Geistigkeit*, we could say, is Freud's attempt to give substance, though that is not quite the right word, to this essence; or to solve the mystery, while preserving it, keeping its miraculous nature intact.

Above all, this achievement of *Geistigkeit* makes the Jewish people of

value *to themselves*. The Jews were not just chosen by their leader, the
qualities his faith bestowed on them gave them infinite worth in their own
minds: 'The "I" feels elated, it takes pride in renouncing the drives.'[110]
Moses, and through him his god, chooses the people. As Yerushalmi points
out, by retaining this from the Bible Freud turns his back on modern secular
Jewish liberalism for which such an idea had become an embarrassment. In
fact Moses does not just choose his people; he *creates* them – Freud is pushing
to its furthest conclusion the argument of *Mass Psychology* that without a
leader the mass cannot exist. Not for nothing does Freud entitle one section
of his work 'The Great Man' (his 'implacability' in dismissing everything
told about other gods as 'lies and deceptions' now becomes 'superb').[111] Like
all good leaders, but going one better, Moses raises the masses in their own
eyes: 'all such advances increase self-esteem, making people proud'.[112]
Through Moses, 'the self-esteem of the Jews' became, uniquely among
faiths, 'anchored' inside their religious belief.[113] We could say, tautologi-
cally, that their proudest possession becomes their pride. This is what gives
the Jewish people their 'toughness'.[114] *In extremis*, the Jews take as their
mantle the narcissism of the group. They become, so to speak, the supreme
embodiment of culture's good opinion of itself: 'The satisfaction that the
ideal gives to those involved in a culture is of a narcissistic nature.'[115] In the
process they become a people in whom Freud himself can likewise once
again take pride. That Yahweh was finally usurped by the god of Moses is
'evidence of a special psychic aptitude in the mass that had become the
Jewish nation'.[116] By the end of *Moses the Man*, the Jews, who make their
first appearance as 'a bunch of culturally backward foreign immigrants', have
completed the transformation from mass into people; they have become an
elite.[117]

Freud therefore turns Moses into an Egyptian, lets the stranger into the tribe.
He castigates the ruthlessness of monotheism, breaks apart the unity both of
the people and their faith. He places murder at the origins of the group. But
this is, finally, no simple iconoclasm. The integrity, the narcissistic unity and
at-oneness of the group, *returns*. Identity, as Jewish identity, reaffirms itself.
How could it not in 1938? In this final essay, Freud leads the Jewish people
into their true inheritance (*Moses the Man* can be read equally as betrayal or as
boast). But he has done so at a time and in the framework of an analysis
which suggests that identity, while it may indeed be necessary for the
survival of subjects and peoples, is no less a danger to both. The problem, not
least for the Jewish people, will not go away. Writing to Gershom Scholem
in reply to his criticisms of her study of Eichmann in 1963, Hannah Arendt
argues: 'the greatness of the people was once that it believed in God, and

believed in him in such a way that its trust and love towards him was greater than its fear. And now this people believes only in itself? What good can come out of that?' She was responding to an assertion by Golda Meir: 'Of course I do not believe in God; I believe in the Jewish people.'[118]

It seems therefore futile to try and decide whether Freud's essay on Moses puts him on the inside or outside of Jewish tradition. The only viable answer must surely be both. Freud defined himself as Jewish in 'essence' even as he feared – and not just for the obvious historical reasons – that psychoanalysis was being seen as a 'Jewish national affair' (ironically given their falling-out, it was only Jung's appearance on the scene that he believed would allow psychoanalysis to escape this danger). What Freud does teach us however, in a struggle present on almost every page of his own text, is how hard it is for any collectivity to avoid the potentially militant self-possession of the clan. Perhaps Freud was trying to do the impossible. How do you save a people at one and the same time from the hatred of others *and* from themselves?

Freud's ideal was Jabneh, the first Torah academy, where the life of learning became the highest aim. 'The fact that Rabbi Jochanan ben Zakkai immediately after the destruction of the Temple obtained from the conqueror permission to establish the first academy for Jewish knowledge', he wrote in a 1938 letter to Dr Jacob Meitlis of the Yiddish Scientific Institute in Vilno, 'was for me always one of the most significant manifestations of our history';[119] Jabneh also appears in *Moses*: 'henceforth it was holy scripture and the spiritual effort that held the scattered nation together'.[120] But Freud also identified with Moses the hero, seeing his life as the founder of psychoanalysis in terms of conquest in a hostile world (the 'Man Moses' in the title restored in this translation redeems the faith). Psychoanalysis offers us the spectacle of a Janus-faced discipline or way of thinking, at once combative and, as it turns to what Freud terms here 'the darkness of the inner life', in retreat.[121]

'A Note on Anti-Semitism', which appeared in a German journal in Paris in November 1938, was, as a gloss appended to the title stated, the first of Freud's works to be published since his exile from Vienna. It consists almost entirely of a long quotation from an article – 'so extraordinary that I selected excerpts from it to use myself' – about whose source, as the last lines of the piece establish, Freud is completely unclear.[122] Commentators have therefore speculated that Freud himself is the author of a critique of anti-Semitism that he has chosen to place in the mouth of a non-Jew. As if to say: in his analysis of Moses he could only do so much; in the end the persecutor must look to himself. But whether these are Freud's own words or not, the effect is the same. Either way, by copiously citing or by inventing, the distinction breaks down, the two fuse. As they must if race hatred is ever to end, Jew and non-Jew speak with one voice, cross over to the other's place. Wonderfully encapsulating the hardest part of his endeavour, this last piece thus performs in the very form of its writing the task whose difficulty Freud proclaims more or less on every page of all these works. Issuing its challenge to the crisis of the times and beyond, the journal in which the article appeared was called *The Future – A New Germany, a New Europe*.

In each of the writings discussed here, psychoanalysis steps outside its own doors, claims its status as fully social analysis, whether between people (empathy, identification, hypnosis and loving) or across the generations (memory, tradition, faith). Even when we dream, we are not alone. Our most intimate psychic secrets are always embedded in the others – groups, masses, institutions and peoples – from which they take their cue, playing their part in the rise and fall of nations. Not to recognise this is, finally, the greatest, most dangerous, illusion of them all.

*First published as 'Introduction' to Sigmund Freud, *Mass Psychology and Other Writings*, Penguin Modern Classics, 2004.

Notes

1 Sigmund Freud, *Mass Psychology and Other Writings*, trans. Jim Underwood, (London, Penguin Modern Classics 2004), p. 17; all quotations, unless otherwise stated, are taken from this edition.
2 See Dennis B. Klein, *Jewish Origins of the Psychoanalytic Movement* (Chicago, University of Chicago Press 1981); Carl E. Schorske, *Fin-de-siècle Vienna – Politics and Culture* (Cambridge, Cambridge University Press 1981); Steven Beller, *Vienna and the Jews 1867-1938* (Cambridge, Cambridge University Press, 1989).
3 Freud, *Mass Psychology*, p. 54.
4 Ibid., pp. 57-8.
5 *The Letters of Sigmund Freud*, selected and edited Ernst L. Freud (New York, Basic Books 1960), cited Marthe Robert, *From Oedipus to Moses – Freud's Jewish Identity*, trans. Ralph Mannheim, Littman Library of Jewish Civilisation (London, Routledge and Kegan Paul 1974), pp. 46-7.
6 Freud, *Mass Psychology*, p. 36, p. 26.
7 Ibid., p. 26.
8 Ibid., p. 22.
9 Ibid., p. 117.
10 Ibid., p. 68.
11 Ibid., p. 69, original emphasis.
12 For a discussion of some of these internal paradoxes see Mikkel Borch-Jacobsen, *The Freudian Subject*, trans. Catherine Porter (Basingstoke, Macmillan 1988), ch. 3 'The Primal Band'; also 'The Freudian Subject: From Politics to Ethics', translated by Richard Miller and X.P. Callahan, in *The*

Emotional Tie – Psychoanalysis, Mimesis and Affect (Stanford, Stanford University Press 1992).

13 Freud, *Mass Psychology*, p. 43, p. 45, p. 47, p. 73.
14 Ibid., p. 47.
15 Ibid., p. 43.
16 Ibid., p. 41.
17 Ibid., p. 42.
18 Ibid., p. 43.
19 Ibid., p. 84.
20 Ibid., p. 45.
21 Ibid., p. 36.
22 Ibid.
23 Ibid., p. 5.
24 For a discussion of Freud in relation to *Haskalah* see Marianne Krull, *Freud and His Father*, trans. Arnold Pomerans (New York, Norton 1986), and also Yosef Hayim Yerushalmi, *Freud's Moses – Judaism Terminable and Interminable* (New Haven, Yale University Press 1991), pp. 62-3.
25 Freud, *Mass Psychology*, p. 98.
26 Ibid., p. 11.
27 Ibid., p. 98.
28 Ibid., p. 220.
29 Ibid., p. 144.
30 Ibid., p. 27.
31 Sigmund Freud, *Civilization and its Discontents*, 1930, trans. David McLintock (London, Penguin Modern Classics 2002), p. 12.
32 Freud, *Mass Psychology*, p. 136.
33 Ibid., p. 152.
34 Ibid., p. 120.
35 Ibid., p. 123.
36 Ibid., p. 122.
37 Ibid., p. 125.
38 Ibid., p. 135.
39 Ibid., p. 160.
40 Ibid., p. 133.
41 Bertolt Brecht, *The Life of Galileo*, 1955, trans. Desmond I. Vesey (London, Eyre Methuen 1963), p. 54, p. 42.
42 Freud, *Mass Psychology*, p. 161.
43 Ibid., p. 150.
44 Ernest Jones, *Sigmund Freud – Life and Work*, vol. 3, *The Last Phase: 1919-1939* (London, Hogarth 1957), p. 375.
45 Freud, *Mass Psychology*, p. 158.
46 Ibid., p. 153.
47 Ibid., p. 162.
48 Letter of 9 October 1918 from Freud to Oskar Pfister, *Psychoanalysis and Faith – The Letters of Sigmund Freud and Oskar Pfister* (London, Hogarth, 1963), p. 63.
49 Sigmund Freud, 'Address to the Society of B'nai Brith', *The Standard Edition of the Complete Psychological Works*, 24 vols (London, Hogarth 1953-73), vol. 20, pp. 273-4 (translation modified); Reik's translation is cited by David

90 THE LAST RESISTANCE

Bakan who discusses the implications of Freud's use of '*heimlich*' in *Sigmund Freud and the Jewish Mystical Tradition*, 1958, (London, Free Association Books 1990), pp. 305-19.

50 Freud, *Mass Psychology*, p. 106.
51 Ibid., p. 162.
52 Ibid., p. 210, my emphasis.
53 Ibid., p. 217.
54 Ibid., p. 288, p. 294.
55 Ibid., p. 210, my emphasis.
56 Letter to Chaim Koffler, cited by Yerushalmi, *Freud's Moses*, p. 13, from *Freudiana: From the Collections of the Jewish National and University Library* (Jerusalem, 1973); letter to Arnold Zweig, from *The Letters of Sigmund Freud and Arnold Zweig* (New York, Harcourt Brace 1970), cited Yerushalmi, *Freud's Moses*, p. 15; letter to Ferenczi cited Jones, *Sigmund Freud*, vol. 3, p. 88.
57 *Freudiana*, cited by Yerushalmi, *Freud's Moses*, p. 13.
58 Ibid.
59 Ibid., p. 3.
60 Freud, *Mass Psychology*, p. 220.
61 Ibid.
62 Ibid., p. 221, p. 178, p. 221.
63 Lydia Flem, *Freud the Man – An Intellectual Biography* (New York, Other Press 2003), p. 159.
64 Freud, *Mass Psychology*, p. 202.
65 Ibid., p. 266.
66 Viktor Shklovsky, 'Art as Technique', 1917, *Russian Formalist Criticism*, eds. Lee T. Lemon and Marion J. Rees (Lincoln, University of Nebraska Press 1965), p. 23, italics original; Shklovsky, *Mayakovsky and His Circle* (London, Pluto 1972), p. 17, emphases mine.
67 Freud, *Mass Psychology*, p. 193.
68 Editor's Note, *Moses and Monotheism, Standard Edition* (1938), vol. 23, p. 4.
69 Freud, *Mass Psychology*, p. 210.
70 For a very strong discussion of *Moses* in relation to the idea of dispossession and dissociation, see Philippe Lacoue-Labarthe and Jean-Luc Nancy, 'The Unconscious Is De-Structured Like a Language', and 'From Where Is Psychoanalysis Possible?' *Stanford Literary Review*, vol. 6, 1991, vol. 8, 1992.
71 Freud, *Mass Psychology*, p. 210.
72 Yerushalmi, *Freud's Moses*, p. 84.
73 Freud, 'The Disillusionment of the War', *Thoughts for the Time on War and Death*, 1915, *Standard Edition*, vol. 14, p. 285.
74 Freud, *Mass Psychology*, p. 167.
75 Edward Said, *Freud and the Non-European*, response by Jacqueline Rose, introduced by Christopher Bollas (London, Verso, with the London Freud Museum, 2003); Jan Assman, *Moses the Egyptian – The Memory of Egypt in Western Monotheism* (Cambridge, MA, Harvard University Press 1997).
76 Freud, *Mass Psychology*, p. 180, p. 181, p. 228.
77 Ibid., p. 182.
78 Ibid., p. 183.
79 Ibid., p. 247, p. 192.

80 Assman, *Moses*, p. 3.
81 Ibid., p. 5.
82 Ibid., p. 21.
83 Freud to Arnold Zweig, 30 September 1934, *The Letters of Sigmund Freud and Arnold Zweig*, p. 91.
84 Freud, *Mass Psychology*, p. 213.
85 Martin Buber, *Mamre – Essays in Religion* (Melbourne, Melbourne University Press 1974), cited Bakan, *Sigmund Freud and the Jewish Mystical Tradition*, p. 117.
86 Freud to Jung, 16 April 1909, *The Freud/Jung Letters*, ed. William MacGuire, trans. R. Mannheim, (London, Hogarth 1974), p. 220.
87 See Bakan, *Sigmund Freud and the Jewish Mystical Tradition*.
88 Freud, 'The Moses of Michelangelo', 1914, *Standard Edition*, vol. 13, p. 213.
89 Marthe Robert, *From Oedipus to Moses*, p. 95; the thesis is central to Robert's study.
90 Freud, *Mass Psychology*, p. 293.
91 Bluma Goldstein, *Reinscribing Moses – Heine, Kafka, Freud and Schoenberg in a European Wilderness* (Cambridge, MA, Harvard University Press 1992), cited Assman, *Moses*, p. 167.
92 Freud, *Mass Psychology*, p. 208.
93 Ibid.
94 Ibid., p. 304.
95 Karl Abraham, 'Amenhotep IV: A Psychoanalytic Contribution Towards the Understanding of His Personality and of the Monotheistic Cult of Aton', 1912, *Clinical Essays and Papers on Psychoanalysis* (London, Hogarth 1955).
96 Freud, *Mass Psychology*, p. 207.
97 Ibid., p. 208.
98 'Dear Prime Minister Sharon', *Ha'aretz*, 19 March 2004.
99 Freud, *Mass Psychology*, p. 208.
100 Ibid., p. 255.
101 Ibid., p. 256.
102 Freud to Zweig, 8 May 1932, *The Letters of Sigmund Freud and Arnold Zweig*, p. 40.
103 Nicolas Abraham, 'Notes on the Phantom: A Complement to Freud's Metapsychology', in *The Shell and the Kernel*, vol. 1, ed. and trans. with an introduction by Nicholas T. Rand (Chicago, Chicago University Press 1994).
104 Freud, *Mass Psychology*, p. 253.
105 Freud, *Totem and Taboo – Some Points of Agreement between the Mental Lives of Savages and Neurotics*, 1913, *Standard Edition*, vol. 13, p. xv.
106 Freud, *Mass Psychology*, p. 275.
107 Ibid., p. 277.
108 Wulf Sachs to Sigmund Freud, 1 August 1938, Archive of the Freud Museum.
109 Freud, *Letters*, cited Robert, *From Oedipus to Moses*, p. 35.
110 Freud, *Mass Psychology*, p. 279.
111 Ibid., p. 223.
112 Ibid., p. 277.
113 Ibid., p. 269.
114 Ibid., p. 270.
115 Ibid., p. 118.

116 Ibid., p. 274.
117 Ibid., p. 179.
118 Hannah Arendt to Gershom Scholem, letter of 24 July 1963, Hannah Arendt, *The Jew as Pariah – Jewish Identity and Politics in the Modern Age* (New York, Grove Press 1978), p. 247.
119 Letter to Meitlis from Jacob Meitlis 'The Last Days of Sigmund Freud', *Jewish Frontier*, vol. 18, September 1951, cited in Bakan, *Sigmund Freud and the Jewish Mystical Tradition*, p. 49.
120 Freud, *Mass Psychology*, p. 277.
121 Ibid., p. 258.
122 Ibid., p. 303.

4

The Hidden Life of Vladimir Jabotinsky*

In 1917, after the British conquest of Palestine, the Jewish Battalion, which Vladimir Jabotinsky[1] had campaigned for since the outbreak of the war and which had participated in several of the battles, was allowed to rename itself the 'Judean Regiment'. Up to that point, under pressure from Lord Rothschild, as representative of those British Jews opposed to any such unit, the British authorities had insisted that no reference to its Jewishness should appear in its title. The newly named 'Judean regiment' chose a *menora* with the Hebrew word *'Kadima'*, meaning 'forward' or 'eastward', as its insignia. This was not the first time that Jabotinsky had used the word. 'Kadima' was also the name of the Zionist publishing house he had founded with a group of friends in Odessa in 1904 (they each contributed 100 roubles), which marked the beginning of Zionist activity throughout Russia. When at the end of 2005, Ariel Sharon left Likud to form a new party, Kadima, a move widely welcomed as creating a fresh middle ground in Israeli politics, he was therefore paying the profoundest tribute to Jabotinsky – Likud's forefather, founder of militant Revisionist Zionism, visionary of the Jewish radical right. As historians have pointed out – notably Avi Shlaim in his famous book *The Iron Wall* – in the Israeli political landscape, Jabotinsky is not a spirit easily left behind.[2]

After Theodor Herzl and David Ben-Gurion, Jabotinsky is perhaps the most renowned, albeit controversial, figure in Zionist history. For the Labor founders of the State of Israel, he was a pariah. He split with the Zionist Organisation on the issue of Jewish self-defence (he was imprisoned by the British in 1920 for possession of firearms and provoking disorder), and of armed struggle against the British in Palestine. He had also proclaimed that the goal of Zionism was the creation of a Jewish state at a time when Zionist leaders preferred to keep quiet about such an aim. 'I, too, am for a Jewish state,' one of his closest collaborators commented, 'but I am against using the *words*'.[3] When he proposed to translate Herzl's *Der Judenstaat* into Hebrew and English in 1919, and to undertake the English translation himself, he was firmly rebuffed by the Zionist Commission. Jabotinsky was ostracised for speaking the truth. Because he recognised Arab national aspirations as legitimate, he had no interest in denying that the Zionist struggle would be violent. According to Jabotinsky, a group of Arabs approached him in 1926: 'You are the only one among the Zionists who has no intention of fooling us'; Egyptian intellectual Mahmed Azi is reported as having thanked him for not disguising his true intentions.[4] In an extended reading of Jabotinsky in his history of Zionist thought, David Goldberg cites Jabotinsky's fundamental ethos: 'Stupid is the person who believes in his neighbour, good and loving as the neighbour may be; stupid is the person who relies on justice. Justice exists only for those whose fists and stubbornness makes it possible for them to realise it.'[5]

Jabotinsky is most famous for the militant youth organisation Betar, which he founded in 1923. Members of Betar saw themselves as warriors opposed to the labouring, agricultural spirit of the first socialist Zionist pioneers (they famously showed up on a sponsorship tour of Europe in 1935 dressed in leather jackets on motorbikes). In his book on Revisionist Zionism, *The Jewish Radical Right*, Eran Kaplan describes how the members of Betar took their inspiration from the early Zionist poet, Ya'acov Cohen:

> In blood and fire Judah fell
> In blood and fire Judah will rise!
>
> War! War to our country, war for freedom –
> And if freedom is forever lost – long live revenge![6]

Today the Betar Jerusalem football team, which names itself after the youth organisation, is known for shouting racist slogans during their games, and anthems in praise of Yigal Amir, currently in prison for the assassination of Yitzhak Rabin (Amir himself professes contempt for them).[7] Although Betar eventually embraced a vision more violent than that of Jabotinsky, and though his position proved too moderate for the founders of the Jewish underground movement Irgun, nonetheless Zionist militarism – notably the creation of Haganah, the first militant unit for Jewish self-defence in Palestine – can fairly be described as starting with him. Jabotinsky was a fighter. His last, posthumously published, book, *The Jewish War Front*, also published as *The War and the Jew*, recounted his attempt to persuade the Allied powers to allow the formation of a Jewish army in the Second World War (creation of a Jewish state would then, he believed, acquire the status of an Allied war aim).[8] 'A nation in our position', he famously wrote in 1936, in response to the Arab riots of 1936, 'must know the ABC and acquire the psychology of shooting, and the longing after it.'[9] It is, however, important to remember that, long before his belligerence was directed towards the Arabs, the target of his rage was the official Zionist leadership. 'I cannot work like you', Chaim Weizmann wrote to him in 1915, 'in an atmosphere where everybody is angry with me and can hardly stand me. This everyday friction would poison my life and kill in me all desire to work.'[10] In 1927 he described the 'hatred' between himself and Labor Zionism as 'organic': 'it is not dependent on our will, and nothing can be done about it'.[11] Jabotinsky's first enemies were other Jews.

Strangely enough, it would be a Labor Prime Minister, Levi Eshkol, who arranged for Jabotinsky's remains to be interred in a state ceremony on Mount Herzl in 1963. Full memorialisation would have to await the election of Menachem Begin in 1977. Celebrations for the 100th anniversary of Jabotinsky's birth were to match the commemoration of first Prime Minister of Israel, David Ben-Gurion. Ten major cities across the country held sound-and-light displays; recitals of Jabotinsky's writings stressed the eternal right of the Jewish people to the whole of Eretz Israel; lecturers were sent out from the Jabotinsky Institute to army units; government-sponsored pamphlets and guides for teachers were issued to schools; stamps were issued in honour of the dissident martyrs of the underground movements, Irgun and Lehi, who had died in the struggle for Israeli independence. It was, as political scientist and anthropologist Myron Aronoff puts it, 'near deification' of Jabotinsky, marking his definitive return to the official Zionist fold.[12] The afterword to a late edition of *The War and the Jew* cites Begin as he recalls the moment he issued the order for the Revolt in 1937 against the British authorities in Palestine: 'it was as though I heard the voice of Jabotinsky commanding me to give it. That is how we all felt. It was under his leadership, even after his death, that the Revolt was carried out. The Revolt succeeded in resurrecting the Jewish State, the Third Jewish Commonwealth, the dwelling place of the Jewish people for all eternity.'[13] (Despite the eulogies, Begin found Jabotinsky too moderate, proclaiming at Betar's World Conference of 1938 that Zionism had to pass into the era of military struggle, whereupon Jabotinsky turned his back, comparing Begin's speech to the sound of a screeching door.)[14]

Jabotinsky's ability to inspire such forms of devotion in his followers is legendary. When a group of Revisionist militants, imprisoned by the British, were unsuccessfully interrogated in 1945, five years after his death, the interrogating officer in Cairo is reported to have commented: '[We were] dealing with a different type of person – a type we are facing for the first time in our careers [. . .]You conducted yourselves as if "someone" were in the room, someone before whom you are on trial [. . .] who is no longer among the living, but who for you is still very much alive [. . .] I see him now before my eyes [. . .] I see him as your idol [. . .] He gave you a religion.'[15] Members of his camp were known as *Khoveve Jabotinsky* (Lovers of Jabotinsky). Each one of them, writes Jabotinsky's biographer Schechtman, had his own 'intimate and captivating *romance* with the man Jabotinsky', a romance whose unwritten formula was 'Jabotinsky belongs to the Jewish nation and to me', or more personally, 'Jabotinsky belongs to me and to the Jewish nation.'[16] Jabotinsky provides a perfect illustration of that strange process described by Freud, whereby an intimate and potentially rivalrous claim to possess the leader on the part of each of his followers nonetheless works to secure the cohesion of the group. According to Schechtman, when Jabotinsky moved from his luxury hotel in Alexandria into the quarantine quarters of Jewish exiles expelled by the Syrian leader from Jaffa during the First World War – an uneasy group of Ashkenazi and Sephardic Jews including Georgians, Bukharians and Spaniards, with twelve languages among them – 'as if by magic, everything changed and the mixed crowd became a single unit, giving the impression of a group that had been educated in the same orderly way. We called this order among exiles "the Jabotinsky regime".'[17]

Jabotinsky expected no less. 'The greatest achievement of a free mass of people', he wrote with reference to Betar, 'is the ability to operate together as one with the absolute precision of a machine [. . .] We would like to turn the entire nation into an orchestra.'[18] Dedication must be absolute: 'Two ideals are an absurdity – like two gods, like two altars, like two temples. I do not want to insult anybody, but a soul that can swallow two ideals and be content is a flawed soul [. . .] An ideal excludes everything peripheral, however beautiful, however pure.'[19]

In this context, the dual reference of *'Kadima'* – to the world of writing and of political action – is illuminating. Contrary to all his best – or one might say 'worst' – rhetoric – Jabotinsky was more than one. In a 1934 letter, on the eve of his split from the official Zionist Organisation, he wrote to a friend: 'There are only three solutions: to conquer the Zionist Organisation, or to convert the Revisionist Organisation into something very "wrathful", or to retire and write novels.'[20] Conquering the official Zionist Organisation was, he acknowledged, impossible ('victory in Zionist elections is almost automatically secured to the party with the biggest war-chest').[21] The second two turned out, however, not to be alternatives. Jabotinsky created his 'wrathful' organisation – the Independent or New Zionist Organisation – that year. But 1935 was also the year in which he completed his last novel

Pitera, or, *The Five* (it had started appearing in instalments in Paris in 1933), translated in 2005 for the first time into English by Michael Katz.[22] *The Five* is the lovingly rendered account of the decline of Russian Jewry in cosmopolitan, turn-of-the-century Odessa told, in the formula of Russian literature specialist Alice Nakhimovsky, with 'irreproducible careless grace'.[23] In his book *Zionism and the Fin-de-Siècle*, Michael Stanislawski, who provides the introduction to the English translation, describes *The Five* as 'the most literarily successful and psychologically revealing of Jabotinsky's adult writings'.[24]

What, we might ask, led Jabotinsky, at the precise moment he casts the die for violent Zionist activism, to turn to his own past (the narrator can be read as a self-portrait), to something 'peripheral', 'beautiful', thereby revealing the division or 'flaw' in his own soul? Jabotinsky's Odessa is a utopia in decline, where 'ten tribes converged', speaking 'one hundred different languages', 'each and every one so fascinating, one more interesting than the next', whose customs 'gradually rubbed up against each other' until they 'ceased regarding their sacred altars in such a serious manner'.[25] The reference to language is important. Throughout his life, Jabotinsky harboured a complex passion for languages. Although he is reputed to have spoken at least nine, he also devoted a significant part of his life as a Zionist to promoting the revival of Hebrew – one language for one people – in both the Diaspora and Palestine. In *The Five*, however, it becomes at least an open question whether the drive of history is towards the purity or rather the confusion of tongues. The narrator who tenderly records this world is a self-doubting Zionist. 'Of course,' he muses, 'I'm in the camp that struggles against disintegration; I don't want neighbours; I want all people living on their own islands; but – who knows?'[26]

Like Herzl, Jabotinsky was a journalist and literary writer before he became a Zionist. At the age of sixteen, he left the gymnasium, which he was attending at great cost to his widowed mother, and presented himself to the editor of the influential liberal newspaper *Odesskiya Novosti* to request a posting to Italy (later he would describe such an act, on the part of a Jew for whom a diploma was a ticket out of the 'Pale', as madness). One of the most renowned journalistic and literary figures in Odessa – something he always cherished was his early translation of Edgar Allan Poe's 'The Raven' into Russian – he turned to Zionism at the start of the new century. Although his involvement predated the Kishinev pogrom of 1905, and his Zionism was also fuelled by the nationalism of the Italian Risorgimento, nonetheless Kishinev was a turning point. 'Once I felt strongly the beauty of the free-lance,' he wrote, 'a man above and beyond the rank and file, having no allegiance, without obligation to anyone on earth, impartial toward his own people and to strangers alike, pursuing the way of his own will over the heads of kin and strangers.' But his new-found Zionist 'faith', like the betrothal of a Jewish woman, requires him to follow the 'cruel but profound' custom of cutting off his hair: 'Perhaps I too could [. . .] sing songs of beauty, bathe in the cheap favour of your applause. I do not want it. I cut off my hair.'[27] Once again the rhetoric is defied by his literary writing. In his first novel, *Prelude to Delilah or Samson the Nazarite*, published in 1926, cutting-off hair brings vengeful retribution, and is no act of pure self-enlightened grace, as if such a gesture were too brutal a repudiation, something that would not finally settle in the author's mind. According to Schechtman, to the end of Jabotinsky's life writing remained his greatest pleasure, the activity in which he felt most contented and at ease. On receiving the first copy of *The Five*, he wrote to his brother-in-law that he was so happy he 'spent the day going from one movie house to another'.[28]

Jabotinsky did not, therefore, give up a literary career for politics, he does not relinquish the false path of fiction for the true Zionist faith. There is more at stake here than the fact that literature was Jabotinsky's first and abiding passion. Nor is it only a matter of the often symbiotic relationship between Zionist literature and politics, the way that for Jabotinsky, as for Herzl, political reality is summoned to meet the dream. 'Sometimes, the era produces the poet. Sometimes one creates the other,' writes Begin in his preface to the 1986 edition of Schechtman's biography, 'but the poetry and the literary works of Ze'ev Jabotinsky preceded an era – he created it.'[29] Lacking the financial resources and institutions of official Zionism, Revisionism was always an ideological, cultural and literary enterprise. Revisionist Zionism can also be described, as Eran Kaplan details in *The Jewish Radical Right*, as an aesthetic project, steeped in the ceremonial and symbolic moulding of the mass mind (it conducted what can be described at the very least as a flirtation with Italian fascism). Even more crucially, as *The Five* so clearly shows, fiction trails Jabotinsky's political acts and rhetoric, belying their conviction, allowing us a glimpse of something darker which that rhetoric will not, or cannot afford to let us, see. For such a diagnosis, Jabotinsky himself provides the terms. 'Every project presents a dark side,' he wrote in *The War and the Jew*, 'every important remedy contains an element which, under other circumstances, would be poisonous.'[30] The note that opens *The Five*, 'Instead of a Preface', concludes: 'I'm a child of my age. I love all its blemishes, all its poison.'[31] Like a confessional, literature becomes the place where Jabotinsky could diagnose the ills of his own life's work.

The implications of this for today are, I believe, profound. As I write, Israel is faced with a democratically elected Hamas government, the legacy of its own brute military policies towards the Palestinians. Behind Hamas's statement that it will not deal with Israel – for which it is isolated and financially starved – we can ironically detect the shade, and perfect logical consequence, of the ethos of Jabotinsky, who famously ended his 1923 essay 'The Iron Wall': 'the only way to reach an agreement in the future is to abandon all idea of seeking an agreement at present' – although, contrary to the unilateral policy of Israel's present leaders, there could, once Zionism was accepted as invincible by the Arabs, be an agreement in time. No negotiation. Jabotinsky elevated inflexibility into political *doxa*. Seen in this context, *The Five* is a discovery. In moments of startling prescience, Zionism appears, not as immutable goal, but as cause for warning or fear. Roughly halfway through the novel, the narrator, a detached cosmopolitan *littérateur* who moves, like the author, between Odessa, Rome and Bern, suddenly understands 'the venomous curse of the emigrant's existence', that uses up the 'soul's juice' in torment. 'But', he continues, 'the soul's juice is not reabsorbed; it accumulates, hardens, and burns the consciousness forever; and if fate ever wills it thus and the exiles *en masse* suddenly return to their homeland and become its sovereigns, *they will pervert all paths and all measures.*'[32]

In Jabotinsky's lexicon, even iron, we discover, is a mixed blessing, or even a curse. At the end of *Samson*, the blind imprisoned hero sends a message to his people: 'Samson thought for a while, and then said slowly: "Tell them two things in my name – two words. The first word is Iron. They must get iron [. . .] The second word is this: a king!"' (he later adds that they must also 'learn to laugh')[33] But in 1925, the year before this novel, Jabotinsky had written a collection of short stories, *A Pocket Edition of Short Stories Mostly Reactionary*, published in Paris and lesser known, which includes the tale of Tristan da Runha, a penitentiary colony of exiled convicts, the most atavistic representatives of the human race, who slowly turn their colony into a model of human dignity and survival, in the words of the observer telling the story, 'a superior, better world than the one left behind'.[34] No metal ores or coal deposits are allowed on the island; when the buildings evacuated by the previous population are destroyed, 'especial care had been taken to remove any trace of metal even such as old nails'. Tristan da Runha is an 'ironless civilisation' – remember this is only two years after 'The Iron Wall' and 'The Ethics of the Iron Wall', both published in 1923.[35] It lacks 'the only materials over which man is absolute master, which he can mould into any shape, and link into infinite combinations to do his will'.[36] In this lies the colony's superiority to the civilised world: 'Metal is the cause of all evil [. . .] It is dangerous for Man to become so absolute a Master of Nature. It is unnatural, and will be avenged [. . .] We who were born into the world of iron shall soon die; and the generations conceived on this island will never know the morbid ambitions, the lust of pawing new things which poison that world.'[37] And then, in lines it is hard not to read once again as Jabotinsky's caution against his own hardening faith (resigning from the Executive he had written to Weizmann, accusing him of 'apostasy'[38]): 'The field of the spirit is the only field where man has the right to conquer, to advance over hedge after hedge [. . .] However high he may soar, his daring will not be avenged, he will not degenerate – so long as he does not attempt to transform spirit into matter, *in the shape of more acres or more power.*'[39] Iron and power are destructive; together they corrupt the spirit of mankind. Jabotinsky, we could say, knew exactly what he was doing, although perhaps not in the way usually assumed, when he evoked the metaphor of the iron wall as the surest path – more acres, hedge after hedge – to the conquest of Palestine.

The Five tells the tragic story of the Milgroms, a successful Jewish grain merchant's family, with five children, whose disintegration, helplessly watched and recorded by the narrator, chimes with the outbreak of revolution in Russia in 1905. From Potemkin Day onwards, a day the narrator does not like to recall, this family 'that had become like my family' is surrounded by a 'dark plague'.[40] The star of the family, the beautiful, flirtatious Marusya – 'I've yet to discover any woman better than Marusya' – dies in a careless domestic fire.[41] Serezha, the 'scamp', is disfigured by acid when his liaison with a semi-incestuous mother–daughter couple is discovered by the former's husband. Marko, who loves Nietzsche but is viewed by his father as a fool, dies when he goes to the rescue of a woman he wrongly believes to be drowning in a frozen lake. Lika, arrested for anti-Tsarist agitation and sent into exile, becomes an agent for the secret police, although the intimation at the end of the book is that she is a Bolshevik and Cheka executioner. Studious Torik, the ideal child in the eyes of his parents, whose library included Graetz's *History of the Jews* – 'the single book with Jewish content in the entire household'[42] – shockingly converts at the end of the novel, although not before graciously warning his father in case he should wish to disinherit him. 'My diagnosis is established irrevocably: disintegration', Torik explains to the narrator, 'The Jewish people is dispersing every which way, and it won't ever return to its previous state.'[43] For Torik, Zion will not exist and Zionism is simply hastening the Jews on their path to assimilation, with 'conversions, mixed marriages, and the complete annihilation of the race': 'only one thing will remain – the desire "to be like all other peoples".'[44] This is in itself heavily ironic, since the desire to be like other peoples, not as assimilation, but through entry into the world of nations, was central to the Zionist drive to become a Jewish state (for that reason, Hannah Arendt would argue that Zionism was in fact the most assimilatory, and dangerous, move that the Jews could make).

The tragedy of the Milgrom family is therefore the tragedy of assimilation and incipient Bolshevism. Although as a young man, Jabotinsky had defined himself as a socialist, and in *The Five* he is clearly on the side of anti-autocratic sedition, he came to loathe the Russian Revolution for tearing the Jews away from other, nationalist, ideals (remember, only *one* ideal). His dismay at the large proportion of Jews among Russian socialists was something he shared with Weizmann. A revolution in another nation was not, as he saw it, worth 'the blood of our old men, women and children'.[45] For similar reasons, he later became – in this unlike Weizmann – a firm advocate of private enterprise, for which he was heavily criticised by the Socialist Zionists. If the novel is in praise of revolt, nonetheless the Milgroms make the fundamental error of believing they can lead a fully Russian life. In his 1906 article, 'Jews in Russian Literature', Jabotinsky addressed an assimilated socialist writer of Jewish origin who 'enthusiastically pledged allegiance to the Russian people and culture [. . .] You went over to the rich neighbour – we will turn our back on his beauty and kindness; you worship his values and have left our little patrimony to rot [. . .] We will exaggerate our hatred to make it help our love.'[46] Once again, such violent repudiation can only be suspect. Placing love in such proximity to hatred is a risky game. Sadism, as Jabotinsky wrote on the subject of anti-Semitism in *The War and the Jew*, cannot bear to lose its object, never lets go.[47] Repugnance is a binding tie. In 1935, the result of such exaggerated, fondly nurtured, hatred would be to return him to the assimilated Jews of Odessa with a passion.

Everyone in Tsarist Russia 'except the Tsar himself', writes Yuri Slezkine in *The Jewish Century*, belonged to a group that was in some way the target of discrimination; nonetheless the Jews were 'first among non-equals'.[48] At the dawn of the twentieth century, the Russian Empire was home to a majority of the world's Jews, who formed the largest and most urbanised group of those who could make no claim to a national home. Although Jabotinsky eventually saw the education he had interrupted (and subsequently completed) as the Jewish ticket out of the Pale, he had in fact, like many of the Jews in Odessa, never been there. Between 1897 and 1910, the Jewish urban population had grown by at least one million, or 38.5 per cent. Between 1853 and 1856 the number of Jewish gymnasium students in the Russian Empire grew sixfold. By 1886, a third of Odessa University's students were Jewish. As was the case throughout Europe, the success of Jews in Russian business, the professions and the arts was accompanied 'by a mastery of the national high culture and an eager conversion to the Pushkin faith'.[49] Jabotinsky was typical as a literary-minded Russian-speaking Jew (although he was apparently exceptional as a Jew who spoke Russian without a trace of accent), with virtually no ties to Jewish tradition or culture. According to Michael Stanislawski, it was far from abnormal for an upper-middle-class Russian Jew to be raised with no knowledge of Yiddish, Hebrew or Judaism.[50] Before he discovered Zionism, Jabotinsky could therefore be described as a Jew who 'passed'. When he eventually introduces a 'religious plank' into the National Zionist Organisation at the Vienna Congress of 1935, the move is as much political as sacred (or rather the two combined). By this stage Jabotinsky's explicit revolutionary aim was to make his organisation the embodiment of the totality of the Jewish people; for this, as he stated, it would be folly to ignore a 'factor of such magnitude as thirty centuries of religious inspiration and thought.'[51] 'We need', he wrote to his son two days after the Congress, 'religious pathos as such.'[52]

But Jabotinsky did not believe in the veracity of the Bible and, as Yaacov Shavit has related, in all his writings, there is not one reference to God's covenant with Abraham, the Exodus, the giving of the Torah on Mount Sinai, or indeed the conquering of Eretz Israel by the Israelites (even if Betar regarded themselves as modern-day Biryonim, the zealots of the Second Temple who rebelled against the Romans). Jabotinsky's Zionism is shorn of Jewishness even when he appeals to sacred tradition as having a part to play in the forging of the national (racial) mind. To this extent it is arguable whether the demise of the Milgroms in *The Five* can be traced to their betrayal of their Jewish identity and spiritual legacy, or whether Zionism itself – or rather Jabotinsky's Zionism – arose at least partially, not just out of the desire to be free of an increasingly violent anti-Semitism, but, para-doxically, also from a longing to leave the Jewish legacy and world behind. Better get out, if a family as beautiful and talented as the Milgroms – carrying the forlorn hope for the Jews of a civilised, European, life – cannot survive. The novel does not judge; it laments. Seen in these terms, Jabotinsky's Odessa is less a prelude to Zion, than its rival – as the publication of this novel in the year he founds the National Zionist Organisation in itself suggests – one that persists in his mind even when its world has vanished. The city rises up as a counter-utopia to his own chosen destiny, lost paradise, rather than a mistake. This gives an added dimension to the acknowledged role of contempt for the Diaspora Jew in Zionism, as it does to the Zionist fantasy of creating an outpost of Western civilisation in the East. 'We have nothing in common with what is denoted "the East", and thank God for that,' Jabotinsky wrote, 'We come to the Land of Israel in order to push the moral frontiers of Europe to the Euphrates.'[53] It was because the Jews could not fulfil the true dream – to assimilate in Europe – that they were so determined to travel *as Europeans* to Palestine.

Might there be, therefore, inside Jabotinsky's project, a core of hatred, as much as love, for the Jews? ('we will exaggerate our hatred to make it help our love'). When the narrator takes up a career in public service ('Secretary in the Temporary Administration of the Society of Sanatorium Colonies and Other Hygienic-Dietary Institutions for the Treatment and Education of Students Suffering from Bad Health from the Indigent Jewish Population in the City of Odessa and its Surrounding Areas'), Marusya offers to accompany him to visit these impoverished, indigent, Jews. 'Would you like to get away from all these Jews?' she asks at the end of a visit which has at once dismayed and exhilarated her, 'Both rich and poor?'[54] And, accompanying her sister Lika into exile in Volgoda, she writes home to the narrator: 'don't forget to remind me when I return to join some political party or other, just as long as there are no Jews in it' (remember, she is the best woman he has ever known).[55] Slezkine tells the story of Esther Ulanovskaia who came to Odessa from a *shtetl* in the Ukraine and joined the Young Revolutionary International: 'the Jews represented the world I wanted to get away from'.[56]

In his autobiography, Jabotinsky cites his first 'Zionist' speech, delivered in Bern in 1898: 'I am a Zionist, without a doubt, since the Jews are a very terrible people, its neighbours justly hate them'[57] (not surprisingly, it was received as anti-Semitic). According to Schechtman, Count Michael Lubiensky once said to him: 'You know that I hold Jabotinsky in highest regard and that my opinion of Weizmann is trimmed accordingly [. . .] Dr Weizmann has all the chances to retain the allegiance of the majority of the Jewish people. Because his entire mentality is identical with that of an average ghetto Jew, while the mentality of Jabotinsky is spiritually nearer to me, a Gentile. I understand him better; he evokes in me a kindred response.'[58] Jabotinsky turned to the assimilated Jews of Russia in 1935, because he still belonged to them. As with his Odessa, so with his Zionism, there was no trace of Pale or ghetto.

If *The Five* tells the other story of Jabotinsky's official Zionism, to read this novel is nonetheless to be struck by how closely these seemingly contrary visions are intertwined. Not just in the sense that the failure of assimilation was in some sense the cause of Zionism, but rather because the question of assimilation was carried over to the issue of the rights of indigenous peoples that Zionism was confronting in relation to the Arabs of Palestine. It is often asked how a people who suffered such persecution could become the oppressors of another people. Faced with Lika's exile, her

father, Ignats Albertovich, 'found many quotations in Heine and Borne to
prove that it's more shameful to be an oppressor than a victim'.[59] But
despite the barely concealed irony at Albertovich's expense, Jabotinsky
showed his own awareness of the link when he proposed for the Arabs the
same minority rights that he himself had promoted at the Helsingfors
Third All-Russian Zionist Convention of 1906 for Russian Jews: Zionism
was 'ready to grant the Arab minority in Eretz Israel every possible right
that the Jews claimed for themselves, but had never achieved in other
countries'.[60] Indeed, the link Jabotinsky proposed from Russia to Palestine
was the basis of one of his disputes with Weizmann: 'We cannot',
Weizmann insisted, 'base our plans on the sad events that occurred in
Russia. There is no territorial programme in the world capable to satisfy
the present needs of the Jewish people [. . .] Zionism cannot be the
answer to a catastrophe. We must proceed slowly.'[61]

For Jabotinsky, Arab national aspirations, like those of the Zionists, were
legitimate. Hence his acknowledgement of the inevitable violence of the
struggle. Antagonism between Jew and Arab therefore veiled a latent
identification. Unlike those Zionists who blithely predicted, with a barely
concealed racism, that the Arabs would relinquish their land when they saw
how the Jewish pioneers made it prosper, he insisted they were a people of
dignity who would not be bought: 'The entire country is full of Arab
memories.'[62] National groupings cannot, therefore, but be at war with each
other. In *The War and the Jew,* he makes a key distinction between the 'Anti-
Semitism of Men', based on irrational, visceral hatred ('a subjective repulsion, strong enough and permanent enough to become anything from a
hobby to a religion [. . .] a constant urge to harm the hated race'), and the
'Anti-Semitism of Things' ('steady, constant, immutable, and therefore
much more formidable'), which follows from the natural desire to protect,
and foster, the interests of one's own kind: 'an instinct which cannot be
criticised, because, after all, it is as natural as preferring one's own children to
one's neighbour's offspring'.[63] Zionist and Arab therefore share a *natural*
hostility to each other. Once again the fiction tells another story. 'It is a good
thing that you should live for a time among the Philistines', Samson says to
one of his followers, 'They are our neighbours, and if men come to know
each other, there is no enmity between them.'[64]

In Jabotinsky's future, Arab and Jew would not be neighbours so much as
carefully differentiated groupings within the body politic of the new state.
We are a far cry from *The Five*'s 'good-natured fraternisation of national-
ities', the 'Babylonian diversity of our common forum', in which the
narrator took such naive but wholesome delight.[65] Arabs might be citizens,
they might even participate in government (once they had submitted, there

could even be an Arab Vice President), but only the Jews would fully belong to the nation. Behind the apparently liberal demand for minority Arab rights lies a plea for the separation of peoples. Jabotinsky has transposed to Palestine the exact arrangement whose utter non-viability for the Jews he knew only too well: 'every possible right that the Jews had never achieved in other countries'. 'The Helsingfors utopia has, of course, never been attained either in Russia or anywhere else', he wrote in his 1930 essay 'Bi-national Palestine', 'I trust that the first country where they will, some day, be fully applied will be our own Palestine – *that is, when we Jews shall have become its masters.*'[66]

If there is an affinity between Arab and Jew, such a form of recognition shows its darker side. The line from Odessa to Tel Aviv, from failed assimilation to national identity, can be run more ways than one. For if there can only be one sovereign people, why would the Arabs, any more than the Jews in Russia, want to stay? Slowly, as Jewish emigration to Palestine from Europe increased throughout the 1930s, Jabotinsky's vision turned towards the transfer of peoples. Not forcibly – he was outspoken against forcible transfer – but nonetheless as the consequence, ironically, of his own belief in Arab nationhood. As Shavit points out, there was an inherent contradiction in the official Revisionist position which rejected the idea of a pan-Arab nation while maintaining that the Palestinian Arabs could be effortlessly absorbed into the larger Arab world (a contradiction all the more intense in that they refused to recognise the Hashemite regime in Transjordan, and hence the Transjordanian nation which was meant to receive them). Somewhat at odds with his own movement, Jabotinsky had no such problem with the larger pan-Arab vision – and, if there was a greater Arab nation, why should they not leave? According to Edward A. Norman, recording a conversation about a possible transfer of Palestinian Arabs to Iraq, Jabotinsky made the 'truly original suggestion' that:

> it would be wise to have the Zionist Organisation openly oppose Arab emigration from Palestine, and then the Arabs would be sure the scheme was not Jewish and that the Jews wanted them to stay in Palestine only to exploit them, and they would want very much to go away to Iraq.[67]

(A deadly repetition of Freud's famous joke of two Jews at the railway station: 'If you say you're going to Cracow, you want me to believe you're going to Lemberg. But I know in fact that you are going to Cracow, so why are you lying to me?' – the *Standard Edition* of Freud's works indexes this joke as 'Truth, a lie'.)[68]

Jabotinsky believed in the power of words. 'Many an observer shares the view', he wrote in his introduction to an English translation of the famous Hebrew poet Chaim Nachman Bialik, 'that among the impulses which have determined the Jewish revival since 1896, the personalities of Herzl and Bialik were the two main factors, more powerful than any "objective" event of those days.'[69] Jabotinsky had translated into Russian Bialik's most famous poem, 'In the City of Slaughter', written in response to the Kishinev pogrom: 'the self-defence organisations which sprung everywhere in Russia to meet the new pogrom-wave two years later, the "Yeomanry" movement in Palestine, even the Jewish Legion which fought for the Holy Land in 1918 – they are all Bialik's children.'[70] To this poem, he attributes almost mystical, telepathic powers. Stanislawski recounts how, in Jabotinsky's rendering – retitled 'Tale of a Pogrom' – the original is stripped of its heterodox, subversive, not to say blasphemous content (the speaker of the poem is an impotent, self-castigating God) as well as of its biblical and Judaic lexicon, to re-emerge as a diatribe against the Jewish people's passivity in the face of suffering, and an invocation to revolt: 'Bialik revolts, and becomes a singer of triumphant, invincible, Manhood, of the arm that wields the sword, of muscles of granite and sinews of steel.'[71] 'The main lesson of the pogrom was shame.'[72] In his 'Letter to the Jewish Community' of 1920, one of two proclamations issued by the 'Prisoners of Acre', he lambastes the 'criminal' British governor, Herbert Samuels, for turning a blind eye to slaughter, condemning the Jewish people to 'moral shame': 'he stifled the outbursts of protest until the impudence of our enemies grew and ripened, and took deep roots, and we became *hefker* [ownerless property] in their eyes.'[73]

For Jabotinsky, therefore, as for many Zionists, militancy was the answer, not just to persecution and injustice, but, as the felt accompaniment of that history, to humiliation. It is a recurrent theme throughout Zionist writing, and I believe the key to much of Zionism's own ruthlessness towards the Palestinians, that persecution of the Jews was experienced as moral disgrace. What is short-circuited in this logic is grief. 'I will harden My heart,' God addresses his 'mournful, slinking' followers in Bialik's poem, 'I will not let thee weep!' 'Thy tear, son of man, remain unshed / Build thou about it, with thy deadly hate / Thy fury and thy rage, unuttered, / A wall of copper, the bronze triple plate.'[74] Bialik has laid on the Jewish people an injunction from which the new nation will not recover – redemption of the people on condition of an inability to mourn. Echoing Bialik at the end of *The Five*, the narrator rages at the funeral of Maruysa against the prayers in praise of 'God-the-offender': 'I'd cast a stone at You, O Lord, if You weren't hiding so far away.'[75]

Maruysa dies when her dress catches fire in the kitchen. In a truly heroic moment, which looks forward to the vision of self-sacrificing Zionist motherhood, she locks her son outside the door and, to avoid any temptation of fleeing and thereby endangering him, throws the key from the window, barring all escape.[76] In an extraordinary hallucinatory passage, the narrator – who claims he never dreams – responds to a strange request she had once made to him, that he should 'dream me'. He relives her last moments, shedding their heroic content, entering into her tunnel of pain, where, we are now told, there was no time to think of her son, because pain is such 'a terribly nasty, completely insane thing': 'Has it ever entered your head that "pain" is a repulsive, demeaning concept? It's the most passive suffering on earth, somehow servile: you mean nothing at all, no one asks you, someone's mocking you' (all pain is inflicted, even with no intent whatsoever behind it, it demeans).[77] On the other hand, Maruysa's father, in response to the tragedy, claims to understand the book of Job – which the narrator has never read – for the first time. Better submit to suffering than rebel against God, otherwise your pain is worthless: 'as if a cart loaded with manure happened to drive by and for no particular reason crushed a snail or a cockroach' (the issue, he insists, is not that of justice or injustice, but that of pride).[78]

The end of The Five suggests that the question of how to respond to suffering was not something Jabotinsky had been able to answer in his own mind. As if the only options were impotent, humiliating, self-sacrifice, or militant, invincible, rage. But unless this deadlock can be broken, with all its dire consequences for the plight of the Palestinians, the conflict in the Middle East has no chance, I believe, of being resolved. To recall, again, Weizmann's letter to Jabotinsky of 1915, in which he asked him how he could bear to be so hated, Jabotinsky seems to have thrived on such hatred, risen to it, as we might say. The Five tells the other story. It allows us to watch his love travelling elsewhere – back to Odessa, in a last fleeting gesture to a world that he was himself playing such a key role in putting the seal on for all time.

In Jabotinsky's writing, Zionism both affirms and doubts itself. What would Israel look like today if the modern leaders who have claimed to take their inspiration from him – Begin, Netanyahu, Sharon and now Olmert, who referred to Jabotinsky in his speech to the first session of the new Knesset in May 2006 – had shown themselves capable of such radical self-questioning?

*An earlier version of this chapter was published in The Nation, 26 June 2006.

108   THE LAST RESISTANCE

Notes

1 Vladimir was Jabotinsky's Russian name but he is best known today by his Hebrew name Ze'ev.
2 Avi Shlaim, *The Iron Wall – Israel and the Arab World* (New York, Norton and London, Allen Lane 2000).
3 Joseph B. Schechtman, *The Jabotinsky Story*, 2 vols (New York and London, Barnes) vol. 2, *Fighter and Prophet*, 1961, p. 37.
4 Ibid., 2, p. 65.
5 Cited David Goldberg, *To the Promised Land – A History of Zionist Thought* (Harmondsworth, Penguin 1996), p. 176. My thanks to David Goldberg for communicating his chapters on Jabotinsky which I read after completing the first version of this essay.
6 Eran Kaplan, *The Jewish Radical Right – Revisionist Zionism and its Ideological Legacy* (Madison, University of Wisconsin Press, 2005), p. xiii.
7 Alon Hadar, 'The Devil's Advocate', *Ha'aretz*, 20 January 2006.
8 Ze'ev Jabotinsky, *The War and the Jew* (New York, Altalena Press 1962, A Chaz-Kalman Book, Tova Press 1987).
9 Schechtman, *The Jabotinsky Story*, vol. 2, p. 444.
10 Ibid., vol. 1, *Rebel and Statesman*, 1956, p. 224.
11 Ibid., vol. 2, p. 236.
12 Myron J. Aronoff, 'Establishing Authority: The Memorialisation of Jabotinsky and the Burial of the Bar-Kochba Bones in Israel under Likud', in M. Aronoff ed., *The Frailty of Authority* (New York and Oxford, Transaction Books 1986), p. 105.
13 Menachem Begin, Afterword to Jabotinsky, *The War and the Jew*, p. 297.
14 Kaplan, *The Jewish Radical Right*, pp. 8-9.
15 Schechtman, *The Jabotinsky Story*, vol. 2, p. 491.
16 Ibid., pp. 178-9.
17 Ibid., vol. 1, p. 204.
18 Kaplan, *The Jewish Radical Right*, p. 101.
19 Shmuel Katz, *Lone Wolf – A Biography of Vladimir Jabotinsky*, 2 vols (New York, Barricade Books 1996), vol. 2, p. 1090.
20 Schechtman, *The Jabotinsky Story*, vol. 2, p. 279.
21 Ibid.
22 Vladimir Jabotinsky, *The Five – A Novel of Jewish Life in Turn-of-the-Century Odessa*, trans. from the Russian by Michael R. Katz (Ithaca, Cornell University Press 2005).
23 Alice Stone Nakhimovsky, *Russian-Jewish Literature and Identity – Jabotinsky, Babel, Grossman, Galich, Roziner, Markish* (Baltimore, Johns Hopkins Press 1992), p. 63.
24 Michael Stanislawski, *Zionism and the Fin-de-Siècle – Cosmopolitanism and Nationalism from Nordau to Jabotinsky* (Berkeley, University of California Press 2001), p. 227.
25 Jabotinsky, *The Five*, p. 198.
26 Ibid., p. 199.
27 Schechtman, *The Jabotinsky Story*, vol. 1, p. 104.
28 Ibid., vol. 2, p. 527.

29 Begin, 'Jabotinsky Set Us Upon the Path to Freedom', Preface to Schechtman, *The Jabotinsky Story*, vol. 1, p. v, original emphasis.
30 Jabotinsky, *The War and the Jew*, p. 148.
31 Jabotinsky, *The Five*, p. 1.
32 Ibid., p. 101, my emphasis.
33 Jabotinsky, *Prelude to Delilah or Samson the Nazarite* (New York, Ackerman 1945), pp. 330-1.
34 Jabotinsky, 'Tristan da Runha', *A Pocket Edition of Short Stories Mostly Reactionary* (Paris, Éditions la Presse Française Etrangère 1925), p. 170.
35 Ibid., p. 174.
36 Ibid.
37 Ibid., p. 200.
38 Katz, *Lone Wolf*, vol. 1, p. 837.
39 Jabotinsky, 'Tristan da Runha', p. 201, my emphasis.
40 Jabotinsky, *The Five*, p. 121.
41 Ibid., p. 25.
42 Ibid., p. 30.
43 Ibid., p. 194.
44 Ibid.
45 Cited Yuri Slezkine, *The Jewish Century* (Princeton, Princeton University Press 2004), p. 157.
46 Schechtman, *The Jabotinsky Story*, vol. 2, pp. 104-5.
47 Jabotinsky, *The War and the Jew*, p. 77.
48 Slezkine, *The Jewish Century*, p. 110, p. 115.
49 Ibid., p. 127.
50 Stanislawski, *Zionism and the Fin-de-Siècle*, p. 123.
51 Schechtman, *The Jabotinsky Story*, vol. 2, p. 285.
52 Ibid., p. 289.
53 Cited Goldberg, *To the Promised Land*, pp. 181-2.
54 Jabotinsky, *The Five*, p. 51.
55 Ibid., p. 63.
56 Slezkine, *The Jewish Century*, p. 171.
57 This is Stanislawski's translation; in his biography, Schechtman renders the lines: 'the enemies of the Jews were not completely wrong, since in dispersion the Jews are a painful abscess in the organisms of other nations'. The original were lines, as Stanislawski puts it, that Schechtman 'could not easily repeat'. Stanislawski, *Zionism and the Fin-de-Siècle*, p. 130, Schechtman, *The Jabotinsky Story*, vol. 1, p. 47.
58 Schechtman, *The Jabotinsky Story*, vol. 2, p. 554.
59 Jabotinsky, *The Five*, p. 64.
60 Yaacov Shavit, *Jabotinsky and the Revisionist Movement 1925-1948* (London, Frank Cass 1988).
61 Schechtman, *The Jabotinsky Story*, vol. 1, p. 304.
62 Shavit, *Jabotinsky and the Revisionist Movement*, p. 254.
63 Jabotinsky, *The War and the Jew*, p. 53, p. 78, p. 75.
64 Jabotinsky, *Prelude to Delilah*, p. 118.
65 Jabotinsky, *The Five*, p. 15.
66 Jabotinsky, 'Bi-National Palestine', Jabotinsky Institute, p. 2, my emphasis.

My thanks to Yisrael Medad for making this and other sources available to me.

67 Schechtman, *The Jabotinsky Story*, vol. 2, p. 325.
68 Sigmund Freud, *Jokes and their Relation to the Unconscious*, 1905, *Standard Edition of the Complete Psychological Works*, 24 vols (London, Hogarth 1953-73), vol. 8, p. 115.
69 Jabotinsky, Introduction to Chaim Nachman Bialik, *Poems from the Hebrew* (London, 'Hasefer' 1924), p. xii.
70 Ibid., pp. xv–xvi.
71 Ibid., pp. xiii–xiv.
72 Ibid., p. xiv.
73 Schechtman, *The Jabotinsky Story*, vol. 1, p. 355.
74 Jabotinsky, Introduction to Bialik, *Poems from the Hebrew*, p. 125, p. 127.
75 Jabotinsky, *The Five*, p. 189.
76 In a review of *The Five*, the distinguished translator Hillel Halkin suggests that Marusya is a self-portrait, her self-sacrifice representative of Jabotinsky's rejection of his own anarchist impulses in favour of the discipline required of him as leader of the Revisionists. Halkin, 'Sacrifices', *The New Republic*, 19 December 2005.
77 Jabotinsky, *The Five*, p. 185.
78 Ibid., pp. 189-90.

5

David Grossman's Dilemma*

In David Grossman's 1998 novel, *Be My Knife*, an antiquarian book-dealer starts a passionate correspondence with a woman whom he has barely caught sight of across a room. The unlikely circumstances of their relation, its strange fusion of intimacy and distance, allows them both to say, or rather write, things which neither one has ever admitted before. It allows them to plumb the depths of who they are. Lost to each other and themselves, mostly they seem out of touch with the world. But just occasionally you get a glimpse of how their peculiar and cherished form of insanity might in fact be inseparable from the nation that spawned their virtual love affair. 'Somewhere in the universe', Yair muses in one of his letters, 'there must be that other world we once talked about – a world of light.' But some people 'unfit for such generous bounty and goodness', would find such a world intolerable and commit suicide. 'Here, where we are,' he asks – 'is *this* the penal colony of that other world?' Perhaps every person here, 'man or woman, it doesn't matter, old or young', has already committed suicide.

For nearly two decades, David Grossman has been turning over in his mind the possibility that Israel, miraculous nation as it likes to see itself, might in fact be a moribund state. 'In order to maintain culture, and especially in order to maintain democracy,' he said in a recent discussion with Amos Oz, 'a certain type of illusion is needed.' In Israel today, the layer of culture has disintegrated 'that makes possible the illusions that are needed to maintain a more or less tolerable fabric of life'. To believe in yourself and your world is an illusion, although it's one we need in order to carry on our daily lives. For Grossman it crumbles definitively the moment you witness flesh tear. From that point on, what you fear, or should fear, most, he seems to be saying, is not that your life might be violently ended at any moment – a fear now real for every citizen in a nation that was meant to make the Jewish people safe – but that you have *already died*. 'An entire nation', he writes in *Death as a Way of Life*, his dispatches from Jerusalem of 2003, 'is in a coma.'

'Six million people have allowed their mind, their will, their judgement to degenerate into infuriating criminal passivity.' 'When we emerge from the cocoon that encloses us, it is liable to be too late.' Grossman's writing offers its answer to all those who argue that it is too easy to criticise Israel from the outside: from the country's most contested, holiest, city, he puts the failing of a nation on record – Israel as a failed state.

Grossman's writing is full of figures who could be described as living a kind of death-in-life. In his most famous novel, *See Under: Love* of 1989, the boy Momik, desperately trying to redeem his family's silence about the Holocaust, creates in his mind the lost story of his grandfather Wasserman who miraculously survived the camps and who shows up at the family home in Israel having been presumed dead for years. In Momik's fantasy recreation, Wasserman becomes the protégé of the camp commandant Neigel after it is discovered that he cannot die. He agrees to tell Neigel stories, the Nazi's deepest and secret desire, only on condition that Neigel makes the attempt, each and every time, to kill him. The story Wasserman then tells (the novel is layer under layer of fiction) is the tale of Kazik, a miracle child discovered by an elderly and barren couple, who proceeds to age and die in accelerated time; he is a withered old man by the time he dies at twenty-two hours. The grandfather cannot die, although death is all he longs for having witnessed the killing of his daughter in the camp. The miracle child dies too soon. Either way death is in the wrong place. Wanting to die because you have suffered too much is one thing. But what to make of a nation – and it is impossible not to read the story of Kazik as an allegory for the birth and growth of Israel – that cannot save its own child?

At the end of *Be My Knife*, Miriam breaks the taboo between herself and Yair, and rushes to his house when, in an unexpected phone call, he starts explaining to her insanely that, after an argument, his son is slowly freezing outside in the rain and that he must break the will of the boy (it is unclear at the end of the novel if either the son or the father has survived). Israel has always seen itself as engaged in a struggle for survival (that is its *raison d'être*). Against the dominant rhetoric, Grossman presents us with a nation that appears – from its violent, stubborn, self-defeating behaviour on the ground – to be hell-bent on destroying itself.

No nation, no democracy can live without illusions. If Grossman is right in the link he makes between the state's ills and those of its children, it is to Israel's youth – its pride – that we should look for the cracks in the surface, and for the sickening of the soul. In December 2004, five teenage refuseniks were jailed for a year by the Jaffa Military Court. It is because they aired their disillusionment so loudly that they became the first refuseniks to be court-martialled (all the others had been given administrative sentences or walked free). But those who serve, and then talk, rend the fabric of civilised life. 'I was carried away by the possibility of acting in the most primal and impulsive manner', Staff Sergeant Liran Ron Furer writes of his experience in Gaza in his book *Checkpoint Syndrome:* 'Over time the behaviour becomes more natural [. . .] it became normative [. . .] without fear of punishment and without oversight [. . .] a place to test our limits – how tough, how callous, how crazy we could be.' A group of 'good boys', he insists, barely out of college, goes wild. Furer became a sadist. Without anything ever being stated, he feels it was what was expected. But no one wants to admit to it; no one wants to see (it was only with great difficulty that he succeeded in having his book published in Israel). 'Perhaps the Palestinian tragedy', Grossman writes in *Death as a Way of Life,* in an open letter to a Palestinian friend at the outbreak of the second *intifada,* is 'that you are facing a tough and complicated partner (one convinced it is the meekest, most malleable, most merciful partner that there is)'. Everything is in that parenthesis. Beware of a people that boasts its own virtue. With a stroke of his pen – and Grossman's writing is full of such moments – he takes Israel's self-image apart at the seams. As far back as *Yellow Wind,* his 1988 collection of interviews with Palestinians, Grossman was already pondering 'how much one must be suspicious of people who testify about themselves morning and night that they are merciful'. Nations, like individuals – and Israel is hardly alone in this – cannot bear to think of themselves as anything other than what they ideally would like themselves to be.

Writing to Theodor Herzl in 1899, the French socialist Bernard Lazare complained that, because Herzl so wanted his people to be a perfect nation, modelled on the West, he could not bear to admit, or include in his vision, the abject, impoverished reality of the Eastern European Jew. For Lazare such idealisation was a form of treachery for which the new nation state, if it ever came into being, would pay a heavy price. Grossman does not, I suspect, share Lazare's anarcho-revolutionary politics, but a century later, he carries something of his legacy in the spirit of truth-telling for which he makes his plea. 'Your ultimate objective', Lazare wrote to Herzl, 'is "not to display our national shames". But I am all for displaying them. We die from hiding our shames [. . .] We must educate our nation by showing it what it is.' 'We need to live a life', writes Grossman, 'that is not ideal, not demonic.'

Although he spent seven months involved in the negotiations leading up to the Geneva accord, for which he wrote the Hebrew preface, it seems important that Grossman puts together *Death as a Way of Life* at a moment when, as he sees it, hope has died and he is on the edge of despair ('something in me is dying', 'there is no hope'). It's as if, against his best, or rather worst, judgement, he still believes that Israel only has to look into its own depths to be saved. Israel is 'cracking down' (an expression he used at Jewish Book Week in 2003). Writing is a type of cure. Like a psychoanalyst, Grossman sets himself up as a doctor of the nation's soul; his vocabulary is full of words such as 'denial' and 'repress'. The average Israeli shuts his mind to everything he most needs to know. He has no idea of the 'depths of Palestinian humiliation and suffering' caused by Israel's action in the Territories. Ignorant of the details, he wrongly believes that Oslo offered the Palestinians a viable state. When Rabin speaks of wanting peace, 'the impression is growing stronger', he writes in 1995 two years after the agreement, that he 'really means an expanded security arrangement that will fence the Palestinians into autonomous areas of confinement, surrounded and separated from one another by a dense network of Israeli roads, roadblocks and settlements'. With striking prescience he predicts in the same essay a renewed *intifada* in the 'strangled, despairing "territories"', this time with violence we have not yet seen'. The Israeli cuts himself off from the Arabs who are living, with their own claim to identity, in his midst. *Sleeping on a Wire*, which Grossman published in 1993, consisted of a set of conversations with Palestinians in Israel: 'The Jews don't know enough about us. They don't even want to know that there is another nation here.'

Worse than all this, and all this is bad enough, the Israeli refuses introspection, dreading the 'disconcerting and menacing emotions' it might provoke. Crucially, the threat is as much political as it is psychological – though in this world the two add up to the same thing. Grossman is not calling for some indulgent, if painful, stroking of the national mind. Introspection is not an alternative to justice, but its *precondition*: 'He dreads that [such emotions] will kindle disquieting questions about the justice of his actions.' 'People listened to the victim and they listened to the politicians', writes Staff Sergeant Furer, 'but this voice that says: I did this, we did things that were wrong – crimes, actually – that's a voice I didn't hear.' The reservists who police the West Bank, Grossman observed back in 1988, have a 'special expression and build: something which projects an unconscious detachment of the man from himself'.

Grossman paints a picture of a world in denial, dissociated, floating in its own fears. Why did Netanyahu's government so often behave as if it were a 'persecuted minority group' as if 'it did not really believe in its own legitimacy'? Sharon's national unity government of 2001, Grossman wrote at the time, will cobble together a compromise 'with no connection to reality' and offer it to the Palestinians: 'Israel will again conduct virtual negotiations among itself and between itself and its own fears.' It is in fact the particular gift of these essays, and indeed of all his writing, that Grossman never underestimates Israel's terrible legacy of fear, but it isn't for him the great silencer and riposte to any critique. Fear is not an endgame; it opens a box. Where does this legacy lead? When Grossman uncovers the wounds of the Jewish psyche, he reveals scar tissue which, as it hardens, will not let the nation breathe.

Spanning the decade since Oslo and published under the government of Ariel Sharon, many of the essays in *Death as a Way of Life* are devoted to charting the rise to power of Sharon, elected and re-elected, Grossman suggests, partly because – in his brute physical reality – he exudes nothing but power: 'Put a toga on him and he will look like a Roman Emperor' ('that image, with its very potent instincts and its brutality and its history, apparently has something that appeals to people'). In December 2001, in response to a suicide bomb, Sharon broke off all negotiations with Arafat whose compound was under siege in Ramallah, and sent planes into the West Bank. In his essay on this strategy, which like everything Sharon does, Grossman situates somewhere between the 'grotesque and the catastrophic', he cites a study published in *Nature* about 'a dangerous mechanism in the human visual system' that allows the brain to refuse to register what the eyes clearly see: 'From the moment the brain decides in favour of a given interpretation of the images it is receiving from the eyes, all stimuli that support any other interpretation simply disappear.' Arafat was being 'blotted out', which means, 'actually, that the Palestinian people had also been blotted out, along with their justified desires and aspirations' (for this process Baruch Kimmerling of the Hebrew University of Jerusalem has coined the term 'politicide'). Sharon is blinding himself – a way of acknowledging, perhaps, that he is, like Oedipus, the perpetrator of a dreadful crime. 'War and violence have blinded our eyes, and have turned some of us into killers, and many others of us into tacit collaborators with murderers.'

'Except for a small number of Israelis (most recently David Grossman)', Edward Said wrote in *The Nation* in February 2002, 'no one comes out and says openly that the Palestinians are being persecuted by Israel.' Grossman has never hesitated in condemning the Occupation as 'deformed, immoral, unjust'. There is no mincing of words. It is again his particular talent to be able to do this at the same time as he acknowledges the flush of pleasure for the young Israeli, even one who has demonstrated against the Occupation, when he first receives his call-up papers. (In the same spirit he evokes the erotic charge of walking into and taking over another people's land: 'the sudden penetration and the breaking of the taboo [. . .] I absolutely remember the physical sensation, the sensation of power'.) You can, he seems to be saying, detach yourself from your own excitement. But it is not easy. Grossman has never underestimated what the internal critic or dissenter is up against. 'In Israel, the reality is that it is easier for a man to change religion, maybe even his sex', he observed drily in *Yellow Wind*, 'than to change in any decisive way his political opinions.' In his summing-up at the trial of the five refuseniks at the Jaffa Military Court, the prosecutor called them 'ideological criminals' – 'the worst kind': 'The fact that they are idealistic people and in many ways positive characters should be counted against them.'

Sometimes Grossman's most powerful indictments of current policy slip out almost as an aside. The concept of a 'ticking bomb', used by the army to justify its policy of targeted assassinations, should apply, he says in passing, only when someone is *on the way to* an attack (instead of which, anyone *suspected* of having planned or of planning attacks, along with any surrounding civilians, is now seen as a legitimate target). In February 2004, the anarchist group Anarchists Against the Wall enjoyed an unwelcome notoriety after one of their members shouted out 'Don't shoot – we're Israelis' before being shot at and seriously injured by the IDF. This shocking cry provoked a crisis of truth – for implying that it is all right to shoot Palestinians (an intention the anarchists fervently deny); for exposing the fact that the army discriminates, although by no means always successfully, between 'blood and blood'.

Death as a Way of Life tells the story of a disaster. By the time we get to the end, Israel is 'more militant, nationalist, racist than ever before'. What kind of victory – since Israel could be said to be winning over the Palestinians – leaves a country 'worse off than it has been for the last thirty-five years' (security, economy, national morale all in decline)? What kind of victory leaves a quarter of Palestinians suffering from malnutrition? To which we can add the increasing numbers of children reported in *Ha'aretz* as risking their lives to slip across the Green Line to become beggars inside Israel. At the end of *Yellow Wind*, Grossman posed one 'last question' which could just as well serve as a coda for his essays: 'Is the feeling that the situation cannot possibly continue forever any guarantee that it will eventually change?'

But Grossman does not simply condemn his own nation (there would of course be something wrong if he did). He is clearly appalled by Arafat – he sees the two leaders as locked in the phantom of their own militancy. While the charges against Israel become louder as he progresses, at the same time the balance of judgement almost imperceptibly shifts. After the outbreak of the second *intifada,* far more atrocities against Israel are listed in the opening notes to his essays than the other way round. The lynching of the two army reservists who lost their way near Ramallah in October 2000 is presented, in Grossman's discussion with Oz, as the breaking point 'for all of us'. One of Grossman's greatest gifts is his precision, the extraordinary lengths he goes to in order to give the other side its voice – both *Yellow Wind* and *Sleeping on a*

Wire are dedicated to that. His account of the expulsion of the Hebron cave-dwellers in December 1999 opens with Mahmoud Hamemdeh: 'I was born in this cave.' Then the language becomes more vague: the Palestinians responded to Sharon's provocative visit to the Temple Mount (al-Haram al-Sharif) with an 'outbreak of unrestrained violence'; 'the riots that erupted the next day resulted in many deaths. The wave of violence that spread throughout the West Bank and Gaza was met with overwhelming force by the Israeli security forces.' Whose deaths? Were the rioters armed? 'Wave of violence' lacks an agent, leaves us in the dark. By April 2002 it is the Palestinians who have 'brought about the current intolerable escalation. It is the outcome of their choice to use the weapon of suicide bombings against Israeli civilians.'

You can condemn the bombings as criminal and counterproductive, but still note that something in the tone gives way (another proof, if proof were needed, that the bombings sap the moral ground of the Palestinians or, in Grossman's expression, 'boomerang'). Compare this from 1997 after the first suicide bombing, but before the strategy had taken hold: 'Today it is hard to speak of the Palestinians having any hope. The majority of Israelis do not realise the depth of Palestinian despair and humiliation caused by Israeli government policies. Under these circumstances it is clear, Israeli lives will be as intolerable as Palestinian lives.' Or this from 1998:

> The Israeli eye is trained to skip over the small items in the newspaper: the Palestinian babies dying at road-blocks, the children fainting from thirst in the refugee camps because Israeli officials control the water supply, thousands of families whose homes are bulldozed on the grounds of being 'illegal construction'. Who can face up to all this nauseating detail? Who can acknowledge that this is actually happening? *That it is really happening to us?*

None of this has changed. If anything it is getting worse, as the pioneering *Ha'aretz* journalist Gideon Levy, amongst others, never ceases to stress. These words from an article written by Levy in December 2003, with their stress on ignorance, could almost have been written by Grossman:

> The suicide bomber at the Geha Junction was from Beit Furik, one of the most imprisoned villages in the territories that is surrounded by road blocks [. . .] on all sides [. . .] At least one woman in labour, Rula Ashatiya, gave birth at the Beit Furik checkpoint and lost her infant. Few Israelis are capable of imagining what life is like in Beit Furik [. . .] Israelis have little interest in knowing the lay of the land from which terror springs

[. . .] Israel counted '81 days of quiet' [. . .] But there is no greater lie than this. The quiet was only here. During this 'quiet', dozens of Palestinians were killed, and almost no one bothered to report it [. . .] There is [. . .] an Israeli price to pay for the many concealed Palestinian dead.

So what has changed for Grossman? Perhaps he feels that his writing has failed: that a decade painstakingly and boldly pointing all this out inside Israel has had precisely no effect. 'I know very well why I joined the Geneva initiative: because I feel that every day that passes without change pushes Israel another centimetre towards the abyss.'

Critics of the Geneva Accords stress that the Palestinians have given up the right of return of the refugees while Israel has taken no responsibility for the creation of the refugee problem in 1948 (as Ilan Pappe has pointed out, it also still leaves the Palestinians with only 15 per cent of their original land). More cynically, some have argued that the only difference between the accord and Sharon's aim of unilateral withdrawal and *de facto* annexation of territories is that the Palestinians are being given the opportunity to agree to the plan. But one criticism of Geneva – that it gives legitimacy to the Zionist character of the state – is worth pausing at. In fact, as Salim Tamari has pointed out, this is not quite right. Geneva does not give legitimacy to Israel as 'the state of the Jewish people', but refers to 'the right of the Jewish people to statehood and the recognition of the right of the Palestinian people to statehood', without prejudice to the 'equal rights of the parties' respective citizens' (an awkward echo of Balfour as he also observes, which famously referred to the civil and religious, but not the *political* rights of the 'existing non-Jewish communities in Palestine').

In *Sleeping on a Wire*, a Palestinian Israeli, Mohammed Kiwan, and a Moroccan Jew, Jojo Abtubal, argue this one out. Kiwan wants autonomy – a canton even – inside the Jewish state. Abtubal is appalled and cannot believe him: 'He doesn't really mean it. He wants security. He wants a way to defend himself. That's what he means when he asks for a canton. He actually wants a lot less than that – equality.' This is 1993 – the quarrel takes place against the backdrop of a two-state solution (the solution also proposed by the Geneva accord). But what this remarkable dialogue illustrates before its time is that the issue of minority status contains within it the question of a binational state: 'Jojo would never give up Israel as the Jewish state. Mohammed would never retreat from his goal of full equal rights with Jojo – that is, that Israel be "a country of its citizens" and "not the country of the Jewish people".' Kiwan, we could say, is trying to make of Abtubal a post-Zionist before post-Zionism. 'Understand one thing,' he expostulates, 'that the minute we repeal all the privileges Jews get here, this country will stop being a Jewish country and will become the country of the people who live in it.' 'Have I ever', Grossman asks in the middle of this poignant, semi-comic encounter which he has himself engineered, 'imagined, down to the smallest living detail, a truly democratic, pluralistic, and egalitarian way of life in Israel?'

'The Jewish majority's explicit desire to retain its numerical superiority', he writes, 'is one that, when it comes down to it, beats in the heart of every nation [. . .] I don't want to be part of a Jewish minority in Israel.' This is, he acknowledges, 'an unresolved discrepancy in the democracy [the Jewish people] desire.' Because of the threat it poses to the irrevocably Jewish nature of the state, Palestinian right of return is Grossman's cut-off point – 'Point of No Return' is the title of the January 2001 essay from which these quotes are taken. 'We must', he says at the end of the essay, try 'to achieve a partial justice for both sides.' We could retranslate: justice is partial. Even if justice is on your side – that is, on the side of the Palestinians, as it so clearly is on this issue under international law – you cannot have it, because it will destroy my dream. That the dream is falling apart or steadily fading, as Grossman so powerfully demonstrates, makes it more not less potent. Israel was a 'marvel and an opportunity'; Israelis today are living on the 'sidetrack of the life that was meant for us'; they need to be reminded of 'what they once were'. 'Are there any Israelis today living the life they want to live?' In phrases like these, it is as if the country had been temporarily diverted from its path: 'this storm that sends our compasses awry', as if violence were a distraction rather than intrinsic, as Grossman was in fact one of the first to acknowledge, to the creation of Israel as a nation state.

Yet, at other moments, the failing, not to say violence, is still endemic: it seems 'as if we Israelis are doomed to make this error by our very nature' (he is talking of Lebanon); 'We are caught in the spiral of violence into which we were born.' In *See Under: Love*, on the walls of Momik's bedroom hang a portrait of Prime Minister David Ben-Gurion and a picture of 'Vultures with their wings spread like steel birds boldly defending the nation's skies'. Across the terrain of the nation, the mind shifts and cannot settle. As a writer, Grossman always has the courage of his own ambivalence. In Israel, we could say, the mind does not know its own place: 'In the Diaspora, we decided we were a people of time. An eternal people. But', he continues in his discussion with Oz, 'even after we came to this place, we were still unable to crystallise for ourselves a feeling of identity as a people of place.'

But what form should, or can, such an identity take? To say Grossman loves Israel is an understatement – the essays in *Death as a Way of Life* often read like the love letters of a man pleading with a lover, who has dreadfully betrayed him, to think again (Yair and Miriam several years down the line). But belonging is something else. Grossman could almost be described as Isaac Deutscher's 'non-Jewish Jew'. When he does feel a sense of Jewish identity, it seems as if it has taken him by surprise. A sense of belonging appears suddenly like an unexpected guest. Every Tuesday he meets with his study group or *hevruta* – a man and a woman – to discuss the Bible, Talmud, Kafka and Agnon: 'In the midst of confusion and the loss that surrounds me, I unexpectedly feel I belong' (he is the 'nonreligious of the three'). When he visits the twenty-six annexed Palestinian villages of Jerusalem, endowed by the governments who seized them 'with the sanctity of biblical Zion', he feels nothing. In 1993, as he travels across a bare-topped piece of countryside where there is neither a Jewish nor Arab village to be seen, 'I had a strange urge to peel this land of its names and designations and descriptions and dates, Israel, Palestine, Zion, 1897, 1929, 1936, 1948, 1967, 1987, the Jewish State, the Promised Land, the Holy Land, the Land of Splendour, the Zionist entity, Palestine.' Could there be a little piece of earth that is 'still free of meaning?' What would remain? In this brief, euphoric moment in 1993, Grossman strips the land of its overburdened significance. Like Virginia Woolf, who once famously said 'I hate meaning', he recognises that only dictators control the world of signs (in *Be My Knife*, Yair reads Woolf in the army). Too much naming, like too much conviction, can kill. At the end of his 2004 novel *Someone to Run With*, a group of thugs discover the cave where the heroine Tamar is nursing her brother back from his drug addiction: 'The Temple Mount is ours', one of them screams as he attempts to seize them, 'Now let's take care of Abraham's tomb.'

In Jewish history, however, language has cut both ways. Again, Grossman's preoccupation with this problem in his writing is precise, historical in relation to the Jews. The peril of resurgent anti-Semitism is that the Jew is being made to revert into a symbol of himself. 'The Jew who came to the Land of Israel and built a state in order to connect [. . .] with a concrete existence', he states in his discussion with Oz, 'has suddenly again become a symbol of something else. After all, the Jew was always a kind of metaphor; he was never perceived as the thing itself.' This threat is existential, but there is no less damage to the Jewish mind. A numbing sense of sacrificial destiny returns and shuts out the world: 'the tragic feelings of Jewish destiny seem to be closing in on us again' (at Jewish Book Week in 2003, Grossman described the Jewish sense of victimhood as a 'temptation'). The collective fossilises and retracts – clings hard and fast to itself. In Israel of all places – intended to restore 'us to the practical, the human, the historical' – Jewish life is failing to become mundane.

Grossman is a universalist. In *Death as a Way of Life*, remarks such as the following – which go against the grain of a central strand of Jewish thinking

– are thrown out almost casually: 'I don't belong to those who believe that the Holocaust was a specifically Jewish event. As I see it, all civilised, fair-minded persons must ask themselves serious questions about the Holocaust. These are not Jewish questions. They are universal questions.' And for all the energy he devoted to the Geneva negotiations, he doesn't really believe in governments: 'There is a no-man's land, a dead place', he writes at the end of *Yellow Wind*, 'dividing personal pain, a man and his feelings, from the place in which things are decided and the agreements and the party manifestos and official eulogies are drafted.' And he hates collectives: 'There are questions', he continues on the Holocaust, 'about the human soul that can so easily be made to stop speaking as "I" and to begin roaring about "we".' Of the campaigning West Bank lawyer and writer Raja Shehadeh he writes in *Yellow Wind*: 'he seems to be one for whom the blind, anonymous Occupation threatens his personal sense of individualism, rather than his Arab or national identity' – as if his struggle for national identity was something from which Shehadeh should be saved. What is left of collective identity, indeed of politics, if – in a classic liberal move that in this case is also a push against the horrors of the world – the individual stands on her own? 'In every person's life', muses Tamar, 'there are situations in which he is solely responsible for saving his own soul.'

Can you be a non-Zionist Zionist? Grossman, I think, comes close. Before being deported, Wasserman in *See Under: Love* was a children's writer, loved above all because he dealt with universal topics and carefully eschewed the requisite and expected Zionist themes (the nation again cramps its child). The teenagers in *Someone to Run With*, all of them artists, trapped and exploited in a vicious refuge for the homeless, sing this song:

> A Star of David broke in two
> Herzl's opinions died with the man.
> Rotten in the grave, with spikes of Sabra fruit.
> But everything goes according to plan.
>
> Like a man to hold a gun in my hand,
> Blow off heads, like a man,
> Like a man, march to my death, all alone,
> And everything goes according to plan.

And then: 'All of a sudden, from all corners of the yard, even from the dance floor, rose the roar: *'Fuck the plan.'* Grossman is devoted to his country, but on condition, it seems, that it reach beyond just about every definition it has ever offered of itself.

Gradually, or rather between the lines, a very different voice can be read from the one that tolls Israel's fulfilment of its worst destiny. This is the voice of Grossman, writer of brilliant fictions which 'dissolve' and 'destabilise' every best defence of his life. Fiction is not consoling: 'it is his very freedom that deprives an artist of comforting illusions'. This makes fiction, intolerably, like war. But it also saves: 'When I write, for a moment *I am not a victim.*' Writing is a cure for dispassion that makes him feel alive again: 'an act of self-definition in a situation that literally threatens to obliterate me'. Above all, literature forces you into other people's minds (Yair's fierce and clumsy accosting of Miriam becomes a metaphor for writing). It forces you to connect. Jerusalem is a city with a centre for lost dogs but not for missing children – it was partly to expose this brute fact about modern life in Israel that Grossman wrote this latest novel. If Tamar saves her own soul, it is not only by saving her brother, but by singing – in a voice that triumphantly swells with its own fear – to strangers on the street: 'I don't have the courage to do this. I am not capable of giving myself up like this, to strangers.' She does. And because she does, and does it so well, her plan to find her brother works. She is picked out and carted off by the criminals who have taken possession of all the child artists of the city, including her brother.

In his fiction, Grossman forces his characters to perform rites of entry that they cannot bear. Everyone goes a bit too far – geographically, physically, psychologically, or all three – as if his fictional characters were atoning for the blindness, or disconnection, of the nation (ignorance and intimacy as the opposite ends of the same pole). 'I must enter the vortex of my greatest fear and repulsion', he wrote as he made his way to the refugee camps in 1988. 'Make room for them within us. How does one do that? It is precisely the thing that we, the majority, forbid them with such deft determination', he asked again in 1993, this time in relation to the Arab Israelis. This is not a call for empathy, but for something closer. A counter to ignorance, but also an alternative to the deadly forms of proximity that characterise a state of war. War after all brings people together like nothing else. Grossman is striving for such intimacy but in a new form. Not by breaking bones – 'Break their bones', Rabin famously cried at the time of the first *intifada*, as Grossman recalls in *Death as a Way of Life*. Not by tearing flesh. But something, oddly, not a million miles away. Like getting into another person's skin. By the time he reaches Tamar, the young boy Assaf, who has been entrusted by Jerusalem City Hall to find the owner of her lost dog, has pored over her diaries. He knows the mind of a young girl who, convinced that nobody will ever understand her, longs above all else to read. Their final encounter merely puts the seal on a link that has been grafted into each of them long before they meet. Although the fiction does not cross the Arab–Israeli divide like the non-fiction, still the challenge is to cross the vortex, to get as far as you can – and whatever the dangers – into the other's place: 'We will see the broken forms in each other', Yair says to Miriam, 'This is what I want, right now. That we will see the darkness in each other.'

Someone to Run With falls into the strange category of adolescent novel. It has been a huge success in Israel, perhaps Grossman's most commercially successful to date, selling 100,000 copies on publication. Since he has been writing about children since the beginning, it seems appropriate that children – or rather not-quite-still-children – should now become his target reading group. Will this generation survive its parents? This is a question for any culture, but one that has its own special urgency in Israel's case. Grossman's Jerusalem is a city of lost souls – runaways, drug addicts, drop-outs, most of whom have left their parents, whether as a consequence of disillusionment or neglect. Once again, the nation fails its child. No one is looking. Parental blindness mimics the shut-down retina of the state. The only seer in the book is Theodora, a Greek nun, who in fact can see virtually nothing as she has been trapped in a house at the centre of the city since she was chosen as a young girl to travel to the Holy Land and wait for the pilgrims of Lyxos (who will never come as the island fell into the sea in 1951). But she is the only one who understands Tamar and Assaf, who find themselves unexpectedly and in turns at her door.

And yet this is one of Grossman's most fiercely optimistic novels: if these children are lost, they have also been set free (we have failed, now it is up to you). Perhaps the mere fact of writing for this group of readers is his way of guaranteeing a future of which he himself – to judge from *Death as a Way of Life* – is increasingly unsure. You would be hard-pressed to recognise the Jerusalem of the essays from this tale. Everything simply moves too fast (one way of saving yourself from political despair, or indeed any kind of despair, being never to stand still). Like a helter-skelter in a fairground, *Someone To Run With* reads as an urgent bid against its own worst fears. Tamar's brother is saved, she finds love and her lost dog. Theodora, at the high point of the drama when Tamar seems in danger, walks out onto the street. Neither 1967 nor the assassination of Rabin in 1995 had persuaded her to move. 'Like a little girl who aged, instantly, without passing through life', Theodora is a reprise of Kazik from *See Under: Love*. The withered, prematurely aged, can find life. The strains of the city will survive – if not what the nation wants for the city (meshing the destinies of Theodora, Tamar and Assaf, Grossman gets close to Joyce's fantasy in *Ulysses* of the 'Greek-Jew').

How much damage can you do to a soul? The question has haunted Grossman from his earlier writing. Can it be repaired? (A different question from asking whether there can be a resolution to the conflict.) In *See Under:*

Love, Neigel tentatively asks Wasserman: 'Are certain passages – I mean – do you think any passages of the soul are irreversible?' (not for him, as it turns out). Grossman addresses the same question as a warning to Gush Emunim, the Block of the Faithful, in *Yellow Wind*: 'Is the soul a modular mechanism in which specific "parts" may be disconnected [. . .] until the danger passes?' 'Some parts of the soul', Grossman asserts more blandly, as a matter of fact, in *Death as a Way of Life*, 'cannot be reclaimed.' Tamar takes up the question again. If a person seals up his soul for a certain mission, can they, when it is all over, go back to being who they were before? But when she remembers and repeats her question at the end of the novel, she is laughing joyously, 'her heart full'.

In *Death as a Way of Life*, Grossman describes Jerusalem as a 'hard city' with 'too much holiness in the air'. 'It's sad to be / the mayor of Jerusalem – it's aweful', writes Yehuda Amichai in one of his most famous poems. Another poem, simply called 'Jerusalem', contains these lines:

> In the sky of the Old City
> A kite.
> At the other end of the string,
> A child
> I can't see
> Because of the wall.
>
> We have put up many flags,
> They have put up many flags.
> To make us think that they're happy.
> To make them think that we're happy.

Grossman is not pretending to be happy. Euphoria can be a measure of bleakness, as well as its counterpoint – *Death as a Way of Life* and *Someone to Run With* appeared together in 2003. Grossman's writing is exuberant, wonderfully sorrowful. It is not a criticism to suggest that at times it feels as if he is the badly let-down child. For me, there is no other Israeli writer, translated into English, who goes so far into the heart of the matter.

*A version of this chapter was first published in the *London Review of Books*, 18 March 2004.

6

Deadly Embrace*

All suicides kill other people. However isolated the moment, suicide is also always an act of cruelty. Anyone left behind after a loved one commits, or even attempts, suicide is likely to spend much of the rest of their life wondering whether they themselves have, or should have, survived. Suicide is rarely the singular, definitive, act it appears to be. The ego, writes Freud, turns onto itself the hatred it feels towards the object. But the object is never spared. No one commits suicide, psychoanalyst Karl Menninger stated in 1933, unless they experience at once 'the wish to die, the wish to kill, the wish to be killed'. You can die, but you cannot commit suicide, on your own.

At the end of Tolstoy's *Anna Karenina*, perhaps the greatest literary exploration of suicide, Vronsky, Anna's lover, responds to her suicide by joining the thousands of volunteers leaving Russia for Serbia to protect the Slavs against the Turks. He had already tried to kill himself when, much earlier in the novel, Anna was assumed to be at death's door after the birth of their illegitimate child. Tolstoy's novel is riddled with suicidal moments. But this final one – since it is clear that Vronsky wishes only to die – is different. These men are sacrificing themselves for a noble cause, as Anna's brother insists when he converges with Vronsky on his way to the war and Levin – the inspired man of the countryside – on the same train. 'But it's not just to sacrifice themselves', Levin responds, 'it's to kill Turks.' Levin will not accept that the 'fine-talking' volunteers and the newspapers reporting them truly speak for 'the will and thought' of the people – 'a thought that expressed itself in revenge and murder'. Sacrifice, even for a noble cause, is an ugly affair. Today in Britain there is outrage, especially among parents, that young men have been sent to Iraq for a lie. We also see the injustice of the tens of thousands of Iraqi deaths, especially those of civilians. But that war is murder, whatever the cause, as Levin insists, is not something that any of us is encouraged to contemplate.

By sending the suicidal Vronsky off to fight in Serbia, Tolstoy brings suicide into the public domain. The last suicide is not that of Anna, convinced she is no longer loved, throwing herself under a train. It is that of a man, already being fêted as a hero by many, who wants to kill and die in the same breath. Suicide bombing is a recent phenomenon, but it is an illusion to believe that only in the culture of Islam has the link ever been made between war and suicide, between murder and martyrdom, between killing the enemy and killing yourself. Samson, arguably the first suicide killer, is the hero of a lovingly rendered novel by the founder of Revisionist Zionism, Ze'ev Jabotinsky. 'The world's first suicide terrorists', writes political scientist Robert Pape in *Dying to Win – The Strategic Logic of Suicide Terrorism*, 'were probably two militant Jewish revolutionary groups, the Zealots and the Sicarii.' From 4 BC to AD 70, they used violence with the aim of provoking a popular uprising against the Roman occupation of Judea (their numerous public assassinations could be described as suicide missions as they regularly led to immediate capture, torture and death).

Suicide bombing is most often considered as a peculiarly monstrous, indeed inhuman, aberration that cannot – or indeed must not – be understood. When Liberal Democrat MP Jenny Tonge observed 'If I had to live in that situation – and I say that advisedly – I might just consider being one myself', the Israeli embassy responded in a statement: 'We would not expect any human being – and surely not a British MP – to express an understanding of such atrocities.' Jenny Tonge was sacked from her party's front bench. I think we can be fairly sure that if she had expressed similar understanding of the policy of targeted assassinations, or extra-judicial killing, in response to suicide bombings, she would not today be out of her job (she was subsequently elevated, or moved sideways, to the House of Lords). The wording she used – 'If I had to . . . ' – is crucial. Jenny Tonge was making a leap of empathetic identification. She was not sympathising; she was trying to imagine what it was like to be a Palestinian in the Occupied Territories (she condemned the bombings). When Cherie Blair said in June 2002, 'As long as young people feel they have got no hope but to blow themselves up you are never going to make progress', Downing Street apologised. What never needs apologising for is the violence of the state. Perhaps there is a logic here. If the case for war is weak (or indeed non-existent), then the ugliness and guilt of war rise perilously close to the surface of the public mind – war, in Levin's words, as murder and revenge. In which case, it helps to be able to point to something far worse, preferably from another culture or world, with which no reasonable human being could possibly identify or empathise. Apart from being evasive, this is politically inept. In the film

The Fog of War, Robert McNamara presents rule number one of his eleven rules of war: 'Empathise with the enemy.'

Suicide bombing kills far fewer people than conventional warfare; the reactions it provokes must reside therefore somewhere else than in numbers of the dead. It is of course feared as a weapon against which there seems to be no protection or viable response (targeted assassinations simply provoke further retaliation and Israel's wall is already showing itself incapable of deterring attacks). The horror it inspires cannot, however, lie in the deliberate targeting of civilians. According to McNamara, 100,000 people were burnt to death at the end of the war in the Allied attack on Tokyo. In *The Natural History of Destruction*, W.G. Sebald describes the 10,000 tons of high explosives and incendiary bombs dropped on the densely populated residential areas of Hamburg in the summer of 1943 (the whole city became a fireball).

The horror would appear to be associated with the fact that the attacker also dies. Dropping cluster bombs from the air is apparently less repugnant, it is somehow deemed, by the leaders of the Western world at least, to be morally superior. Why dying with your victim should be seen as the greater sin than saving yourself is unclear. Perhaps, then, the reason lies partly in the unbearable intimacy shared in their final moments by the suicide bomber and her or his victims. Suicide bombing is in itself an act of passionate identification – you take the enemy with you in a deadly embrace. As Israel becomes a fortress state, and the Palestinians are shut into their enclaves, with less and less possibility of contact between the two sides, suicide bombing might be, tragically, the closest they can get. 'I will never cease embracing you. / And I will never release you', writes Mahmoud Darwish in his poem 'He Embraces His Murderer' (he is not talking about suicide bombing but of the hateful intimacy between the two sides of the conflict).

There is a historical aspect to that proximity. By fostering Shia resistance, Israel's invasion of Lebanon in 1982 created the space for Hizbollah, who carried out the first suicide bombings in the early 1980s. Israel began supporting Hamas from the late 1980s after a deliberate decision was made to strengthen Islamic groups in order to weaken Arafat and divide the Palestinians among themselves. The Islamic University of Gaza was created with the approval of the Defense Ministry; when cinemas in Gaza were stormed by Islamic groups and restaurants set on fire for selling alcohol, Israeli soldiers stood by and watched. All this is detailed in Christopher Reuter's *My Life Is a Weapon* of 2004. Hizbollah in turn would get a permanent foothold inside Israel when it offered vital support to the 415 leading cadres of Hamas and Islamic Jihad, expelled into Southern Lebanon by Yitzhak Rabin following the abduction and murder of an Israeli soldier in

December 1992. It has always been a paradox for Western observers that Hizbollah, which promotes an Iranian-style Islamic revolution for the whole of the Middle East (the organisation was created following the arrival in Lebanon of 1000 Iranian Revolutionary Guards in the early eighties), is also the most efficient provider of welfare and support for displaced Palestinians in Lebanon and in the Occupied Territories, sometimes with what might seem unlikely effects. One widow of a suicide bomber, under pressure to move into the household of her father-in-law, was enabled by Hizbollah to live with her children on her own.

That Israeli policy engendered suicide bombing was acknowledged by Rabin. Having originally promoted indiscriminate bombing of South Lebanon 'until there's nobody left there' – he was Defense Minister at the time – he was finally led to conclude that 'terror cannot be finished by one war; it's total nonsense'. Replacing 'PLO terrorism' with 'Shi'ite terrorism', they had done 'the worst thing' in the struggle against terrorism. 'No one PLO terrorist', he observed, 'has ever made himself into a live bomb.'

According to Eyad El-Sarraj, psychiatrist and the founder and director of the Gaza Community Mental Health Programme, those committing suicide attacks today are the children of the first *intifada*. Studies show that during that uprising, 55 per cent of children witnessed their fathers being humiliated or beaten by Israeli soldiers. Martyrdom – sacrificing oneself for God – increases its appeal when the image of the earthly father bites the dust. 'It's despair,' Sarraj states baldly, 'a despair where living becomes no different to dying.' When life is constant degradation, death becomes the only source of pride. Kamal Aqeel is the acting mayor of Khan Yunis in Gaza. 'In 1996,' he explains, 'practically all of us were against the martyr operations. Not any longer [. . .] We all feel that we can no longer bear the situation as it is; we feel that we'd simply explode under all this pressure of humiliation.' Martyrs are saying to their own people, writes Reuter, the cause is greater than our (and your) lives. To the outside world, they are saying: we fear humiliation more than we fear death.

It is a widespread religious belief, by no means exclusive to Islam, that life begins after death. But for those wishing to denigrate suicide bombers and their culture, which is not the same thing as condemning the act, it is easy to degrade that belief. Humiliation can, it seems, pursue its quarry into the afterlife. Most often we are told of the seventy-two virgins proffering their favours in the skies. In fact the virgins reputedly awaiting the martyr in Paradise are symbols of purity and innocence – this is more a sacred utopia, a late, exalted, compensation for the wretched of the earth, than a second shot at worldly pleasures. 'Thoughts of Paradise', writes award-winning *Ha'aretz* journalist Amira Hass, 'embody the evaporation of the dream of a Palestinian state.' Or in the words of psychologist Shalfic Masalqa, interviewed by Barbara Victor in *Army of Roses* of 2004: 'To be tempted to go to Paradise means that life on earth is hell.'

There are other myths that need to be challenged, such as the idea that the families of the suicide bombers only celebrate the martyr's death. 'The barrage of communications continued unabated, and the shouting and speeches being staged in the street made sure there was no room for tears and sadness', writes Donia ElAmal Ismaeel in 'Dates and Bitter Coffee', her short story in the 2006 collection *Qissat: Short Stories by Palestinian Women* about the family of a suicide bomber, 'closing the door on people's humanity' – the family are stunned and grieving when Islamic Jihad arrive and start the barrage in the street. Or that there is never any doubt and can be no change of heart. In Hany Abu Assad's Oscar-nominated 2005 film, *Paradise Now*, one of the two men on a suicide mission changes his mind, and the other is challenged by a woman friend in the longest dialogue in the film on the destructiveness and utter futility of such acts.

The mythology, however, suggests a contradiction. On the one hand, suicide bombers are beyond the pale of understanding. On the other, what goes on inside the mind of a suicide bomber can somehow be uncovered in its most intimate detail, both in this world and beyond. Reuter opens his book by asking: what motivates a suicide bomber? Or rather, what 'kind of people' are they? He knows there is no answer. Suicide bombers are not a species. He also knows that his question is loaded. If suicide attacks are political, then they call for a political response. If they stem from 'perversity', then the perpetrators can be isolated as 'a criminal sect'. Behind the argument that suicide bombers should not, or cannot, be understood lies a subtext of racist dehumanisation. When El-Sarraj is asked if it is true that Palestinians do not care about human life, even their own flesh and blood, he replies: 'How can you believe in your own humanity if you don't believe in the humanity of the enemy?'

Writing about suicide bombing therefore poses a serious question of genre. It is not just, as Avishai Margalit puts it, that every statement is liable to be contested. Nor just the disputed vocabulary (describing these attacks as 'suicide bombing' is already to beg the question). What is at issue is something more like an ethics of form. Reuter has chosen to write a history, or perhaps a geography, that meticulously traces the beginnings of today's attacks to the child battalions of Khomeini, cannon fodder who went into battle with a key to Paradise around their necks, through Syria to Lebanon and Israel–Palestine (those child battalions give the lie that sending children into battle is something only Palestinians have ever done). This in itself allows him to defuse the concentration on the Palestinians, stops them from appearing like freaks of nature (or culture), places them inside a legacy which stems from the realpolitik of modern times, for which of course the West bears more than a share of responsibility (Britain supported Saddam Hussein in the war against Khomeini).

What is unique about the suicide attacks of the second *intifada* is that they come '*from* the people *for* the people', in Reuter's phrase, unlike the more sect-based cults of the Tamil Tigers or the Kurdistan Workers' Party. This makes them almost impossible to defeat. If suicide attacks arise from below, as the reaction to an invading or occupying army, the simple conclusion is that, when those armies pull out, so the strategy will cease. Following the Israeli withdrawal from Lebanon, enthusiasm for suicide attacks has dramatically declined. Sheikh Fadlallah, *spiritus rector* of the most radical Lebanese Shi'ites, was one of the first high-ranking Islamic scholars to condemn the attacks of 11 September 2001. In Iran today, the idea of killing oneself in order to enter Paradise has all but disappeared. There is a lesson here. It is not military intervention – 'the preferred (and not terribly successful) method of Israel and the United States vis-à-vis their Palestinian and Al-Qaeda jihadist foes' – but the internal development of Iran itself, the growing desire for democracy after two decades of theocratic experiment, that has made the difference. Reuter was writing before the election of Ahmadinejad, which has put back the cause of democratisation, and advanced that of theocracy, to say the least. Nonetheless, against the violent Manichaean rhetoric of the times, and its brute interventionism, Reuter offers a counter-narrative. Suicide attacks in Israel–Palestine will stop when Israel withdraws from the Occupied Territories. More generally across the region, notably in response to 9/11, the West should keep out.

Robert Pape's *Dying to Win* is based on a database he compiled of every suicide attack around the world from 1980 to 2003. 'What nearly all suicide terrorists have in common', he writes 'is a specific secular and strategic goal: to compel modern democracies to withdraw military forces from territory that the terrorists consider to be their homeland.' (To the charge that this does not apply to Al-Qaeda, Pape points to Osama Bin Laden's repeated public statements that his actions were designed to remove the American presence from the Persian Gulf.) If this is true, then US strategy in relation to Afghanistan and Iraq is likely to provoke the very onslaughts it is intended to resist: 'The sustained presence of heavy American combat forces in Muslim countries is likely to *increase* the odds of the next 9/11.' 'Our actions', he concludes, 'may well end up helping terrorist leaders recruit many more suicide terrorists to kill us.'

As Reuter also points out, the Palestinians are strangely in tune with their messianic counterparts in Israel, one of the farthest outreaches of Zionism, in aligning nationalism with religious fervour. There are voices on both sides in the conflict for whom the struggle over Palestine constitutes a holy war (for Pape, fundamentalism is not the cause of suicide bombing, but the presence of religious differences between occupier and occupied greatly increases the chances of the strategy taking hold). Torah scribe Elitzur Segal, from Ofra, a hilltop settlement in the West Bank, is the author of a *halakhic* article dealing with the concept of *mesirut hanefesh* (self-sacrifice) during war, entitled 'Suicide for the Sake of Heaven', cited by Nadav Shragai in *Ha'aretz* in December 2004. 'In every war,' he writes, 'situations arise in which a person must knowingly place himself in a situation where his death is certain, and anyone who volunteers for such an operation is a holy hero [. . .] It is permitted to carry out an action that causes death, as people in the outposts in Sinai did in the Yom Kippur War and in other wars in which they fought the enemy to the death, even though they could have saved themselves, or as the holy person Dr Baruch Goldstein did in Hebron, but it appears that even a more certain death, such as blowing oneself up with a hand grenade together with the enemies – a case in which death is certain – is also without a doubt permitted and a commandment.' On 25 February 1994, Baruch Goldstein shot and killed twenty-nine Muslim worshippers at a Hebron mosque before being killed by other potential victims at the site. In his article on extremism in Judaism, Christianity and Islam, John Shepherd cites the rabbi at Goldstein's funeral, who eulogised him as a 'holy martyr [. . .] from now on our intercessor in heaven [. . .] he heard the cry of the land of Israel, which is being stolen from us day after day by the Muslims [. . .] The Jews will inherit the land not by any peace agreement but only by shedding blood.' After the funeral, the army provided a guard of honour at the tomb. Attorney Naftali Wertzberger, who regularly represents Kach members and hilltop residents who fall foul of the law, refers to him as a *shaheed* or martyr for the cause. Goldstein's grave at Hebron, visited today by Jews from all round the world, is a shrine.

How, then, should you write about suicide bombing? To consider this question and its difficulties, we might pass from Christopher Reuter, who has written a history, to Barbara Victor, whose *Army of Roses – Inside the World of Palestinian Women Suicide Bombers* reads more like a novel or short-story collection (she is a novelist, as well as a journalist with more than twenty years of experience in the Middle East, and the author of a study of Hanan Ashrawi). As the subtitle suggests, her desire is to enter the world of the women suicide bombers, and to tell their stories. Empathy here is in no short supply. 'She tries to understand, even to feel' (the words of Christopher Dickey, *Newsweek* Paris bureau chief and Middle East editor, who writes the foreword). For many in the West, the female suicide bomber is the most inhuman, since she violates the woman's role as the bearer of life. Victor's aim is to redeem her: 'This book tells the story of the women who died for reasons that go beyond the liberation of Palestine.'

Above all she *narrates*, uncovering the most private, indeed frequently humiliating, details of these women's lives – six at the time of Victor's book, more since. On 4 October 2003, Hanadi Jaradat blew herself up at Maxim's restaurant in Haifa on the eve of Yom Kippur killing nineteen Israelis and injuring many others. From a privileged Palestinian family, on the verge of opening her own law practice in Jenin, Jaradat had been the witness to the killing by the Israeli army of her cousin Salah and her brother Fahdi, when they were sitting together in a café the previous May. Without preamble, the soldiers drew up alongside them and shot them. According to Victor, a bomb-laden car that Fahdi was to drive into Haifa the next day was parked only a few feet away. Jaradat fled but 'ran directly into the arms of Yasser Obeidi, one of the most wanted men in the West Bank', a twenty-nine-year-old married man and the military commander of Islamic Jihad in Jenin (Literally into his arms? Was he standing on the street corner? This sounds like something out of the film *Notting Hill*). A very different account by Kevin Toolis in the *Observer* states that she was in fact in Jordan shopping for Fahdi's wedding when he was killed but returned to Jenin to identify him in the morgue. Victor's story – as may already be clear – is a story of romance, passion and cynical intrigue. In her version, Jaradat is cruelly manipulated by Obeidi who persuades her to become a martyr – 'he became her lover, mentor and one-way ticket to Paradise', where they would find 'eternal happiness as man and wife'. The source for this narrative is not given. In fact, as it emerges, there are conflicting stories as to how and why Jaradat ended her life. For the Palestinians, it was to avenge the deaths of her cousin and brother. For the Israelis, she was a woman depressed at her lack of marriage prospects at the age of twenty-nine: 'Allegedly she intimidated men because of her good looks and education.'

This gives the issue of empathy a new twist. The Israeli reading of Jaradat's motives should warn us that, whether what it attributes to her is true or false, personalising the female martyr can be a way of denying the abuses of the army – in addition to the killing of her brother and cousin, Hanadi's father had been denied permission to attend a hospital in Haifa for his illness – and of silencing the Palestinian political case. In November 2006, a picture of the latest woman suicide bomber was on the front page of *Ha'aretz*, Fatima Al-Nejar, described as a fifty-seven-year-old mother of nine – in fact she is sixty-eight – with no mention of the fact that one of her grandsons had been killed in the conflict. Rory McCarthy of the *Guardian* interviewed her family: ' "Some people say she must have been depressed", says her daughter Fathiya, "But it wasn't true, she was a religious woman. She did this to fight the Israelis and get them out of our land." ' Here the distinction between suicide and martyrdom becomes crucial. According to Islam, it is a sin to commit suicide. Your life belongs to God and is only his to dispose of. Martyrdom is, however, something else. 'If a martyr wants to kill himself because he's sick of being alive, that's suicide. But if he wants to sacrifice his soul in order to defeat the enemy and for God's sake – well, then he's a martyr', explained the late Abdul Aziz al-Rantisi, second-in-command of Hamas until he was killed by the Israelis in 2003. (As Reuter stresses throughout, this also shows Islam as requiring interpretation.)

In Victor's analysis, the only possible explanation for the woman suicide bomber is that she is sick of life; the back cover refers to their 'blighted inner lives'. Wada Idris, the first woman suicide bomber, was in despair after being divorced for diagnosed infertility; Darine Abu Aisha was determined to avoid the fate of marriage; Zina, accomplice of Izzedine Masri who detonated himself in Sbarro's Pizzeria in Jerusalem in August 2002, interviewed by Victor in prison, had her illegitimate child taken away from her: 'Without exception, every woman and young girl who attempted to or succeeded in blowing herself up had been marginalised by Palestinian society.' Victor is protesting the place of women in the Muslim world. She also sees herself as fighting a 'misguided feminist movement': 'We die in equal numbers to the men.' The problem is that the more she generalises her analysis to all women in the culture, the more its power to explain individual cases starts to decline: if life is unbearable for women under Islam, then why *this* one woman? Slowly and painstakingly, Victor has turned these women from martyrs into suicides. Some, such as Ayat al-Akhras, are described as taking their destiny into their own hands – she acted in order to redeem her father who had been accused of collaborating with the Israelis and to save her family from disgrace (challenging the gender division, this is exactly the motivation attributed to Said, one of the two characters on a suicide mission in *Paradise Now*). But the overall message is clear. Not one of these women is truly the political agent of her own life.

Why, we might also ask, should there be only one motive? Is a political act degraded by being drawn from the deepest wellsprings of an individual life? Does a personal story forfeit its quality as personal if it finds its way, through the complex detours of history, to a political act? 'This story has no moral, it is not a parable, no lesson can be drawn from it', writes Shulamith Hareven in her 1993 essay 'Portrait of a Terrorist', about Mohammed Abu-

Nasser, not a suicide bomber, but, in his own words, a *hablan* or saboteur – he refuses the word *mehabel* or terrorist of her title – jailed for twenty years after throwing a grenade at a queue of soldiers in Jericho (he was told how noble it was to sacrifice yourself for the cause). Hareven befriended him in the 1980s after they were introduced by El-Sarraj who was treating him after he had come out of jail. His family had been exiled in 1948, his father killed by the Israelis, he had entered Bir Zeit University, returning to a life of militancy when it was shut down by the Israeli authorities and El-Sarraj and his wife left Gaza temporarily for England. He was finally shot by the IDF in a street. 'Each man and his circumstances. His case does not teach us very much, except that maybe there is no such thing as a single motive, the motive of eternal hatred of Israel, as the more paranoid among us would like to believe; rather there is a cluster of motives.' Nasser was a child of Gibalia refugee camp in Gaza, 'in whose life all windows were barred'.

This is far cry from *Army of Roses*, where empathy starts to look like a cover for prejudice. The Palestinian Zina – anonymous by family request – has, writes Victor, 'a history of problems'. Whereas Israeli Malki Roth, killed by the Sbarro bomb Zina played her part in planting, was a 'well-balanced, wholesome teenager'. Rachel Levy, killed in March 2002 by Ayat al-Akhras in a grocery store in the Jerusalem neighbourhood of Kiryat Yovel, was finally, after the family returned to Israel from California, adjusting to the 'rhythms of teenage life'. In fact these young Israeli women are living in, and acutely suffering from, a society that encourages them to be blind. Rachel Levy's mother never discussed the political situation with her children; it was too terrifying. Rachel would come home and turn off the television: 'She just didn't want to know.' These are dangerous and frightened lives. In a letter to God written for the Jewish New Year, Malki Roth ended with the hope 'that I'll be alive and that the Messiah should come'.

Although Palestinian suffering under occupation has a central place in *Army of Roses*, at moments Victor comes close to an idealisation of Israel not far from the myth that the nation continues to promote about itself. More simply, the Israelis are better people. Faced with loss, they do not commit suicide, or kill, but care for their families, carry on with the business of living. The violence of the state is pushed aside. Life continues. Suicide bombing, on the other hand, involves abandoning limits 'as we understand them with the democratic mind'. Is it finally empathy at all if you enter a person's – a whole culture's – mind, only to make such a clean and confident exit?

One way of underscoring the precarious nature of such distinctions is to look back in time. Towards the end of *Galoot* (*Exile*), the remarkable documentary of Israeli filmmaker Asher Tlalim, Ariella Atzmon, former lecturer in philosophy and education, recalls her life as the daughter of militant Jewish nationalists who arrived in Palestine in the late 1930s. She was named after Arie Itzhaki, who made bombs in his cellar. He blew himself up, crying 'Death to the British' as he was about to be arrested, on the day she was born. As a child she sang songs to Shlomi Ben Yosef, member of Etzel, or Irgun, the pre-state paramilitary organisation which carried out attacks on Arab marketplaces. He became a martyr when he was executed by the British after a failed attack on an Arab bus (Ben-Gurion believed that Etzel wanted him hanged). 'She will sit and weep, this woman who mourns for her son, so dear, so great.' We did not want peace, she says. The Palestinians will want peace when they have a country.

For years Israeli secret service analysts and social scientists have been trying to build up a typical profile of the suicide 'assassin', only to conclude that there isn't one. The further you reach into the depths of the mind, the harder it is to generalise. Finally you might be forced to conclude that your desire to solve the problem is creating it, that burrowing into the psyche of the enemy, far from an attempt to dignify them with understanding, is a form of evasive action designed to blind you to the responsibility for their dilemma that is staring you in the face. One thing nobody will disagree with: the story of suicide bombing is the story of people driven to extremes. 'Children who have seen so much inhumanity', states El-Sarraj, 'inevitably come out with inhuman responses.' We need to find a language that will allow us to recognise why, in a world of rampant inequality and injustice, people are driven to do things that we hate. Without claiming to know too much. Without condescension.

*An earlier version of this chapter appeared in the *London Review of Books*, twenty-fifth anniversary issue, 4 November 2004.

PART II

After Disaster

7

The Body of Evil:
Arendt, Coetzee and 9/11*

The wind of faith is blowing to remove evil from the peninsula.
> Osama Bin Laden, statement broadcast
> on al-Jazeera television, 7 October 2001

Out of the shadows of this evil should emerge lasting good.
> Tony Blair, Labour Party Conference, 2 October 2001

The way of the wicked will be defeated, those who profess evil will not prosper.
> Ariel Sharon, cited *The Sunday Times*, 10 March 2002

Evil, as these quotes suggest, is a moveable feast. It has the strange characteristic of being at once an absolute, and something far closer to what linguistics calls a 'shifter'. Pronouns, famously the pronoun 'I', are purely indexical signs which refer only to the moment they are spoken. They only work for any one of us because they can be appropriated by everyone else. Hence 'shifter'. Their meaning resides in their capacity to move. There is of course something deeply unsettling about this – after all the pronoun 'I' is the word in which we invest our most fundamental sense of self. Evil has something of the same aura. When people use the word 'evil', it is very unusual to question whether they in fact know what they are talking about. And yet, in the above quotes, 'evil' refers alternately to the United States, to Al-Qaeda, and to suicide bombers in Israel/Palestine. Read them out without identifying the sources, as I did at a debate organised by the *London Review of Books* in May 2002: 'The War on Terror – Is There an Alternative?', and people are hard pressed to say, not only who is being referred to as evil but, more interestingly, who is *speaking*. People using the term 'evil' all sound the same.[1]

In considering evil, we should perhaps start by noticing this contradiction. Surest of terms, invariably invoked with the most passionate if at times desperate conviction, evil also spins on its axis, loses its way. It behaves like that part of language which fatally, if invisibly, undermines the certainty of our speech. Evil is also mobile in another sense. Like all words for 'immediately' which gradually degrade into meaning something like 'in a while', 'evil' has a remarkable capacity for extending and diluting itself. The *Oxford English Dictionary* lists as the meanings for 'evil': 'wickedness, moral depravity, sin', then 'whatever is censurable, painful, malicious or disastrous', and finally 'any particular thing that is physically or morally harmful'. Provided it is unwelcome, evil can be *any particular thing*. A void opens waiting to be filled. During his first election campaign (so before 11 September), Bush commented on the enemies of America: 'We're not so sure who they are, but we know they're there.' More recently, Defense Secretary Donald Rumsfeld explained the Pentagon's shift from a 'threat-based strategy' to an offensive 'capabilities-based approach' in terms of the need 'to defend our nation against the unknown'. (As Frances Fitzgerald puts it: '[this] means simply that the Pentagon can ask for whatever it wants without having to justify its requests by the existence of even a potential enemy').[2] In this essay, I want to pursue the radical instability, or vacuity, of evil – as distinct from the 'banality of evil' – to take and remake Hannah Arendt's famous phrase.

Since 11 September 2001 evil, as one might say, is in the air. In an interview I conducted with Noam Chomsky for a television film on Israel, he described how Turkey, Israel and the United States are referred to in the Egyptian press as the 'axis of evil': 'plenty of evil', he continued, 'in this case a real axis, not an invented one'. Similarly, as Russian Formalist Boris Tomachevsky pointed out in 1925, new literary schools, opposing an older aesthetic, nearly always proclaim themselves, one way or another, more 'realistic' or attuned to reality than the one that went before. The issue here is not who has the greater right to make the claim, but the contested nature of its grounds. Sometimes vocally, more often silently, there is an argument going on whenever 'evil' is proclaimed. Chomsky is in fact making a very simple point. He is suggesting that those who brandish the epithet 'evil' post-11 September, notably Bush in his 'axis of evil' speech, ignore the uneven distribution of power (it was not, Bush has repeatedly insisted, America's power that was the target but her freedom). Choosy and yet indiscriminating, evil becomes the supreme and unjust equaliser between men. When you accuse someone of evil, history disappears. In the great and uneven distribution of the world's resources, it becomes strictly irrelevant where or who they are.

In the report of South Africa's Truth and Reconciliation Commission, the commissioners point to a striking disparity – the 'magnitude gap' – between the perception of violations of human rights under apartheid by the victims and by the perpetrators of the crime.[3] For the victims, such action either exceeds the range of the comprehensible, enters a realm of mystery, or it is 'deliberately malicious', 'sadistic', 'an end in itself' (Gillian Slovo's account of the amnesty hearings of the man responsible for her mother's death was entitled by the *Guardian*, 'Evil has a Human Face').[4] 'Each party', writes Susan Neiman in *Evil – An Alternative History of Philosophy*, 'insists with great conviction that its opponents' actions are truly evil, while its own are merely expedient.'[5] Either way, the act deemed evil is beyond the pale; it fails to enter a world in which anyone would choose to recognise him- or herself. In South Africa, for the perpetrators their acts were the rational consequence of historical necessity, the nation defending itself by all available means from a Communist threat. As Archbishop Desmond Tutu puts it in his introduction: 'The supporters of the previous regime have been at great pains to insist that the reason they did many of the unsavoury things that have since some to light was largely because they were fighting an evil and predatory Communism.'[6] The disparity is eloquent of the way evil 'shifts' in another sense – more 'shifty', as one might say. 'I' am never evil; only 'you' are. In this respect the term 'evil' perversely mimics the first-person pronoun in reverse. No one wants to wear it; unlike the 'I' which each human subject spends a large part of their life rushing – however ruthlessly – to claim. But it may be too that the South African experience can help us understand one of the reasons why Arendt's 'banality of evil' was such a controversial phrase. If evil, it must be total. No part of the personality must escape. 'Evil', states Elizabeth Costello in J.M. Coetzee's essay/short story on this topic – 'The Problem of Evil' – which will be the focus of much of this essay, 'would not be true evil if it can be exited and entered at will.'[7] Evil accepts no qualifiers. You can't do evil partly (it is never something you 'sort of' do). Reduce the force of evil one iota, and the perpetrator of atrocity has won the argument. His actions just might be reasoned, necessary. Or, simple, banal, they make up the colours of the day. For the victims, the commissioners comment, the experience was sheer 'horror'; for the perpetrators, more often, 'a very small thing'. 'Perpetrators', they continue dryly, 'tend to have less emotions about their acts'.[8]

What seems to be at stake then is the issue of how much, or rather how little, it is permissible to feel. The worst outrage is for someone to have committed an atrocity without the requisite affect. In Gillian Slovo's memoir, *Every Secret Thing*, she describes her encounter with the man who organised the murder of her mother as a moment of mutual dissociation: 'Our meeting', she writes, 'had been an exercise in dissociation from which I'd emerged in a stupor that had sent me straight into a dreamless afternoon sleep.'[9] Craig Williamson is incapable – syntactically incapable – of recognising what he has done. Read the pronouns in this sentence when Slovo presses whether Ruth's death weighed on him:

> 'Yeah,' he said grudgingly, 'I said that you'll never get rid of. You can wish it or regret it or do as much as you like but you can't change it. What's done is done and if you try to analyse why it was done and how it was done and what the strategy and belief behind it was [. . .] it's difficult to believe that it could have been done but it was.'[10]

The 'I' hardly figures here, nor indeed the crime: '*that* you'll never get rid of'. I spend some time arguing with my students on a course I teach on South African writing, whether that last sentence – 'it's difficult to believe that it could have been done but it was' – indicates a subject struggling to enter his statement, acknowledging that he is faced with something too dreadful to be thought, or is merely the voice, in Slovo's words, of 'a huge mountain of a man, all oil, and lies, and half-excuses'.[11]

We could perhaps ask, then, whether it is the action that is the worst evil or the perpetrator's refusal to recognise the horror, to identify psychically with his victim or, in simpler language, to 'connect'. It was Arendt's insistence that neither the intention of the perpetrator nor his affectivity should be deemed relevant in measuring the magnitude of the crime (Eichman's apparent lack of evil intent should not exonerate him). One of the wagers of South Africa's Truth Commission was to make victims and perpetrators go the distance and recognise each other across what the commissioners themselves describe as an almost insurmountable abyss. In the trial of Ruth Ellis who murdered her lover in 1950s Britain (she was the last person to hang in this country) or in the response to social worker Marietta Higgs who had scores of children she suspected of being victims of abuse in Midlands Britain in the 1980s withdrawn from their homes, the worst outrage was the lack of emotion both women displayed. Higgs was of course wresting children from a crime many would classify as 'evil', Ellis was technically on the other side. And yet the screaming outrage against these two women, partly one suspects because they were women, put something graphic on display. Anyone brushed with 'evil' must, for *us* to survive *their* encounter, lose or appear to lose control of their minds. 'Evil' is unbearable or it is nothing. Like death, it is something from which you don't return.

In 2002, I attended a conference in Tilburg entitled 'Evil', the second of a series organised by the Nexus Institute called 'The Quest for Life'. J.M.

Coetzee accepted the invitation on condition that he could deliver his paper in fictional form. Returning to the format of his Tanner Lectures of 1998, published as *The Lives of Animals*, now republished as *Elizabeth Costello*, Coetzee chose this occasion to revive the character of Elizabeth Costello, feminist, vegetarian and campaigner who, in her first appearance, had given a prestigious series of literary lectures on the somewhat unexpected topic of animal slaughter (she was invited as the famous author of a 1969 novel about Molly Bloom, the wife of Leopold Bloom, 'nowadays spoken of in the same breath as *The Golden Notebook* and *The Story of Christa T* as pathbreaking feminist fiction').[12] In this instance she has been invited to Amsterdam to address a conference on evil. Once again Coetzee doubles his character with his own position as speaker (although the immediacy of this is lost in the published version of the text). The story turns on a crisis. Costello has come to speak about a book – Paul West's *The Very Rich Hours of Count von Stauffenberg* – a book whose depiction of evil has deeply repelled her and led her to question the ethical limits of the writer's craft and task, only to discover that Paul West is attending the conference. For Costello, the issue is precisely how or where to place evil in her mind. *The Very Rich Hours of Count von Stauffenberg* tells the story of Hitler and his would-be assassins in the Wehrmacht, above all of their execution which is described in a physical and mental detail which she finds obscene. West goes too far into a realm where she now feels, as a result of the effect on her of reading this book, writers perhaps should not tread: 'in representing the workings of evil, the writer may *unwittingly* make evil seem attractive and thereby do more harm than good' (that 'unwittingly', in italics in the text, is a concession – Costello knows by now that West is in the audience).[13]

The story is wonderfully self-defeating, because its central proposition will only work if we enact in relationship to Elizabeth the very form of fictional identification she is now cautioning against. That is to say, it only works if we find ourselves, without let or inhibition, entering Elizabeth's own mind. A mind which includes, not just the horror of reading the book and the ethical protest it provokes on her behalf, but also the memory – reluctant but overwhelming – of a scene of sexual violence to which she was subjected as a young girl. As well as, in perhaps the most powerful moment of the essay, an instant where, in a shocking identification, Elizabeth looks at her own naked body and imagines herself as one of those women victims of the Nazis 'at the lip of the trench into which they would, in the next minute, the next second, tumble, dead or dying with a bullet to the brain'.[14] In an ironical twist which makes her objections more not less poignant, it is Elizabeth, not Paul West, who – we might say – does the best line in forced identifications, throwing the reader into the arms of evil, or into the pit.

The point is that her critique of the power of writing only works because of the power of her own; because she does to the reader – through the strength of her ability to convey her experience – exactly what she objects to having had done to her by Paul West's book. Of course, being in a story by Coetzee, she is only too aware of this. Costello argues with herself: 'Yet she is a writer too. She does the same kind of thing, or used to' (that 'used to' is sleight of hand since Costello – Coetzee as writer – is doing it to the reader *now*).[15] Writing forces unexpected, often unwelcome identifications, or it does nothing. Coetzee knows well that scenes like the one where Elizabeth was assaulted, however repugnant, will be compelling to the reader. Designed to shock, they make the reader intimate with fear. In this case there is an added pull because the violence is conveyed as an almost reluctant memory, the narrator's private musings on an event which she has never communicated before. We are the hidden, privileged, party to a confession of something so devastating it has never, until now, made the passage into words. Nineteen years old, she has just been picked up by a docker and goes back to his room:

> 'I'm sorry,' she said, 'I'm really sorry, can we stop.' But Tim or Tom would not listen. When she resisted, he tried to force her. For a long time, in silence, panting, she fought him off, pushing and scratching. To begin with he took it as a game. Then he got tired of that, or his desire tired, turned to something else, and he began to hit her seriously. He lifted her off the bed, punched her breasts, punched her in the belly, hit her a terrible blow with his elbow to her face. When he was bored with hitting her he tore up her clothes and tried to set fire to them in the waste-paper basket.[16]

And so on . . . 'It was', Costello comments, 'her first brush with evil.'[17] She is convinced that he liked hurting her more than he would have liked sex. 'By fighting him off, she had created an opening for the evil in him to emerge.'[18] I should perhaps add, as it will be relevant later, that while I am happy – although 'happy' is not the right word – to reproduce these lines here, I found it very difficult and then impossible to read them out at the annual Conference of the Council for College and University English in Oxford and then at the conference honouring Gillian Beer on her retirement in Cambridge in 2003 (it gets worse).

It would, I think, be fair to describe such a moment as obscene (in the sense of what it wants to be). In fact Costello saves this epithet for the description of the bodies of the plotters on the point of execution, above all for the way the executioner humiliates and terrifies them, taunting them with the physical details of what is to come. Can there really, she asks, have been witnesses who wrote this down in such detail? Or is it West's fantasy: his passionate identification with the victims, but no less – of necessity if he is to render the scene faithfully – with the executioner, 'the butcher with last week's blood caked under his fingernails', whom he brings so intensely to life? ('Terrible that such a man should have existed, even more terrible that he should be hauled out of the grave when we thought he was safely dead.')[19] This is, for Costello, 'obscene'. Although it is not clear in the following sentence whether it is the grim abjection of the plotters or the no less grim perversity of the executioner which oversteps the bounds: '*Obscene. That is the word*, a word of contested etymology that she must hold on to. She chooses to believe that *obscene* means off-stage. To save our humanity, certain things that we may want to see (*may want to see because we are human!*) must remain for ever off-stage.'[20] To rephrase: obscenity must remain off-stage because, as humans, we want to see it so much. This, I would suggest, comes very close to making evil, if not the essence of writing, then no more than an exaggerated, or a kind of worse-case, embodiment of what compels us to read. Like evil, writing is enticing: 'He made her read, excited her to read.'[21] We want to get inside other people's skins even if they are about to be fleeced alive. In the throes of identification – with victim *or* executioner – there is no limit to how far people are willing to go. What Costello seems to be objecting to is not evil so much as its *temptation*: 'she had gone on reading, excited despite herself'.[22]

The idea of evil as tempting has a long history (from the beginning, as one might say). One of the ways of thinking about the horrors of the last century – to leave aside for the moment those unfolding today – is as a transmutation in the age-old connection between these two terms. 'Evil in the Third Reich', writes Hannah Arendt in her famous *Eichmann in Jerusalem – A Report on the Banality of Evil* of 1963, 'had lost the character by which most people recognise it – the quality of temptation.' (She is writing about the same history as West's book.)[23] In civilised countries, she continues, the law assumes that the voice of conscience instructs its citizens: 'Thou shalt not kill': 'even though man's natural desires and inclinations may at times be murderous'. But under Hitler, when the law changes sides, temptation follows suit: 'Many Germans and many Nazis, probably an overwhelming majority of them, must have been tempted *not* to murder, *not* to rob, *not* to let their neighbours go off to their doom [. . .] and not to become accomplices in all these crimes by benefiting from them, but, God knows, they had learned how to resist temptation.'[24]

Imagine then a situation where the law instructs you to commit acts you would barely entertain in your wildest dreams. In Freudian terms, the law is always a problem because our psychic enforcer, the superego, draws its energy from the unconscious it is meant to tame; which is why the superego's edicts often seem fierce or cruel. Laced with perversion. But this is something else. Now the superego is instructing you to let the most terrifying components of your own unconscious go stalking. Faced with such an edict, the voice of conscience pales, becomes a ghost of its former self. Tempting, but impotent. Like the memory of someone you might once have been. But it would be wrong to think that this is anarchy, a release into freedom, no holds barred. The strength of Arendt's analysis is that she recognises that there is something deadly in the law. Hence her repeated emphasis on the 'reason of state' and its inherent violence: 'the rule of law, although designed to eliminate violence and the war of all against all, always stands in need of the instruments of violence in order to assure its own existence'.[25] Likewise Chomsky, against the dominant rhetoric on terrorism, relentlessly charts acts of Western-sanctioned state terrorism in the modern world.

Perhaps we are tempted by evil, find its literary representation so compelling, because evil is not just an outsider, nor just our guilty secret – the word 'transgression' won't do here – but belongs at the heart of the very mechanisms we deploy in order to restrain it. Violence is never more terrifying than when it believes itself justified by the highest law (Bush has stated quite clearly that he has known his divine mission since 11 September). In Coetzee's story, it is the law – brazen, mocking – that produces the excessive energy which Costello describes as obscene: 'In his gibes at the men about to die at his hands there was a wanton, an *obscene* energy that exceeded his commission.'[26] This energy is contaminating, 'like a shock, like electricity'.[27] If it weren't, Costello as reader would have no reason to object. West has thrust her, not just into the horror of what is still for many the worst atrocity of the twentieth century, but into its *mind*. Fiction's greatest offence becomes its ability to turn us into perpetrators, each and every one.

In their chapter on 'Concepts and Principles', the South African commissioners feel the need to justify their exploration of the 'Causes, Motives, Perspectives' of the perpetrators which appears in the final volume of 'Findings and Recommendations'. Understanding can be seen as exonerating. Trying to get into the mind of the perpetrator is too risky : 'Without seeing offender accountability as part of the quest for understanding, the uncovering of motives and perspectives can easily be misunderstood as excusing their violations.'[28] Far from fiction, even in the most sombre conditions of political assessment and analysis, to allow a mind to the perpetrators of atrocity is, it seems, to risk one identification too far (as we have seen in the previous essay on suicide bombing). In fact in the chapter itself, the perpetrators emerge as oddly without character. Psychological analysis is more or less eschewed: 'In such situations, people act primarily in terms of their social identities rather than personal attributes.'[29] 'Political frameworks provide the fuel for atrocities.'[30] One by one, the report rules out the argument from human nature (regression into atavistic behaviour), the argument from psychopathology (no psychological dysfunction), the argument from authoritarianism (a collective phenomenon, not a person- ality type). In fact in a report that has been severely criticised for its emphasis on individual actors at the expense of a critique of state power, it is striking how in this chapter the whole analysis scrupulously, repeatedly, swerves in the direction of what Freud famously called group (or 'mass') psychology. Under apartheid, crime became the law: '[To paraphrase Hannah Arendt],' write the commissioners at the end of the opening chapter on the historical context, 'Twentieth-century law in South Africa made crime legal.'[31] The perpetrators are best understood in terms of social coercion or 'binding' ('compliance', 'identification', 'internalisation').[32] Only acts, not individuals, can be described as 'evil': 'While acts of gross violations may be regarded as demonic, it is counterproductive to regard persons who perpetrated those acts as demonic.'[33] In a strange mimicry of what collective identification is presumed to do to individuals (take away their personalities), it is as if there is *nobody there*.

And yet, by the account of the commissioners themselves, these explana- tions are unsatisfactory. There is a factor that escapes. On authoritarianism: 'But does this offer an explanation for a predisposition to commit atrocities? Evidence is really rather thin'; on social identity: 'It may be noted that social identity theory does not explain violence itself, but the preconditions of violence'; on group identification:'while these processes begin to explain why we become bound into groups, institutions and authorities, they do not yet suggest violence'.[34] 'Do not *yet*' – something has to wait. Without final cause, atrocity resists explanation, draws a blank. Attempting to explain the demonic, the Commissioners find something invisible, unnegotiable, sinister (demonic?) at play. Evil, it seems, is not just an absolute, not just a shifter; it is an empty place. This may seem like a failure of explanation. Or it may take us, I want to suggest now, to the heart of the matter. In her famous exchange with Gershom Scholem over her book on Eichmann, Arendt writes:

It is indeed my opinion now that evil is never 'radical', that it is only extreme, and that it possesses neither depth nor any demonic dimension. It can overgrow and lay waste the whole world precisely because it spreads like a fungus on the surface. It is 'thought-defying', as I said, because thought tries to reach some depth, to go to the roots, and the moment it concerns itself with evil, it is frustrated because *there is nothing*.[35]

To describe evil as a 'fungus' is to remove from it even the faintest trace of sublimity. It also means, as Susan Neiman suggests, that the sources of evil do not reach to a depth 'that would make us despair of the world itself'.[36] But might there also be a connection, I want to ask for the rest of this essay, between evil as nothing, and evil as subject to, or even as the violent, intransigent – obscene – embodiment *of*, the highest law?

Arendt's analysis of Eichmann suggests there might be. She is best known for describing him as petty, banal (her phrase is cited by the Commission). Arendt continues the quote above: 'That is its "banality"'. But in a less commented moment early in the book when she is introducing her main character, she tells of how he saw his birth as an 'event to be ascribed to "a higher Bearer of Meaning", an entity somehow identical with the "movement of the universe".' She writes: 'The terminology is suggestive. To call God a *Höheren Sinnesträger* meant to give him some place in the military hierarchy, since the Nazis had changed the military "recipient of orders", the *Befehlsempfanger*, into a "bearer of orders", a Befehl*sträger*, indicating, as in the ancient "bearer of ill tidings", the burden of responsibility and of importance that weighed supposedly upon those who had to execute orders.'[37] Eichmann is dismissive of metaphysics – the moment is passed over – but it is nonetheless central to Arendt's analysis that Eichmann's ' "boundless and immoderate admiration for Hitler" ' (in the words of a defence witness) played a major part in his accepting that Hitler's *word*, without having to be written, had the force of law.[38] Hitler, or rather love of Hitler, comes close to the sacred. Evil is tempting because the devil, however despicable to the sanguine mind, takes on the aura of a god. There may be something mysterious, resistant to final explanation, in people's ability to commit evil acts, although to say that is already to run the risk of mystification – hence Arendt's insistence that evil must be understood (Neiman identifies two traditions on this issue, one from Rousseau to Arendt for which morality demands we make evil intelligible, the other from Voltaire to Jean Améry for which morality demands that we don't). But mystery might also be intrinsic to the process which enables individuals to violate, even in the name of legality, the bounds of all human law. In *The Brothers Karamazov*, the Grand Inquisitor says to Ivan Fyodorovich:

> There are only three powers, only three powers on earth, capable of conquering and holding captive for ever the conscience of these feeble rebels, for their own happiness – these powers are miracle, mystery and authority.[39]

Without depth – Arendt continues her letter: 'Only the good has depth, can be radical' – evil relies on transcendence. This is of course to invert the normal order of things in which the devil is presumed to exert all his power from below.

To pursue this a little further, I shall take a detour, before returning to Coetzee, via a moment which for many has become the new century's embodiment of evil. 'Fear is a great form of worship, and the only one worthy of it is God' – these words are from 'Atta's Document', the document released by the FBI that was found in the baggage of Mohammed Atta, the suspected ringleader of 11 September, thought to have piloted the first of the two planes into the Twin Towers. The original Arabic text has not been released, and only four of five original pages have been made available for translation.[40] Although its authenticity has been questioned by some (why wasn't his baggage on the plane?), and critiqued as a violation of Islam by others, it is such a bizarre mixture – in the words of the *Observer*, who published it on 30 September 2001 – of the 'apocalyptic', 'dramatic', 'sometimes downright banal', that it is hard to imagine it invented even by someone, post-9/11, intent on the most violent slandering of Islam. In fact three copies were found – one more in the wreckage of the plane that crashed in Pennsylvania, another in a car abandoned by the hijackers outside Dulles Airport. 'It is [therefore] unlikely', write commentators Kanan Makiya and Hassan Mneimneh, 'that many of the hijackers did not know the suicidal nature of their mission.'[41] The document is, as they put it, 'an exacting guide for achieving the unity of body and spirit necessary for success'.[42] That God is the instructor is unsurprising. Returning to the spirit of the Prophet, to the brief period of his rule between 622 and 632, the manual calls for a return to the path of *ghazwah*, to be understood as a raid on the path of God:

> Consider that this is a raid on a path. As the Prophet said: 'A raid . . . on the path of God is better than this World and what is in it.'[43]

Most striking, however, is the way the words work, as divinely sanctioned performatives to be repeated at every stage: 'Recite supplications', 'Remind yourself and your brothers of the supplications and consider what their meanings are', 'Recite repeatedly the invocations to God (the boarding invocation, the invocation of the town, the invocation of the place, the other invocations)', 'When you arrive and see [the airport], and get out of the taxicab, recite the invocation of place', 'Recite the supplication', 'Wherever you go and whatever you do, you have to persist in invocation and supplication.' Like the God to whom they are addressed, these supplications are infinite but invisible: 'It should not be noticeable', 'If you say it a thousand times, no one should be able to distinguish whether you were silent or whether you were invoking God.'[44]

The preparation for the body is no less crucial than that of the mind: 'Shave excess hair from the body and wear cologne', 'Shower', 'Tighten your shoes well, wear socks so that your feet will be solidly in your shoes', 'Tighten your clothes' – in square brackets we are told by the *Observer* translator, Imad Musa: 'a reference to making sure his clothes will cover his private parts at all times'. [45] ('A ritual act of self-purification', as Bruce Lincoln puts it, 'that helps secure salvation' – the process brings to mind the link Freud posited between religious observance and the compulsive actions of the obsessional.)[46] The body must be perfectly in place so that it can most perfectly forget or let go of itself: 'True selflessness', comment Makiya and Mneimneh, 'requires an acknowledgement of the flesh-and-blood self in order to become estranged from it.'[47] If slaughter is, chillingly, a gift, it is not an act of aggression because there is precisely no-body there, only God: 'Fight for the sake of God those who seek to kill you, and do not commit aggression. God does not favour those who aggress.'[48] This is for the commentators the most frightening aspect of the document because it inserts into the Muslim tradition the idea of the martyr who, void of any communal purpose, acts solely to please God (there is no mention anywhere of any wrongs to be redressed):

> Martyrdom is not something bestowed by God as a favour on the warrior for his selflessness and devotion to the community's defence. It is a status to be achieved by the individual warrior, and performed as though it were his own private act of worship.[49]

Instead of which, they observe, martyrdom in the Muslim tradition is always subject to stringent forms of judgement about the communal benefit at stake (the tradition is 'being turned on its head').[50]

Later developments of Islam relegate the most extreme forms of fear as worship to mystical experience, but here the martyr is driven by a fear of God which empties him of any personal intent. The document tells the story of Ali Bin Abi Talib (companion and close friend of the Prophet Mohammed) who, when spat on by a non-believer in battle, did not kill him immediately but raised his sword: 'After he spat at me, I was afraid I would be striking him in revenge, so I lifted my sword.' Only when sure of his purity of purpose, did he go back and kill the man. Without qualities – remember Arendt on Eichmann: 'he had no motives at all' – the document offers us an image of someone who purifies mind and body in the cause of slaughter: 'you must make your knife sharp and must not discomfort your animal during the slaughter', and then heads, in both senses, for the skies.[51] If Eichmann, in Arendt's account, lacked intention, in the case of 11 September, the intention on the contrary could not have been more absolute – 'a maximalist intention' in Lincoln's phrase (the hijackers are instructed to endlessly renew their plans).[52] 'The description of evil as thoughtless', writes Susan Neiman, 'captured so many cases of contemporary evil, that we were unprepared for a case of single-mindedly thoughtful evil.'[53] But in both cases, something has to be emptied for a higher, deadly, purpose to be fulfilled.

'It is tempting', writes Lincoln, 'in the face of such horror, to regard the authors of these deeds as evil incarnate [. . .] Their motives, however, were intensely and profoundly religious.'[54] Jane Smith, professor at Hartford Seminary, Connecticut, and author of *Islam in America*, comments: 'Apparently one can assume that what was done was done by people out of a genuine and sincere belief that they were helping bring about the will of God. And that, in turn, may be the most frightening thing about it.'[55] Or in the words of John Esposito, director of the Center for Muslim–Christian Understanding at Georgetown University, 'We have a certain need to explain what somebody does as totally irrational [. . .] the fact that they might come out of a pious background stuns us.'[56] In fact, if martyrdom has become an individual path to transcendence, then piety has deformed itself (one reason among many for not seeing 11 September as the embodiment of Islam).

As we have seen in the essay on 'Mass Psychology' (Chapter 3), Freud was eloquent on the subject of group insanity. But what would he have had to say about a superego carved so closely to the features of a monotheistic God that it would destroy half the world in His name? (It is a question, one should add, as relevant to Evangelical America as to fundamentalist Islam.)[57] Or was he already sentient of the dangers: '[in the history of religion] human beings found themselves obliged in general to recognise "intellectual [*geistige*]" forces – forces, that is, which cannot be grasped by the senses (particularly by the sight) but which none the less produce undoubted and extremely powerful effects'?[58] In *Civilization and its Discontents*, he gave what remains today perhaps the most persuasive account of fear as the driving force of social life. The child lives in fear of a superego whose aggression knows no bounds simply because it has inherited all the aggressiveness which the child would like to use against it. There is something unavoidably craven, abject, masochistic – self-abolishing – in every subject's relationship to the law. When we read Atta's Document alongside Freud's text in an MA class in 2001, it seemed as if there was only one step from his analysis to the idea of obedience as a form of divinely sanctioned fear. 'Fear', Freud writes, 'is at the bottom of the whole relationship.'[59] In the link between superego and ego, the link we rely on for entry into our social identities, fear is key. At the very least Freud seems to be suggesting that our worst acts – in the West as much as anywhere else – are driven by a tendency to worship what we are most frightened of.

In his essay on 'The Structure of Evil', British psychoanalyst Christopher Bollas describes evil as a form of transcendence. 'The killer finds a victim who will die his death.' The killer murders his victim, as it were, on his own behalf. Enacting death, he avoids his own subjection to its law. Every time the killer strikes, it is his own death that he avoids. In this analysis, murderousness is based on a passionate if involuntary identification. Like the term evil itself, killing serves to get rid of something felt as too threatening; you hand it over to someone else and then destroy it so that you can wipe your hands of the affair. Evil represents 'the unconscious need to survive one's own death'.[60] Onto the other you slough off this mortal coil. If we go back to Costello, we could therefore say that every time fiction ushers us into a world of evil, it is at least partly our own death that we escape.

Transcending one's own death might be a fair description of Atta's Document. But Bollas's article can also take us back to Elizabeth Costello. If we return to the passage where she finds herself identifying with the women victims of Nazism at the edge of the pit quoted earlier, we see that it is a very specific body – the ageing, flagging body – that Costello finds herself in identification with:

> If there were a mirror on the back of this door instead of just a hook, if she were to take off her clothes and kneel here before it, she, with her sagging breasts and knobbly hips, would look little different from the women in those intimate, those over-intimate photographs from the European war, glimpses into hell, who knelt naked at the lip of the trench.[61]

In 'The Problem of Evil', ageing and its humiliations are something of a refrain: 'Twenty million, six million, three million, a hundred thousand: at a certain point the mind breaks down before quanta; and the older you get – this at any rate is what has happened to her – the sooner comes the breakdown'; 'She does not know how old Paul West is [. . .] Might he and she, in their different ways, not be old enough to be beyond embarrassment?'; 'She does not like to see her sisters and brothers humiliated, in ways it is so easy to humiliate the old, by making them strip for example, taking away their dentures, making fun of their private parts.'[62] This is at the heart of the most offending, *obscene*, chapter from West's book:

> fumbling old men for the most part [. . .] their false teeth and their glasses taken from them [. . .] hands in their pockets to hold up their pants, whimpering with fear, swallowing their tears, having to listen to this coarse creature, this butcher with last week's blood caked under his fingernails, taunt them, telling them what would happen when the rope snapped tight, how the shit would run down their spindly old-man's legs, how their limp old-man's penises would quiver one last time?[63]

If this is the ultimate degradation, whose writing, it seems fair to ask – Paul West's, Elizabeth Costello's or J.M. Coetzee's – is repeating the offence?

Is the ultimate evil then a dying body that no ablution or supplication can save? Is such a body – which of course means all bodies – the real disgrace? In Coetzee's prizewinning novel of that title, the central character, David Lurie, meets with his estranged wife after his sexual harassment of a young student has driven him from his university position: ' "Do you think", she asks, "a young girl finds any pleasure in going to bed with a man of that age? Do you think she finds it good to watch you in the middle of your . . . " ' Lurie muses: 'Yet perhaps she has a point. Perhaps it is the right of the young to be protected from the sight of their elders in the throes of passion.'[64] Again it is a refrain. Lurie takes tea with his daughter when he has just arrived at the farm: 'He is aware of her eyes on him as he eats. He must be careful: nothing so distasteful to a child as the workings of a parent's body.'[65] Explaining to her later why he will not appeal against his dismissal: 'After a certain age one is simply no longer appealing, and that's that.'[66] And perhaps most tellingly in the first chapter of the book:

> He ought to give up, retire from the game. At what age, he wonders, did Origen castrate himself? Not the most graceful of solutions, but then ageing is not a graceful business. A clearing of the decks, at least, so that one can turn one's mind to the proper business of the old: preparing to die.[67]

We might note too in passing that in *Disgrace* Lurie – following a violent assault by a group of black youths during which his daughter, Lucy, is raped – is forced to ask, when Lucy will not speak to him: 'do they think that, where rape is concerned, no man can be where the woman is?' and then later to take his own question further: 'He does understand; he can, if he concentrates, if he loses himself, be there, be the men, inhabit them, fill them with the ghost of himself. The question is, does he have it in him to be the woman?'[68] In *Disgrace*, the answer is that he doesn't. Lurie is never allowed to enter Lucy's violated experience and space.

But in the story of Costello on evil, Coetzee defies his own caution. He gives us Elizabeth's scene of sexual violence, puts us in the room with her, goes – one might say – to places where, by his own previous account in the earlier novel, the man should not, or cannot, tread. Is the worst offence of this story, therefore, not West's forcing us to enter – body and mind – into Hitler's executioners and the hangmen, not Costello letting us into a moment of sexual violence from her past, but Coetzee as author entering this time the mind of his female character at the very point which, in *Disgrace* – and it is not an aside, it is absolutely central to the dilemma explored by the novel – was not possible or permissible for the man? Is Coetzee, advertently, or perhaps in this instance inadvertently, indicting himself?

Coetzee's preoccupation with the ageing dying body gives us the other face – or underside – of transcendence. It suggests that the issue, in *Disgrace,* but not only in *Disgrace*, is not just one of moral turpitude but also of physical turpitude, a turpitude of the body, utterly effaced in Atta's Document, taken on – tremulously, obscenely – by Coetzee, to which one morality, *in extremis* as it were, may be a possible reply. *Disgrace* ends with Lurie, having dedicated himself to the care of abandoned and stricken dogs, handing one of them over to die. Lurie's connection to these dogs is the key to his transformation in the book. Earlier, in a crucial moment of dialogue with Lucy, Lurie – with obvious allusion to white treatment of the blacks in South Africa – had made his view of the place of dogs in the scheme of things very clear: 'by all means let us be kind to them. But let us not lose perspective. We are of a different order of creation.'[69] Lucy on the other hand is willing to envisage herself returning in her next life as a dog. (She is a Rawlsian – she knows that if there is to be any chance of justice in the world, then you are obliged to imagine yourself in the weakest place.)

Previously, like many other readers, I saw the last moment of the book as an act of compassion or mercy on the part of Lurie towards a degraded species: 'Are you giving him up?' 'Yes, I am giving him up.'[70] Now I am more inclined to see it as an act of mercy towards himself. Nor do I think we can read this as simply a metaphor for a dying white South Africa and its language although both can be read into the book (a reading confirmed by the fact that on his retirement in 2002 Coetzee left South Africa). Through Lurie and Costello, I see Coetzee as giving us one of the barest accounts, for someone for whom transcendence is no option, of the dilemma of a body – an ageing, dying, body – that is repelled by itself. They are on a continuum: if you cannot secure a path to God, travel down the chain of being in the opposite direction. Lie down with the animals (the first book in which Costello appears, making her plea against animal slaughter, was called *The Lives of Animals*).

Coetzee is not alone. Jean Améry, author of one of the most harrowing accounts of life in Auschwitz, went on to write a book on ageing, *On Ageing – Revolt and Resignation*. Ageing appears as an experience of horror – '*horror and angor*', 'fear, *angor, angustiae*, constriction, anguish' – that, shockingly he insists, nothing of his experience in the camps can match.[71] To die in the camps would have been to be brought down by an enemy – 'the good death by murder that didn't want to know me at all' – whereas ageing comes from within, a sheer degradation that alienates us from our bodies while bringing us closer to their 'sluggish mass than ever before'.[72]

At a seminar organised by Pittsburgh University for its visiting students in London to mark the first anniversary of 11 September, seven minutes of footage were screened, footage only shown once on American and British television and then pulled as too disturbing by CNN. It consists mainly of bodies – visible, almost recognisable – plunging from the burning buildings to their deaths. There is, commented one participant in the seminar, a taboo on death in American culture. (In Russia, the image shown repeatedly was of people in the building waving white flags, an image never shown on US television, presumably because it could be seen to signify surrender.) Above all a body must not be seen to die. Bodies that fail and fall. To efface, or pre-empt, such images George Bush – with the full backing of Tony Blair – went to war against Iraq. The infinitely superior killing machines of the West took to the skies. Another way of saying, perhaps, that the greatest evil lies within ourselves.

*An earlier version of this chapter was published in *New Formations, Intellectual Work*, vol. 53, Summer 2004.

Notes

1 For a discussion of the symmetry between Bush and Bin Laden's rhetoric, see Bruce Lincoln, 'Symmetric Dualisms: Bush and Bin Laden on October 7', in *Holy Terrors: Thinking About Religion After September 11* (Chicago, University of Chicago Press 2003).

2 All quotes from Martin Kettle, *Guardian*, 12 September 2002.
3 *Truth and Reconciliation Commission of South Africa Report*, 5 vols, (London, Macmillan 2003), vol. 5, p. 272.
4 Ibid.; Gillian Slovo, 'Evil has a human face', *Guardian*, 31 October 1998.
5 Susan Neiman, *Evil – An Alternative History of Philosophy* (Princeton, Princeton University Press 2002, new edition 2004), p. xv. For a philosophical survey of evil, see also Peter Dews, *The Idea of Evil* (Oxford, Blackwell, forthcoming).
6 *Truth and Reconciliation Commission*, vol. 1, p. 13.
7 Coetzee's essays in the voice of Elizabeth Costello were subsequently published as *Elizabeth Costello – Eight Lessons* (London, Secker and Warburg 2003). The text of the original lecture has been slightly modified in the published version in which this quotation no longer appears.
8 *Truth and Reconciliation Commission*, vol. 5, pp. 271-2.
9 Slovo, *Every Secret Thing – My Family, My Country* (London, Little, Brown 1997), p. 267.
10 Ibid., p. 268.
11 Ibid., p. 266.
12 J. M. Coetzee, *The Lives of Animals* (Princeton, Princeton University Press 1999), p. 16.
13 Coetzee, *Elizabeth Costello*, p. 164.
14 Ibid., p. 178.
15 Ibid., p. 179.
16 Ibid., p. 165.
17 Ibid.
18 Ibid.
19 Ibid., p. 158, p. 168.
20 Ibid., pp. 168-9, original emphasis.
21 Ibid., p. 179.
22 Ibid., p. 178.
23 Hannah Arendt, *Eichmann in Jerusalem – A Report on the Banality of Evil* (New York, Viking 1963; revised edition Harmondsworth, Penguin 1977), p. 150.
24 Ibid., p. 471, original emphasis.
25 Ibid., p. 291.
26 Coetzee, *Elizabeth Costello*, p. 177.
27 Ibid., p. 176.
28 *Truth and Reconciliation Commission*, vol. 1, p. 130.
29 Ibid., vol. 5, p. 228.
30 Ibid., p. 282.
31 Ibid., vol. 1, p. 42.
32 Ibid., vol. 5, p. 292.
33 Ibid., p. 274.
34 Ibid., p. 286, p. 289, p. 292.
35 Arendt to Scholem, letter of 24 July 1963, in Arendt, *The Jew as Pariah – Jewish Identity and Politics in the Modern Age* (New York, Grove Press 1978), p. 251, my emphasis.
36 Neiman, *Evil*, p. 303.
37 Arendt, *Eichmann*, p. 27.

38 Ibid., p. 149.

39 Fyodor Dostoyevsky, *The Brothers Karamazov* (London and New York, Quartet 1990), p. 255.

40 In *Holy Terrors*, Bruce Lincoln states that the first page of the document has never been made available.

41 Kanan Makiya and Hassan Mneimneh, 'Manual for a "Raid"', *Striking Terror – America's New War*, ed. Robert B. Silvers and Barbara Epstein (New York, New York Review of Books 2002), p. 303.

42 Ibid., p. 304.

43 Ibid., p. 306. All citations from the version provided in *Striking Terror*, which can be compared with the translation published as an Appendix in Lincoln, *Holy Terrors* and in the *Observer*. In *Holy Terrors,* these lines appear as 'Remember that this is a battle for the sake of God', p. 96.

44 Makiya and Mneimneh, 'Manual for a "Raid"', pp. 321-4.

45 Ibid., p. 321.

46 Lincoln, *Holy Terrors*, p. 94.

47 Makiya and Mneimneh, "Manual for a 'Raid'", p. 312.

48 Ibid., p. 315.

49 Ibid., p. 317.

50 Ibid. For a discussion of the tension between the Islam of Mecca and Medina, see Kenneth Cragg, 'The Finality of the Qur'an and the contemporary Politics of Nations' in R. Greaves, T. Zeldin, Y. Haddad and J. Idelman, eds, *Islam and the West post-9/11* (Aldershot, Ashgate 2004), and interview with Al-Afif Al-Akhdar, Ehud Ein-Gil, 'The Roots of Jihad,' *Ha'aretz*, 17 March 2006.

51 These lines appear in both the *Observer* version of the document and in Lincoln but not in the version published in Makiya and Mneimneh.

52 Lincoln, *Holy Terrors*, p. 12.

53 Neiman, *Evil*, p. 285.

54 Lincoln, *Holy Terrors*, p. 16.

55 'Atta's Document' and commentaries, *Observer*, 30 September 2001.

56 Ibid.

57 For a discussion of the proximity between Islamic, Christian and Jewish fundamentalism, see Karen Armstrong, *The Battle for God* (London, HarperCollins 2001), and John Shepherd, 'Self-critical Children of Abraham? Roots of Violence and Extremism in Judaism, Christianity and Islam', in Ron Greaves, Theodore Zeldin, Yvonne Haddad and Jane Idelman, eds, *Islam and the West Post-9/11* (Aldershot, Ashgate 2004).

58 Sigmund Freud, *Moses and Monotheism*, 1938, *Standard Edition of the Complete Psychological Works*, 24 vols (London, Hogarth 1953-73), vol. 23, p. 114.

59 Freud, *Civilization and its Discontents*, 1930, *Standard Edition*, vol. 21, p. 136.

60 Christopher Bollas, 'The Structure of Evil', in *Cracking Up – The Work of Unconscious Experience* (New York, Hill and Wang 1995), pp. 189, 193.

61 Coetzee, *Elizabeth Costello*, p. 178.

62 Ibid., p. 159, p. 163, p. 178.

63 Ibid., p. 158.

64 Coetzee, *Disgrace* (London, Secker and Warburg 2000), p. 44.

65 Ibid., p. 61.

66 Ibid., p. 67.
67 Ibid., p. 9.
68 Ibid., p. 141, p. 160.
69 Ibid., p. 74.
70 Ibid., p. 220.
71 Jean Améry, *On Aging – Revolt and Resignation*, 1968, trans. John D. Barlow (Bloomington, Indiana University Press 1994), p. 116, p. 117.
72 Ibid., p. 118, p. 127.

8

Freud and the People,
or Freud Goes to Abu Ghraib[*]

Ever since the fall of Baghdad, when looters went rampaging through the city, there has been a barely spoken, but centuries-old, assumption about 'the people' running beneath the ghastly aftermath of the war. And that is that the 'people', meaning 'people *en masse*', are incapable of restraining themselves. In this case, two further assumptions are at play. People freed from the yoke of oppressive dictatorship are most at risk – the excesses of the Iraqi populace are laid at the door of Saddam Hussein at the very moment when he loses his power to control them, and not, for example, seen as the responsibility of the occupying armies. Second, the Iraqi people are especially prone to such behaviour because they fall outside the civilising processes of the West. Thus underneath Donald Rumsfeld's magnificently evasive 'Stuff happens' – the formula allows us to think for a second that such things might happen to anyone, including presumably us, or even him – we glimpse a much harsher, discriminatory, form of judgement. Between dictatorship and barbarity, Iraq stands condemned; one reason no doubt why democracy, if that were ever the motive of the war, has to be imported and cannot be entrusted to the Iraqis themselves. Even while the images that poured out of Abu Ghraib prison suggest that there is no foundation whatsoever in reality for such fine, self-serving, discriminations between them and us.

Perhaps one of the most shocking things Freud did in *Mass Psychology and the Analysis of the Ego* in 1921 was to cut from an image of the 'masses', not far from that of an uncontrollable mob, to the church and the army in which the most passionate, not to say sacred, group identifications are formed. As I discussed in more detail in Chapter 3, Freud's word is '*die Massen*' which, until the latest translation by Kafka translator Jim Underwood as 'masses', has always been rendered as 'group'. Certainly '*die Massen*' is ambiguous – a translation more faithful to its spirit might be 'collectivity', since Freud's question, throughout the texts which from 1914 onwards deal with this issue, is what moves individuals together, leads them to bind themselves into entities of more than one. But 'collectivity' sidesteps the problem, since it avoids the awkward but politically productive blurring of boundaries between masses and groups. Or, say, between looters and the army. Or, between Iraqis running wild in the street, and American and British soldiers in Baghdad jails obeying with unchecked enthusiasm vicious orders from their superiors.

'We don't feel like we were doing things we weren't supposed to do, because we were told to do them', says Lynndie England. The fact that such orders can be traced back through the highest chain of command, from Abu Ghraib to CIA manuals, and on to Guantanamo, as well as back to British training in Oman and Northern Ireland, did not stop efforts to make her a scapegoat in the United States and England alike. The process is not of course exclusively attached to crimes of war. Outrage at events that are genuinely appalling seems to contain its own sting. 'I have no doubt', stated Judge Elizabeth Butler-Sloss as she granted lifelong protection to Jon Venables and Robert Thompson, convicted of the murder of two-year-old James Bulger in 1993, 'they were in serious danger of being killed or at least severely beaten.' Sadism will be met with sadism. One letter sent to Maxine Carr, ex-girlfriend of Soham murderer Ian Huntley, on her release from prison, told her she would be dead in six days. It is hard to keep moralism on a leash. In the case of Iraq, the stakes are even higher because the violations are not those of one or two individuals whom it is easy to hate, but of a group – a group moreover that is meant to embody our national pride: 'it's hard to believe that this actually is taking place in a military facility', stated Senator Dianne Feinstein in the *Guardian* in May.

At moments it felt as if exposing this reality, rather than the reality itself, were the worst offence. This is presumably why Geoff Hoon, and not only Geoff Hoon, seemed to think the most important issue was that some of the photographs were faked (as if discrediting the image would make the problem go away). Lynndie England and her partners in crime were despised, less one suspects for the appalling things they have done than for shattering the complacency of Western values, for letting the world see. By the end of this sorry tale, what would be left standing? Not our belief in our government as the guarantor of human rights. Nor in the ethical credibility of the army. Nor even the idea that, in a democracy, the people are restrained by the rule of law – if that were true Huntley, Venables and Thompson, to which we can add Mary Bell, as well as Maxine Carr, would not have to be effectively 'disappeared' for the sake of their own protection. Not one of these pillars of Western self-imagining can remain intact. In fact the net should be cast even wider. The lone criminal can be distanced, but not the policies of state. After all, these are the institutions of a government that, democratically elected, represent each and every one of us. We cannot palm our atrocities off on a dictator.

The people can be cruel; our institutions vicious. Knowing this, however, may not in the longer term make any difference. It might even make matters worse. According to Freud, it is when people's self-love is threatened that they resort to extremes. Far from being humbled, they are far more likely to lash out in narcissistic self-defence. We are in a vicious circle if it is true that there are no limits to what people will do to hold on to their belief in themselves.

It is not a coincidence that Freud's first extensive analysis of people *en masse* came after his study of narcissism, which had obliged him to transform completely his model of the mind. It was impossible for him to hold on to his early distinction between love and hunger, the move towards the other and towards the self, once he discovered that people can be their own preferred object, that our most passionate commitment might be to maintaining our best image of ourselves. A group is nothing if not the struggle to preserve its own ideal. This is not, however, an 'ideal' as in the sense of the ideal of democracy invoked so often in justification of an illegal war, the sort of ideal that is set in front of us as something to which we, and the world, can aspire. After Freud, things are ethically more complicated, in that such an apparently unobjectionable ideal can be seen as cover for something far less disinterested. What if, in struggling, say, to impose democracy (an oxymoron if ever there was one), we are in fact servicing an ideal, superior, version of ourselves?

It is surely no coincidence that Freud was led to this analysis of narcissism at the outbreak of the First World War. The war was a collective disillusionment – 'The Disillusionment of the War' was the title of Freud's first essay in *Thoughts for the Time on War and Death* of 1915. What was being shattered by the war, along with the lives of the people over which it trampled, was the self-idealisation of the West. Then, the greatest shock was that war could break out between the civilised nations of Europe. Freud was not talking about the pre-emptive warfare of America's New Century against the countries of the East, but his idea of what war should be like – a belief falling to pieces as he wrote – bears repeating. 'We saw [such a war]', Freud writes, 'as an opportunity for demonstrating the progress of comity among men since the era when the Greek Amphictyonic Council proclaimed that no city of the league might be destroyed, nor its olive groves cut down, nor its water supply stopped.' 'There would of course', he continues, 'be the utmost consideration for the non-combatant classes of the population [. . .] And again, all the international undertakings and institutions in which the common civilisation of peace-time had been embodied would be maintained.' Such a war would have produced 'horror and suffering' enough, he recognises, 'but it would not have interrupted the development of ethical relations between the collective individuals of mankind – the peoples and states'.

In a strange way, warfare becomes the deadly repository of our most tenacious and precarious self-idealisation. Because it is so ugly, it must be good: civilised in its conduct and civilised in its aims. In psychoanalytic terms, you might say that narcissists are so frantic and demanding because of the extent of the internal damage they are battling to repair. Paradoxically, it is because war is so awful that we invest with such ferocity in the belief that it can be the bearer of civilisation to all peoples. Either way, it seems significant that Freud elaborates his theory of narcissism in mourning ('Mourning and Melancholia' is also written in 1915) when the self-love of Europe seems lost.

Freud's bruising catalogue of the reality of the war in which such hope had been so naively invested is worth quoting at length:

> Then the war in which we had refused to believe broke out, and it brought – disillusionment [. . .] It disregards all the restrictions known as International Law, which in peace-time the states had bound themselves to observe; it ignores the prerogative of the wounded and the medical service, the distinction between the civil and military sections of the population [. . .] It tramples on all that comes its way as if there were to be no future [. . .] It cuts all the common bonds between the contending peoples and threatens to leave a legacy of embitterment that will make any renewal of those bonds impossible for a long time to come.

Even more crucial perhaps is what this conduct of the war does to the relationship between the citizen and the state. It is precisely because the state is the representative of the people, precisely because we are a democracy, that the disillusionment is so intense. What is falling apart is the belief in the virtue of representative institutions. It is starting to cross the minds of the citizens that states might embody the very evils they use to justify the wars against other – totalitarian or what today are called 'rogue' or 'failed' – states. 'Peoples', Freud continues, 'are more or less represented by the states which they form, and these states by the governments which rule them.' But today the citizen is faced with the dawning recognition – the 'horror' to use Freud's term – that 'the state has forbidden to the individual the practice of wrongdoing, not because it desires to abolish it, but because it desires to monopolise it, like salt and tobacco'. (Freud uses the same word, '*der Schrecken*', horror or terror, to categorise both war and the people's loss of faith.) A belligerent state not only breaks the law in relation to the enemy; it violates the principles which should hold between itself and its citizens: 'A belligerent state', Freud writes, 'permits itself every such misdeed, every act of violence as would disgrace the individual.' No surprise then that, faced with the disclosure of such misdeeds as those at Abu Ghraib, the state will rush to return them to the citizen precisely as 'individual disgrace'. Furthermore, the state uses secrecy and censorship to rob its citizens of the critical defences with which they might be able to deal with the reality of war. Truth, we have so often been told, is the first casualty of war. We tend to understand this as referring simply to the censorship of information, but Freud is making another point. Numbing its own citizens' capacity for judgement is one of the chief war aims of the modern state.

This is I think one of Freud's most radical moments. Of course we can read these essays at least in part as his response to his own disillusionment in finding his own nation on the wrong side of the First World War: 'We live in hopes that the pages of an impartial history will prove that that nation, in whose language we write and for whose victory our dear ones are fighting, has been precisely the one which has least transgressed the laws of civilisation.' 'But at such a time,' he continues, 'who dares to set himself up as judge in his own cause?' But inside this personal lament is one of his fiercest defences of the people against the democratic state's monopoly and abuse of violence. For it is not just that the state demands of its citizens a form of virtue from which it so blatantly abstains itself; or that it suppresses the critical faculties of the people at a time when they are more in need of the freedom to exert them than ever; or that it has broken a bond of trust between itself and its citizens at a time when, in the name of patriotism, it is demanding ever more sacrifices. All this is bad enough. Worse however, like an insane parent – passing over for the moment that all parents are a little bit insane – who insists it is being cruel to be kind, the state insists that its worst belligerence is a virtue.

The greatest sacrifice the people are being asked to make on behalf of the state is to give up their right not to believe in it. If there is one thing worse than disillusionment it is not being allowed to recognise that disillusioned is what you are. (As psychoanalyst D.W. Winnicott once said, it doesn't matter what children feel provided they are allowed to feel it.) There is a lie at the heart of democracy if the state will sacrifice its citizens' freedom to take dissent to the limit, and indeed its relationship to them, for the sake of its own violently enacted and no less violently preserved self-regard. Tony Blair's increasingly desperate statements of conviction would then simply be an inflated example of the trend. 'I believe in myself' is the last great performative of an idealist on the rocks. It also exposes the lie since, believing in himself and himself alone, he clearly neither believes in, nor belongs to, the people. 'It is crucial', Winnicott argued in his paper 'Discussion of War Aims' of 1940 that 'we should win a military and not a moral victory': 'If we fight to exist we do not claim to be better than our enemies.' How many times have we been told, as though it should make us feel better, that the soldiers' activities in Abu Ghraib 'do not compare with Saddam Hussein's systematic tortures and executions'? As Ahdaf Soueif put it in the *Guardian* article of May from which I take that quote: 'This torture started from the very top.' 'Hussein is now the moral compass of the West.'

Humiliation is a central component of torture. In Abu Ghraib, as many commentators have pointed out, this humiliation is targeted deliberately at Muslim sensibilities of sexual decorum and pride – a sure sign that these instructions come from the educated corridors of power and not from the blacks and 'poor white trash' being sent to do the dirty work of the war. Behind the humiliation there also lies a very carefully thought-out policy of psychic abuse. 'The purpose of all coercive techniques', states the *Human Resource Exploitation Manual* produced by the CIA for Honduras in 1983, 'is to induce psychological regression [. . .] Regression is basically a loss of autonomy.' The manual is an updated version of the *Kubark Counterintelligence Interrogation Manual* of 1963, according to which such regression has to be traumatically induced: 'There is an interval [. . .] of suspended animation, a kind of psychological shock or paralysis. It is caused by a traumatic or sub-traumatic experience which explodes, as it were, the world that is familiar to the subject as well as his image of himself within that world. At this moment the source is far more open to suggestion, far likelier to comply.'

This is psychologically very precise. It is almost exactly the scenario laid out by psychoanalyst Christopher Bollas in his 1995 article on 'The Structure of Evil' which describes the 'psychic death' or 'radical infantilisation' that the serial killer imposes on his victim: 'With the total collapse of trust and the madness expressed by sudden dementia of the real, the victim experiences an annihilation of adult personality structures and is time-warped into a certain kind of infantile position, possibly depending now for existence itself on the whim of incarcerated madness.' Incarcerated madness will do nicely for Abu Ghraib. Crucial in both cases is that the subject is made to regress to a state of childlike dependency, at the same time as losing all the reference points that would allow the victim to find her- or himself even in this massively regressed, infantile, world. The key, as the CIA manual puts it, is 'loss of autonomy'. 'This structure', writes Bollas, 'is part of the unconscious knowledge of the West.'

Far from raising the world to heights of civilisation, the ruling powers of the new century seem to be spending a lot of energy trying to turn both citizen and enemy into children.

Wandering the streets of Paris in 1885, Freud was dismayed by the 'people' (he took none of the pleasure of the *flâneur* of Walter Benjamin). Writing to his fiancée's sister, he described them as a 'different species', as 'uncanny', knowing the meaning of neither 'fear nor shame': 'the women no less than the men crowding round nudities as much as they do round corpses in the Morgue'. It would not be until the year after the war, in 1919, that he would formulate his theory of the uncanny as something repressed that returns to haunt us, that is, as something provoking disquiet because it is a piece of ourselves. But, even as he takes his distance in this letter of 1885, he is already recognising that the people have access to a truth about the civilisation, from which he excludes them, and to which he believes himself to belong. If the 'people' are shameless and fearless – 'utterly different' as he continues in his letter to Minna Bernays – it is because their vulnerability, their place outside privilege, at once gives them licence and increases their vision. 'Too helpless, too exposed to behave like us'; in their 'lack of moderation' they are compensating for being 'a helpless target for all the taxes, epidemics, sicknesses and evils of social institutions'. In this early letter, the people lose all moderation because they have nothing to lose, no illusions to maintain – in this they are way ahead of the disillusioned citizens of war-torn Europe of 1914. Why on earth should the people believe in the benign powers of social institutions? (They do not have to be told that the state monopolises tobacco and salt.)

The people expose the evils of social institutions, the injustice of culture (what he refers to elsewhere as 'our present-day white Christian culture'). That is why they are so loose and licensed – they strip the façade. In doing so, they reveal unconscious desires that, however shameless (indeed because they are so shameless), implicate us each and every one. In *Mass Psychology*, as discussed at more length in Chapter 3, he describes the mass as laying bare 'the unconscious foundation that is the same for everyone'. Go back to those nudities and corpses in the morgue from the letter of 1885: 'the women no less than the men crowd round nudities as much as they do round corpses in the Morgue'. It is uncannily resonant of the images of grinning soldiers crowding round the abjectly sexualised inmates of Abu Ghraib. These images are pornographic, as has been pointed out, but in a very specific form. *In extremis*, they trade on the unconscious association of sex and death. You do not have to accept Freud's vision of the mob, since that is after all what it is, a vision in which we can recognise all the stereotypes of bourgeois fear, to notice that he has run a line from perversion to truth. Civilisation is unjust (in *The Future of an Illusion* of 1927, he will state that a culture that fails to satisfy so many of its participants will not, and does not deserve to, survive); our most venerated social institutions are evil; be wary of pointing the finger at the individual who disgraces us, since we are all of us perverts in our dreams.

'Well may the citizen of the world of whom I have spoken', Freud writes in 'The Disillusionment of the War', 'stand helpless in a world that has grown strange to him.' But, he adds, 'there is something to be said in criticism of his disappointment' – 'It is not justified, since it consists in the destruction of an illusion.' At this unexpected turning point of his essay – Freud was nothing if not a great dramatist in his writing – we discover that what he means by 'disillusionment' is not quite what we have been led to expect. It is not the disappointment, say, of a gravely let-down man, but something far closer to 'disabuse'. Our mistake, it turns out, was to have believed in the first place. In this context, war, at the very moment when the state is doing its utmost to subdue the critical judgement of citizens, might be a rare opportunity. Like 'the people', who of course need no such prompting or crisis, we can now see things, see human beings, as they really are. 'In reality, our fellow-citizens have not sunk so low as we feared, because they had never risen as high as we believed.' This is not, finally, a narcissistic lament ('how have we fallen' or 'this does not represent the America that I know' to cite Bush's more recent phrase); it is something at once more modest and more devastating. 'White Christian culture' should stop kidding itself.

Much follows from this. There is no such thing, Freud states, as ' "eradicating" evil' ('eradicating' is in scare quotes). Bush and Blair could perhaps take note. Travelling through Yugoslavia in 1936 and 1937, Freud's contemporary, Rebecca West, also found herself contemplating the question of evil. In Slav culture, she suggests, we are confronted with the 'seeming paradox of a fierce campaign against evil with a tolerance of its nature'. 'We cannot', she muses, understand this in the West, 'where we assume that sincere hostility to sin must be accompanied by a reluctance to contemplate it and a desire to annihilate it'. For Freud, on the other hand, the impulses that constitute the 'deepest essence' of human nature are 'neither good nor bad' in themselves. He will condemn actions but never the drives from which they stem. It is a central tenet of psychoanalysis that if we can tolerate what is most disorienting – disillusioning – about our own unconscious, we are less likely to act on it, less inclined to strike out in a desperate attempt to assign the horrors of the world to someone, or somewhere, else. It is not, therefore, the impulse that is dangerous, but the ruthlessness of our attempts to be rid of it. This might be one reason why illegally occupying armies, who can neither settle nor face their own conscience, become so brutalised – it is their own discomfort they are trying to erase. For historian Richard Overy, this is the lesson of Abu Ghraib, which confronts us with 'the standard behaviour of troops under pressure, fighting a war whose purpose is hard for them to understand'. In the case of Iraq, the brutality requires a further explanation: 'The chief culprit is Bush's war on terror [. . .] the division in the Bush/Blair view of the Middle East into putative "democrats" or terrorists has created a climate of fear.' The soldiers are the victims of the government's projections: 'Ultimate responsibility lies at the top.'

If it is the ideal that is dangerous, it follows that we need to be more wary of collective identifications (no 'saving ideals'). 'What psychoanalysis seeks', writes Moustapha Safouan – the Paris-based Egyptian psychoanalyst and translator of *The Interpretation of Dreams* and of Hegel's *Phenomenology* into Arabic – is to 'reduce identifications to the minimum requisite for the exercise of our responsibilities.' Keep the proper distance. In setting this as the goal, analysis does not aim to 'shelter [the patient] from passions, but from joining in those collective passions in which the intelligence of human groupings normally founders'.

Freud knew that the fierceness with which a group builds and defends its identity was the central question of modern times. But unlike the leaders of our 'present-day white Christian culture', he also knew that no group is safe from the dangers of conviction, and that a nation that frees itself from doubt and refuses to question its own motives can place the whole world in peril.

*Originally delivered as the Freud memorial lecture at Essex University, 21 May 2004; published in the *London Review of Books* as 'In Our Present-Day White Christian Culture', 8 July 2004, and in *Harpers*, October 2004. In order to avoid repetition, I have based the present essay on the version published in *Harpers*.

9

On Being Nadine Gordimer*

Whether or not it will actually happen, it seems clear that America is planning for its next global intervention on behalf of the new century to be in Iran. As with Iraq, the ostensible motive or pretext will be disarmament. Despite the catastrophe of the Iraqi adventure, the United States government has not wavered in its belief that the question of which countries, or rather which rulers, have the right to destroy other countries – and possibly the whole world – is one it alone must decide. 'The direst of all threats in the world's collective fear', the narrator comments roughly halfway through Nadine Gordimer's *Get A Life*, 'beyond terrorism, suicide bombing, introduction of deadly viruses, fatal chemical substances in innocent packages, Mad Cow Disease – is "nuclear capability".' This does not mean of course that the USA, as 'the power with a foot on everyone's doorstep' is on the side of non-proliferation, unless it suits its ambitions. Popular protest against nuclear energy is not something which the industrialised world as a whole tends to support. A danger from Iran may be a welcome opportunity for multinational expansion – to be promoted at all cost – in the new South Africa. Uneven development, one might say. Centring her novel around these contradictions, Gordimer brings her writing firmly into the twenty-first century.

Gordimer is not of course the first to have noted the insanity of living in an era 'where there are wars going on over who possesses weapons that could destroy all trace of it'. In the course of the novel, this sentence is repeated more or less verbatim three times, each one with reference to archaeology whose artefacts, miraculously preserved and unearthed from the ancient past, silently reproach our modern-day recklessness. What of our own era will be available for such loving, fastidious attention? What, if anything, will survive? This may be Gordimer's question about her own legacy as a writer, or about her role after the end of apartheid which has given so much of her writing its finest, if desperate, rationale. But by taking up this issue, Gordimer is paradoxically staking a claim to a future none of us can be sure of. In her previous novel, *The Pickup*, she as writer, or her central characters, left South Africa for an unnamed Arab country. Returning in this novel to the country she herself has never been able to leave – 'I have never felt not at home here', she stated in the 1970s – she makes it once again globally central (even while those double negatives evoke a more ambiguous belonging).[1] The forces struggling over the future of the new South Africa are those that will decide the destiny of the planet. For Gordimer, unlike Coetzee, South Africa is still the epicentre of the world.

In *Get A Life*, Aids and the strong arm of globalisation seize their mainly black victims. Gordimer has always been a writer predominantly read by whites, her grandeur – she won the Nobel Prize in 1991 – viewed by some black critics in South Africa with suspicion (although after being awarded the prize, she was greeted on her return from a visit abroad by black writers from the Congress of South African Writers, an ANC delegation and by Walter Sisulu as speaker at a later welcoming ceremony). Her talent, and importance, has been to turn disabling white privilege into fiction. 'The white artist', she wrote in her 1979 article 'Relevance and Commitment', 'is the *non-European* whose society nevertheless refused to acknowledge and take root with an indigenous culture. He is the *non-Black* whom blacks see as set apart from indigenous culture.' 'He does not know as yet', she continues, in words still resonant in today's burgeoning and stricken South Africa, 'whether this is a dead-end or can be made a new beginning.'

Get A Life is not the first of Gordimer's writings in which power plants are the political focus. In her 1984 novella *Something Out There*, four ANC revolutionaries hide out in a house set on several acres in a satellite country town, with AKM assault rifles, bayonets and limpet mines, from where they conduct a successful strike against a power station (the episode is based on a real event). Although Gordimer never engaged in such acts of militancy, the experience of one of the two white characters has strong echoes of her own: 'She would not have been here if she had not found her own re-education, after the school where she had sung for God to save white South Africa.' Placing the tale of the terrorists in tandem with that of an escaped baboon from a zoo, she mocks the racist fears of the white population in the same breath as she exposes a government rhetoric against 'terror' which bears uncanny resemblance to that of Bush and Blair: the Prime Minister 'was able to call upon support from all sections of the community to meet the threat from beyond our borders that was always ready to strike at our country'.

On 15 March 2006, Gordimer put her name to a letter in the *Guardian*, signed by 407 writers, urging the closure of Guantanamo – the letter refers to the '*so-called*' war on terror. Gordimer has always been suspicious of the public rhetoric of the United States – which she has referred to variously as a 'brutal society' and as the 'harshest country in the world' – and more broadly that of the 'West'. 'In the ditches of El Salvador, in the prisons of Argentina and South Africa, in the roofless habitations of Beirut', she wrote in her 1982 essay, 'Living in the Interregnum', 'are the victims of Western standards of humanity.' Editing the piece for the *New York Review of Books*, Bob Silvers objected to the unqualified critique of Western capitalism: 'Won't you keep in mind the Western reader who might not want to cross the slag heaps with you?' (She felt he had edited the piece into a 'mild, unchallenging plea'.) With its focus on the dangers posed to South Africa by the intent of the developed world, *Get A Life* is therefore recycling an abiding preoccupation. Certainly there is no evidence here for the strange conclusion of Gordimer's new biographer, Ronald Suresh Roberts, that Gordimer has responded to the end of apartheid by relaxing 'on her historical oars as if crossing an historical finishing line'. (Statements like these might be one reason that Gordimer, having originally given the biography her support, now wholly dissociates herself from it.)

Something Out There is one of Gordimer's most radical stories. Today, its clear, exhilarated, support for the militants would be likely to place her on the wrong side of the new UK law against glorification of terrorism (though in South Africa this was not one of her three banned books: *A World of Strangers*, 1958, *The Late Bourgeois World*, 1966, and *Burger's Daughter*, 1979). According to Suresh Roberts, Gordimer's advocacy of armed struggle predated that of Nelson Mandela. She once described as a 'calumny' the suggestion that she promoted the violent overthrow of the state, but in 1988, she appeared as a witness in mitigation of sentence at the trial of Mosiuoa Lekota, Popo Molefe and Moss Chikane, stating under interrogation – and to gasps from the gallery – that she supported Umkhonto we Sizwe, the ANC's armed wing. Terrorism was, she wrote in a 1960s essay, 'The Price of a White Man's Country', the 'deadly logical outcome' of the situation: 'They felt useless as they were, and so became what they were not.' This is just one of her many striking formulations that can be profitably transferred across to other conflicted parts of the globe. Here is another, taken from her 1940s jottings, which would do well for the children of the Palestinian *intifada*: 'The natives: For many years [. . .] they asked for bread, and we gave them a stone. Now they have found a use for these stones; we are getting them back – thrown. Thrown at trains, at police, at white men's cars.' Note the 'we'. By her own analysis, Gordimer has always been a legitimate target.

Paul Bannerman, the central character of *Get A Life*, is a campaigning ecologist who, when the novel opens, is suffering from a cancer whose treatment has left him radioactive. In these circumstances, only his parents, regardless of the danger of the fall-out to their own health, are capable of the 'missionary' grace involved in caring for their child. 'I am', he says, 'my own experimental pebble-bedded nuclear reactor.' Recovered, he picks up, together with a black comrade, Thapelo, his campaigns against such a nuclear reactor, a dam-building venture, and a mining project on the sand dunes of Pondoland. The mines require forced removals reminiscent of apartheid – 'many are illiterate and some have lost their cattle and sheep as a result of being forced to move' – although this is not the analogy that springs to Gordimer's pen: 'There have been different commands for this type of thing. *Juden heraus.*' Gordimer's relationship to her own Jewish background is complex. In her first semi-autobiographical novel of 1953, *The Lying Days*, Helen Shaw has her key relationship with, but is not herself, a Jew. But Gordimer has always seen the links binding her Jewish legacy to apartheid South Africa. In the fifties, she condemned the 'incipient Hitlerism' of South Africa, describing apartheid as an 'avatar of Nazism'; in *Something Out There*, one of the militants forges a clarinet out of jam tins and the ring-pulls from beer cans, reminding another of 'the ingenuity of objects displayed in the concentration camps of Europe'. In post-apartheid South Africa, Nazism, she seems to suggest, is taking the guise of the International Biodiversity Strategic Action Plan. Gordimer, we could say, never shies from an analogy. In 2000, she commented – to some anger – that Israel had taken over from Britain 'the colonial position of an occupying power'. (A year later, she urged Susan Sontag not to accept the Jerusalem Prize.)

Bannerman is, in his own words, a 'conservationist'. This makes him at least partly a throwback to Gordimer's 1974 novel of that title, a negative pastoral focused on a dissociated, nihilistic, white South African, Mehring, who spends his weekends on a farm over which he slowly but surely loses all control: the novel opens with the unearthing of an unidentified black body on his farm and ends with a flood of apocalyptic dimension in which the earth drowns. He is also a child molester. Reread this novel today and it is hard not to see Mehring as the forerunner of Coetzee's dysfunctional and/or sexually abusive male characters (although he is not an Afrikaner); hard, too, not to be impressed by Gordimer's literary transvestism: 'Do I really want to be a man?' she wrote to Katherine White, fiction editor of the *New Yorker*, in 1958, 'I can't believe I do.' But this allusion to the earlier work, whose title was heavily ironic, acts as a caution against the more romantic dimensions of Bannerman's quest, which only occasionally threaten to overwhelm Gordimer's later novel. It is one of the productive tensions of *Get A Life* that Gordimer looks to the earth, whose political control has never ceased to be her topic, for redemption against the evils wrought on it by politics. In *The*

Lying Days, Helen Shaw describes the illusion of being happy in South Africa as 'like having a picnic in a beautiful graveyard where the people are buried alive under your feet'. The earth cries out; or worse, as in *The Conservationist*, it throws up its dead silently, as a prelude to the end of the world. Gordimer once stated that the idea of being attached to the land was meaningless:

> The only attachment that makes claims valid in human terms is some sort of vital attachment to the people; you cannot be 'attached' to soil and thorn trees, because these do not respond, you can kiss the earth in bliss or be hanged from one of the trees in terror – the landscape is totally unaffected by either.

The great mistake of Afrikaner ideology was to take attachment to the land as proof of title, 'some kind of right that is entirely separable from behaviour, social behaviour'.

There is, then, no land to speak of outside of the social relations embedded within it. This is no less true in today's South Africa than under apartheid, as the struggle over mining, dams and reactors at the core of this novel makes clear. Gordimer does not ignore the ethical and political complexities of these developments. Australian-based Mineral Commodities offers the mining option to a black-empowerment company that represents, in Bannerman's words, 'the very community, the traditional leaders we counted on, the people *we've* been lobbying to protest misuse of their land'. 'So? We don't want rural blacks to have a share in the growth of economic power?' Gordimer can, however, only go so far down this path. She cannot, unlike Zakes Mda in his brilliant novel of 2000, *The Heart of Redness*, trace the dilemma back into the land of the forefathers. In his rendering of the same clash between development and tradition, Mda has the amXhosa of Qolhora reliving the conflict that tore apart their community at the time of the great mid-nineteenth-century cattle slaughter. (Would killing the animals free the people from the whites, as prophesied, or was it a colonial plot?) Gordimer can empathise: Bannerman can *see* the problem. But you cannot conjure ancestors out of the dust.

If Gordimer can be described as apartheid's 'lyrical analyst', in Suresh Roberts's phrase, she also remains the writer who offered the most trenchant, unforgiving, analysis of why under apartheid lyricism had no place. In the 1990 *My Son's Story*, it is the black man, Sonny, suddenly intolerant of his own sensuousness, who rails against the white man's domain of 'quiet and beauty, screened by green from screams of fear and chants of rage, from the filth of scrap-heap settlements and the mashed symmetry of shot bodies. He had no part of it. He did not know what he was doing there.' Here, surely, there is also a critique of the sensuousness of Gordimer's own prose, of her inability or unwillingness to let apartheid thwart her writing's own love affair with itself (in *The Conservationist*, the lushness of the prose often jars against the novel's overall message of distaste). Sensuousness in writing, inadvertently or not, places its hush upon the world. At times, Gordimer's writing can feel too tolerant of its own literary weight. Today the scrap-heap settlements have not disappeared. Although 1.8 million houses have been built for the poor since 1994, according to official figures, cited by Rory Carroll in the *Guardian* on 22 February 2006, up to a quarter of the population – twelve million people – live in shacks, a rise of 50 per cent in the last ten years.

And yet in *Get A Life*, land, without or despite human intervention, oblivious to the social behaviour of its inhabitants, becomes its own redemption, spontaneously renews itself. The Okavango, an inland delta in Botswana, 'could never have been planned on a drawing-board by the human brain. Its transformation, spontaneous, self-generated, could not have been conceived.' This is not, the narrator insists, 'evidence to be claimed by religious or other creational mysticism, either', but the innovation of matter, greater than any collective mind or faith. Perhaps 'whatever civilisation does to destroy nature, nature will find its solution in a measure of time we don't have'. In *The Conservationist*, a couple, Mr and Mrs Loftus Coetzee, drown when their car is carried by the flood to a pit between disused mine dumps 'that had long been a graveyard for wrecked cars and other obstinate imperishable objects that will rust, break and buckle, but cannot be received back into the earth and organically transformed'. Gordimer's concern with renewal – and with mines (she was brought up in the mining town of Springs) – has a long history. Nonetheless, *Get A Life* involves a big shift of perspective – cosmic, precisely. Afrikaans writer Antje Krog, at the end of *Country of My Skull*, her agonised story of the Truth and Reconciliation Commission, rejoins a love of her country that apartheid had threatened to place under permanent duress: 'How vast, how desperately beautiful this country is. My eyes lick the horizon clean.' Gordimer has to travel further. Faced with the continuing failures and corruptions of the world post-apartheid, we should, it seems, be looking back at earth from outer space. Against her own harsher insights, she gives herself permission to renew the poetic licence of the earth.

In a famous comment, Adorno wrote: 'The illusory importance and autonomy of private life conceals the fact that private life drags on only as an appendage of the social process.' Gordimer apparently underlined this phrase in the 1970s, and – one might argue – has carried it with her as inspiration and burden throughout her writing life. The belief in a domain of privacy that can somehow jump free of historical process is at once a prayer and a form of decadence under a system where the spoils of privacy, or even the chances of privacy, are so unevenly and unjustly spread. In one of the most powerful moments in *July's People*, Gordimer's 1981 projected tale of post-revolutionary South Africa, the white woman, Maureen Smales, now at the mercy of her black servant who has rescued her family from the insurrection and taken them to his village, realises that her sense of self – the person she has taken for granted in the most intimate core of her being – has relied on the physical dimensions of a room. The recognition tears into the white liberalism in which she had taken such misjudged pride: 'The absolute nature she and her kind were scrupulously just in granting to everybody was no more than the price of the master bedroom.' (It is a type of racialised version of Virginia Woolf's plea on behalf of women in *A Room of One's Own*.)

And yet Gordimer also believes that there is an unreachable core of our being which moves, like the tectonic plates of the earth – like, say, the mutations of Okavango – in the depths: 'It is not the conscious changes made in their lives by men and women', Helen Shaw ponders in *The Lying Days*, 'which really shape them [. . .] but a long, slow mutation of emotion, hidden, all-penetrative [. . .] This gives a shifting quality to the whole surface of a life.' This slowly mutating world is, for Gordimer, the privileged domain of the writer, the domain of 'unconscious reality' as she puts it in a letter to Stephen Clingman, a domain to which the writer, unlike the intellectual, has unique, almost mystical, access. 'Even if he writes about a great public event, or war or revolution', she stated in her acceptance speech for the 1961 W.H. Smith Prize for *Friday's Footprint*, the writer's 'view is as private as when he writes of an incestuous love affair.' This is the realm of inner 'commitment' which struggles on the page with 'relevance', the writer's unavoidable political task: 'Relevance has to do with outside events; and commitment comes from within.' This is of course a fairly traditional view of the role of the artist. But in the context of South Africa, the claim on behalf of privacy acquires a new urgency, becoming at moments – *pace* Adorno – a type of retreat ('unget-at-able at' to use Gordimer's phrase). As if, in such politically destitute times, there is nowhere else to hide. Aesthetic privilege then becomes the only form of privilege Gordimer feels licensed to grant herself with impunity.

It would be wrong to suggest therefore that the pull of the earth against the worst of history in *Get A Life* is entirely unexpected. Rather, it inherits in new guise one of the central political and aesthetic tensions of Gordimer's writing and her life. Gordimer has always been eloquent on the ethical dilemma of privilege. 'I should be a liar', she wrote to Katherine White in 1965, when the numbers detained without trial reached 950, 'if I said we were unhappy.' Her critique of liberalism as 'hopelessly inadequate' to the realities of apartheid – she once called it the 'great aunt of empire-building' – is also a form of self-indictment. 'Please do not call me a liberal,' she insisted in an interview with *The Times* in 1974, 'Liberal is a dirty word.' The test is universal franchise: 'I want it; the liberals don't' (the South African Liberal Party she described as a 'Noah's Ark for whites'). Liberals make promises they have no power to keep. They pay but they won't fight – although paying of course helps. Gordimer was scathing about the sudden flurry of fund-raising for Israel in 1967 among South African Jews who had made no contribution to the Anti-Apartheid Defence Fund: 'Where were all the fur coats and family silver, then?' In fact, as Glenn Frankel narrates in *Rivonia's Children*, Jews were central to the struggle against apartheid; nonetheless, from the beginning, Gordimer was dismayed at the number wooed by the National Party into apartheid's privilege of whiteness – the party had been rabidly anti-Semitic until its narrow election victory of 1948.

As the situation of the blacks steadily worsened throughout the 1970s and 80s, this critique intensified. It was also given added charge by the emergent black consciousness movement of the 1970s which rejected the contribution of whites like Gordimer and, with it, a multiracial vision of a new South Africa. But as early as the 1940s, Gordimer had been implicating herself in 'the failure of the liberal attitude'. The only difference, she observed in 1944, between the civic guard who want to imprison 'kaffir' servants for brewing illegal beer, and their employers who want to protect them, is that the latter do not want to have to go to the trouble of finding new servants. 'Even to live here', she stated in her 1959 essay 'What is Apartheid?', 'is to acquiesce in some measure to apartheid – to a sealing off of responses, the cauterisation of the human heart, as well as to withholding the vote from those who outnumber us eight to one.' 'We whites', she wrote in 1982, 'have still to thrust the spade under the roots of our lives.'

In this context, the radioactive condition of Bannerman, the campaigner against nuclear power, at the start of *Get A Life*, is not only an allusion to the fall-out of apartheid, but a way of reiterating a fundamental political point. You may, as one of the advantaged, choose to side with the wretched of the earth, but you will always be the bearer of the ill you are trying to cure.

There were of course whites who went much further than Gordimer knew she had gone. Compared with Ruth First and Bettie du Toit, both campaigning activists who put their lives on the line, she always felt that she had not been brave enough: 'She was so fearless', she wrote of Ruth First, 'that she made one feel ashamed.' 'In comparison', she wrote in her preface to du Toit's autobiography, 'how the rest of us have writhed and squirmed through the years, seeking accommodations contorted between conscience and self.' That 'self' is expressive; Gordimer still believes somehow that the self can, or should, float free of the assaults it weathers from the outside world. 'Our lives have been totally invaded by the effects of politics', she wrote, again to Katherine White, in 1965. In 1989, she talked of her increasing involvement with – 'not politics, but the things that politics do *to* people' (my emphasis). There is always the danger, for the white liberal imagination, that politics simply *spoils* matters. Helen Shaw's first love affair is destroyed by the 'restless depression' that descends upon her lover as he increasingly feels the contradiction between his part in the struggle for black emancipation and his daily work trying to ameliorate black lives. 'Well,' she insists plaintively and to no avail, 'I don't see why one can't do both.'

Gordimer's writing is at its best for me when she transmutes this core anxiety, which stretches across the corpus of her work, into the substance of her fiction. At the opening of *The House Gun*, perhaps her most successful post-apartheid novel to date, the Lingards, progressive liberal whites struggling to do their bit in the new South Africa, are informed that their son has been arrested for murder. Violence from which they had wrongly considered themselves immune erupts into their private space. Claudia Lingard is a doctor who protects the body from pain: 'She stands on the other side of the divide from those who cause it.' On occasion, Gordimer succeeds in pressing the dilemma into the syntax of a single sentence. The Lingards have just discovered that a black lawyer will be defending their son:

> She's not one of those doctors who touch black skin indiscriminately along with white, in their work, but retain liberal prejudice against the intellectual capacities of blacks.

Stop at the first comma and Claudia Lingard is not a doctor who touches black skin; read on, and she is not one of those whites who refuse to accept blacks as real equals *even though* they are all too happy to touch black bodies, in a purely professional capacity of course. It is a split second of self-incrimination. How much has really changed? White liberalism – white prejudice – dies hard.

For the past few years, Gordimer has given active support to the South African Treatment Action Campaign (TAC), an HIV/Aids advocacy group that works to promote literacy on Aids and to increase access to antiretroviral drugs (at least five million South Africans are currently estimated to be living with Aids, more than any other country; an equivalent percentage in the US would mean thirty million people). The organisation was founded in 1998 after the death of anti-apartheid gay rights activist Simon Nkoli, who died from Aids at a time when antiretroviral therapy was available to wealthy South Africans. Today Aids is one of the most contested issues in South Africa (the gap between access to drugs for rich and poor is inequality's deadly new face). Mbeki is famous for having questioned the link between HIV and Aids and for playing down the pandemic; at a conference in 2004 organised by the South African embassy in London to celebrate ten years of democracy, Aids was barely mentioned. Such reticence, to which TAC has come as the dramatically effective response, is not wholly surprising. Aids is a gift for those who relish the prospect of a failing black-ruled South Africa (or worse, see black Africa as the primordial, world-contaminating, source of the disease).

In 2001, TAC successfully sued the government for not ensuring that drugs enabling the prevention of mother-to-child transmission were available to pregnant mothers (35,000 HIV-positive babies are born each year). More recently, TAC has proceeded with litigation against the Minister of Health for allowing German vitamin-maker Matthias Rath to distribute unregistered medicines and advertise unproven remedies for Aids. At the end of his biography, Suresh Roberts inexplicably turns on Gordimer for supporting TAC – he appears to brook no criticism of Mbeki – as well as attacking Edwin Cameron, the High Court judge whose public admission of his own positive status has been crucial in reducing the stigma of the disease (Mandela wrote the preface to his book, *Witness to Aids*, which came out in 2005). Gordimer has also collated and edited an anthology of short stories by international writers, *Telling Tales*, the profits from which go to Aids-preventive education and treatment. She invited the authors to contribute without payment, and persuaded the publishers to take production costs only. 'Have we perhaps not abused our contingent freedoms', she asked in 1996 in an essay on the pandemic, 'moving about the world, taking as our right a disregard for the social and sexual mores of other people, seeing concourse across borders and classes not as an exchange of cultures but as a sweeping aside of them' (Roberts reads this as indicting the impoverished as much as the privileged, whereas the 'we' surely makes it clear who is the target of blame). In *Telling Tales*, she reminds us of such brutal crossings by choosing as her own contribution, 'The Ultimate Safari', which relates the flight of a Mozambican family through the Kruger Park to South Africa – the only story she has written from inside the mind of a black child.

In *Get A Life*, Aids makes the uneasy passage into Gordimer's fiction. Paul Bannerman's mother, Lyndsay, adopts a three-year-old HIV-positive orphan and rape victim as the novel comes to a close (with the reactor halted, and the birth of a new baby to Paul and his wife on the last page, the final note is up-beat). This unexpected turnaround follows another: her husband, Adrian, at the end of the archeological trip to Mexico they had long promised themselves on his retirement, announces he is leaving her for their thirty-five-year-old Norwegian tour guide. The reader shares the double shock not least because it was the son, not the self-sacrificing parents – the grey background to his sick radiance – that this novel, or so it seemed, was meant to be about. In a much earlier short story, 'Sins of the Third Age', a husband similarly tells his wife, just as they are about to move to the house in Italy they have been preparing for their retirement, that he has 'met someone' – the wife moves out to Italy nonetheless and the story ends with the estranged resumption of their lives. Gordimer was therefore writing about the third age long before she got there – the theme does not appear here for the first time as autobiographical mirror to her own life. Rather it retrieves the 'slow mutation of emotion, hidden, all-penetrative' evoked by Helen Shaw in *The Lying Days* (retirement would then be the great myth of stability, rarely addressed in fiction not because of its tedium but because of its threat). But the unanticipated, extravagant, nature of the gesture – its staginess – also serves to make an ethical and political point. To be surprised, or even shocked, by Lyndsay's adopting of the orphan might be a way of registering the distance: between continuing white privilege and the world, say, of Khayelitsha, the township on the outskirts of Cape Town, designed under apartheid to purge blacks from the settlements but still there today, whose population has been decimated by Aids. 'Those living in affluence', Cameron writes in *Witness to Aids*, 'often do not see, still less have any contact with, people suffering from preventable illness, avoidable hunger, and remediable destitution.'

White woman saves black Aids orphan: the trope hovers perilously close to patronage (abandoned wife also finds a new cause). An act of atonement for apartheid, with disquieting echoes of Coetzee's *Disgrace*, in which a white woman who is raped during an assault on her and her father by blacks becomes pregnant and resolves to keep the child. As if to forestall objections, Gordimer allows the character to voice her own internal critique: 'Her own motives were suspect to her.' Who is saving whom? And yet Gordimer knows from TAC that individual acts of redemption, as opposed to state intervention, will not save South Africa from Aids. 'I was taking the drugs', Cameron writes of the antiretroviral drugs that saved him, 'only because I could afford them.' In *Get A Life*, the battle with the pharmaceutical companies over drugs is invisible: 'There was a good chance, said the paediatrician Lyndsay took the child to, that her HIV-positive status would correct itself shortly.' HIV redeems itself. This is surely where the critique of corporations – the son's struggle – is most needed. One half of the novel has lost the other's political spirit. Aids belongs to the heart. Once again the saving, private, domain carries the burden of political fear. Having the child be a rape victim also sidesteps the key issue of mother-to-child transmission (while, also like *Disgrace*, evoking the spectre of black rape, and, at the same time, considerably raising the black-child-as-helpless-victim stakes). 'If I were to sum up in a word what is the most striking feature of South African society,' Gordimer wrote to Harry Levin in 1976, 'I would say without hesitation "ambiguity".' In this context, however, ambiguity is of limited value. Here, Charlene, the Aids worker who first took Lyndsay to the orphanage, is talking of her work among HIV and Aids sufferers:

- What happens to the babies? Many die? And if they survive, with treatment. They do get treatment?
- Many die. What can you do. They've been left in public toilets. Some in the streets, the police find them and bring them in.
- The mothers?
- Nobody knows the mothers, who're the fathers.

The child – Lyndsay calls her Klara – is one of thousands of abandoned Aids orphans, 'found without a name', 'a child of unknown parentage, abandoned no one knows by whom'. Is the mother or the rape the source of the disease?

When I teach Nadine Gordimer, I always start with a 1950s short story, 'Which New Era Would That Be?', in which a young white liberal woman visits a Johannesburg printing shop and confronts the three men, black and coloured, with her own well-meaning pretension. At the climax of the story, one of the men relates how he was made to sit out on the stoep for his lunch during a visit to a trade union boss with a white colleague, after they had all shared a drink together. 'I feel I must tell you', she says as she is leaving, 'About that other story – about the lunch. I don't believe it. I'm sorry, but I honestly don't.' It was, the narrator comments, 'the final self-immolation by honest understanding [. . .] She would go to the length of calling him a liar to show by frankness how much she respected him.' After she has left, one of the men kicks the chair he had cleared for her to sit on and sends it flying. The story is an allegory of white writing. Its genius is the way it portrays the complete breakdown of understanding between black and white – 'These were the white women who, Jake knew, persisted in regarding themselves as your equal. That was even worse, he thought, than the parsons who persisted in regarding *you* as *their* equal' – even as Gordimer goes inside the thoughts of the black characters to make her point. 'There is no representation of our social reality', Gordimer replied to a hostile questioner at a conference on 'Culture and Resistance' held in Botswana in 1982 (black writers could not meet in South Africa), 'without that strange area of our lives in which we have knowledge of each other.' The implied symmetry is, however, misleading, as the early story makes clear. For while it may be true that the oppressed knows the oppressor (she/he has to), how can the oppressor – without repeating the basic offence – ever claim knowledge of the oppressed?

In South Africa, it is Gordimer's portrayal of her black characters which causes the most objections. It is one of the reasons she has never enjoyed there the status she has outside Africa. Her portrayal of Thapelo in *Get A Life* sways between empathy and condescension, the exact combination she had made her own target in 'Which New Era Would That Be?' In his use of mother-tongue slang, Thapelo is still living the street life of blacks: 'It's not what he's emancipated from, it's what he hasn't, won't leave behind.' In a stroke, Gordimer frames, or even corners, the progressive bilingualism of her own text (there is a glossary for Thapelo at the end). The 'won't' carries the ambivalence. Although I do not think this is what Gordimer intends, it allows the sentence to be read: Why won't the blacks grow up, give up the past, enter the colonial tongue? Bannerman 'teases him; in appreciation'. There is still the sense in Gordimer that empathy, or – today – appreciation, should be enough, even while she charts the reasons why empathy must fail, will never on its own be sufficient. But if she had been true to the insight of the earlier story, it is not clear that she would have been able to write about South Africa at all.

If, finally, we put back together the two halves of *Get A Life* – the mother's regressive benevolence, the son's struggle against nuclear development – we can recognise the central dichotomy of Gordimer's work: as the one appeals to a liberal solution of ills which the other shows to be way beyond liberalism's reach. Over the past half-century, no writer has done more to explore this dilemma. Gordimer is of course not the only writer, nor indeed person, who cannot quite accept what she knows. In her latest novel, she communicates once again how much she both wishes, and doesn't wish, that she could have been something else.

*First published in the *London Review of Books*, 20 April 2006.

Note

1 Quotations from Gordimer's correspondence and journals, unless otherwise stated, are taken from Ronald Suresh Roberts, *No Cold Kitchen, A Biography of Nadine Gordimer* (Johannesburg, STE Publishers 2005), from which Gordimer has publicly dissociated herself.

10

Specimen Days – On
Michael Cunningham and Walt Whitman*

At the centre of Michael Cunningham's 2005 novel *Specimen Days*, in the second of its three tales, Cat, a black woman police investigator in New York, has the job of receiving and recording the calls of people threatening to blow themselves and others to pieces. Only because these deranged stories have become too familiar does she miss the one who really means it, a young boy, one of a harmless breed she thought, who, without forewarning or apparent motive, goes up to a stranger in Central Park, embraces him and explodes. He is part of a cell, or 'family', of drifting boys taken up by an old woman who goes by the name of Walt Whitman – whose poetry they all cite and whose vision they share. 'We don't die. We go into the grass. We go into the trees.' 'Of your real body and any man's or woman's real body,' Whitman wrote in 'Starting from Paumanok', 'Item for item it will elude the hands of the corpse-cleaners, and pass to fitting spheres.' No doubt with his mind partly on 9/11, but with striking resonance for London in July 2005, Cunningham brings suicide bombing, via Walt Whitman who haunts all three of the stories, into the visionary heart of America.

In the wake of the London bombings, we were once again fed the endless mantra that we should neither excuse nor seek to understand – as if these were somehow the same thing. ('Those who find ways of justifying terrorism,' Peter Mandelson said after the Madrid bombings, 'who can talk of understanding the motives of terrorist actions, need to think hard and think differently.') To read Whitman in this context, and Cunningham's Whitman, is edifying. At the end of this second tale, which is called 'The Children's Crusade', Cat walks off, after a second attack, into an unknown future with a third child from the family, 'irreparably damaged', deformed and abandoned as a baby. Without sentimentality – she knows he is a potential killer – she decides to adopt him: 'She and the boy were hurtling towards the day when [. . .] the boy she had rescued would decide that he finally loved her enough to murder her.' 'O you shunned persons,' Whitman writes in 'Native Moments', 'I at least do not shun you [. . .] I will be your poet,/I will be more to you than to any of the rest.' Whitman's famous expansiveness stretches to slaves, vagrants, criminals, prostitutes, people with venereal disease, dwarfs and thieves. This is not, however, charity. It is not just observant kindness, or vigorous compassion at a distance. It is a form of becoming: 'I am the hounded slave. I wince at the bite of the dog.' Whitman was not a patriot, insists the NYU academic whom Cat goes to consult in order to understand the mindset of the 'family', since that implies 'a certain fixed notion of right versus wrong': 'I make the poem of evil also, I commemorate that part also, I am myself just as much evil as good, and my nation is' ('Starting from Paumanok'). Rather, he was an ecstatic. Refusing to respect or police the appropriate boundaries, the poet embraces – hurls himself into – everything he sees.

Such moments of becoming recur in Cunningham's writing. Often they take the form of a slippage when the mind suddenly loosens, and gives itself over, surprised. In *Flesh and Blood* of 1995, something rises up in Will that 'he would never understand'. As he briefly leaves himself to become his lover, he feels, 'in the ongoing rush and clatter of being Harry', not just his hopes and fears but 'something else': 'The sum of his days.' At the opening of *The Hours* (1999), Virginia Woolf lies drowned at the bottom of the river while the scene unfolding on the bank slowly enters the wood and stone of the bridge above her from where it passes into her body: 'Her face, pressed sideways to the piling, absorbs it all.' In the first story in *Specimen Days*, 'In the Machine', set at the height of New York's industrial revolution, the young boy Lucas stands watching as smoke pours out of a sewing factory, and one of the young female workers throws herself from the window (shades again of 9/11): 'With every breath, Lucas took the dead inside him.' Sex or death are normally the trigger, but sometimes the reaching-out is even more uncanny, not quite held to the proper species. Waiting in the hallway of his dead brother's fiancée, Lucas thinks he sees a goat's skull on a discarded oil can: 'He went into the skull. He became that, a bone grinning in the dark.'

It would be possible to read *Specimen Days* as a novel orchestrated by moments such as these, with Whitman as the unconscious maestro of Cunningham's earlier books. With its three movements, this novel repeats the structure of *The Hours,* whose abiding presence across the generations was Woolf. Once again, Cunningham turns Harold Bloom's famous 'anxiety of influence' – his theory that all writers are haunted by their literary ancestors – into the stuff of fiction. Woolf dictated the text of the characters' lives in *The Hours*, just as Whitman does for those in *Specimen*

Days. But now Cunningham has upped the stakes. We do not just move from Sussex to Los Angeles to New York, from 1923 to 1949 to today. We stay more or less in the same place, but we travel much further back and forwards in time, from the industrial revolution, to post-9/11, to a moment pitched 150 years into the future when New York is peopled by interstellar visitors and by clones. The form of haunting has become at once more elliptical and more intense – we know it is the same characters in each story, but their connections – more widely stretched and less exactly charted – are wilder. And Whitman, in some of the novel's least felicitous moments, walks straight into at least two of the tales. Above all, he is not just read, as Laura Brown read Woolf in *The Hours*, making but not quite making Woolf's tragic story her own. Or named, as Clarissa is named for *Mrs Dalloway*, making her New York party for the Aids-stricken Richard a reprise. In fact, in *Specimen Days*, Whitman is not read at all. He is spoken, his words endlessly cited by the central character of each of the three tales. They cannot help it. Whitman takes over their voice. 'He hadn't meant to speak as the book,' we are told of Lucas, 'he never did.' 'I'm sick', states Simon in the last story, 'of spitting out lines of verse I don't even understand [. . .] I hate it.' In this way, Cunningham brings a central question of his past novels to a hallucinatory pitch. What does it mean, exactly, to enter into the mind, or body, of somebody else? (Or when, as the reverse of the coin, we say to someone, in apparently flattering recognition, that they have taken the words right out of our mouth?) Is this generosity or terrifying invasion? After all, as critics have often pointed out, there is also something imperious and coercive about Whitman's insistence on making everyone's experience his own: 'I have embraced you', he writes in lines not cited here from *Leaves of Grass*, 'and henceforth possess you to myself,/And when you rise in the morning you will find what I tell you is so.' Cunningham, it seems, wants us to be persuaded, but also astonished, or perhaps even alarmed, by his own aesthetic principles – that you can walk without let or hindrance into the mind and body of someone else.

It is easy to appropriate Whitman. In the past few years, as Whitman scholar Ed Folsom has related, he has made some unlikely public appear-ances: a gift from Clinton to Monica Lewinsky (which led some commen-tators to read him as an oral sex manual); the harbinger, after 9/11, of America's spirit of civic and national resolve; and for neo-conservatives in May 2003, the spirit of the 'motivating hopefulness of America' when Bush was confidently declaring the end of the Iraq war. None of these readings of course are exactly wrong, but behind the idea that Whitman can be all things to all people lies a more productive tension. For Whitman, American democracy was in harmony with the openness of the nation's citizens towards each other. 'Boundless sympathy' – 'this terrible irrepressible yearning', as he puts it his own *Specimen Days*, the memoir from which Cunningham takes his title, is democracy's affective charge. 'Endless streams of living, pulsating love and friendship' are the foundation of the 'universal comradeship' that is 'so fitfully emblematic of America'. As with its citizens, so with the nation. Whitman's belief in the Union, or the 'TOTALITY' – his capitalised term in *Specimen Days* – is unqualified, drawing much of its force from the traumas of his experience as a nurse to the wounded and dying in the Secession War. (Neo-conservatives would do well to read his unrelenting and graphic account of that conflict: 'the real war will never get into the books'.) Crucially, this is not a conquering vision: 'I'd rather anything should happen to us', he wrote to his disciple Horace Taubel, 'than that we should add one inch of territory to our domain by conquest.' Nonetheless there are moments in Whitman's writing that tip over into something more troubling – we will build 'an enlarg'd, general, superior humanity', he writes in *Specimen Days*. In 'Salut au Monde!', his most translated poem, he moves effusively across the globe, winging his way towards 'you all, in America's name'. At what point does a nation's exuberance start to obstruct its vision? 'Sharing', as we have seen only too clearly in relation to Iraq, can be a form of domination, being lavish with one's own values can be a cover for power. 'As nature, inexorable, onward, resistless, impassive amid the threats and screams of disputants, so America', Whitman wrote to Emerson, 'Let all defer.'

By starting in Whitman's era, and ending in the long-distant future, Cunningham has made his novel a barometer, or touchstone, of this ambiguity in the poet's work. For the old woman in 'The Children's Crusade', he was 'the last great man who truly loved the world', living at a time when the machinery which devours and destroys its workers in the first story (called 'In the Machine') had just begun. Behind democracy, there is inequality – 'a problem and puzzle in our democracy' as Whitman put it in *Specimen Days*. In 'Like Beauty', the last tale, Nadians who reached Earth on 'Promise Ships' are being exploited as migrant labour. 'Simulos' or clones, built to be projected into infinite space, are now being exterminated as their unpredicted complexity (they are capable of dreaming) interferes with their function. This is the era after the meltdown which appears to have been the apocalyptic finale to the Children's Crusade. Christians have just won the election ('not good news for simulos'); one president has converted, another is in jail. It is a vision not unlike that of Robert Bly in his recent poem 'After Reading "The Sleepers"':

> The corporate criminal sleeps in his cell,
> Our dim-witted president, out of touch with reality, sleeps
> [. . .]
> The Iraqi whose house was destroyed sleeps
>   in a room elsewhere with fifty others.

In Cunningham's America, it is appropriate to live in a permanent state of fear: 'Why exactly', Marc, a simulo, asks Simon in 'Like Beauty' just before he is obliterated by government drones, 'do you think we *shouldn't* be nervous all the time?' The first suicide attack in 'The Children's Crusade' takes the lid off the naivety of the everyday, by simply reminding New York's citizens that 'we all humped along unharmed because no one had decided to kill us that day'. Not that you could possibly know, Cat muses, 'as we hurried about our business, whether we were escaping the conflagration or rushing into it'. When the old woman finally offers her analysis, it is at once deranged and trenchant: 'Look around. Do you see happiness? Do you see joy?' Americans have never lived so long in such health throughout history, yet a tenth of US citizens are in jail, food has to be sealed so it won't be poisoned, ten-year-olds are on heroin or murdering eight-year-olds or both: 'We are bombing other countries simply because they make us nervous [. . .] Would you say this is working out? Does this seem to you like a story that wants to continue?' In *Specimen Days* America is living in a state of violent perplexity. The message is clear. There is no danger from outside (the visitors from another planet are refugees). America is in greatest danger from itself. The novel is a lament. Whitman is the hero, but his hopes, partly under the impetus of the very force he so welcomed for the nation, have run away with themselves, gone to extremes. The poet stalks a world beyond his worst imagining.

There is another way of reading *Specimen Days*: as Whitman meets Freud. A psychoanalytic narrative weaves its way through all of Cunningham's novels, which not just formally, but also psychologically, are often arranged in threes. 'We needed all three points of the triangle', Bobby muses of his domestic arrangements with Jonathan and Clare in *A Home at the End of the World* of 1990, which more or less mutate all possible sexual combinations between them (the tripartite pattern of *The Hours* and of *Specimen Days* begins here with their alternating voices). At moments, Cunningham seems bent on a progressive rewriting of the classical Oedipal narrative – all combinations are fine: 'Whitman liked boys, didn't he?' Cat muses as she pages through *Leaves of Grass*. You are allowed to be sexually whatever or whoever you are. In the last analysis, and however tautological, intimacy is the only thing we can share. At other moments, Cunningham seems bent on giving the basic psychoanalytic story a stranger and darker twist. In most of his novels, a child dies too soon: Bobby's brother in *A Home at the End of the World*, in shards of piercing glass, during a party thrown by his parents to celebrate the spring return of the sun; Zoe, the preferred daughter, and Ben, the grandson, in *Flesh and Blood*; Richard who dies before his mother in *The Hours* which ends with her awkward, but determined and articulate, grief. *Specimen Days* opens when Lucas's brother Simon has just been devoured by the factory machine (perhaps with a gesture to James's *The Ambassadors*, Cunningham never names the commodity for which these workers toil). Cat's son had died at three of a misdiagnosed complaint, years before the story begins.

This makes Cunningham a type of Freudian ghost writer. Only occasionally are there the signs of a crude psychoanalytic aetiology: was Richard's mother's suicidal moment when he was a child somehow the cause of both his homosexuality and his death? (Along with Whitman and Dostoyevsky, Cat reads Winnicott and Klein.) But for the most part, these deaths – less meaningful, more significant – serve to make life urgent and translucent. They colour and shape their world. For French psychoanalyst Serge Leclaire, killing off the inner child is a key part of psychic life (as he also points out in *A Child Is Being Killed*, Oedipus's father, Laios, had tried to have him killed before the main action begins). Killing off children can, then, be a way of simply asking everyone to sit up internally and take note of themselves – of what they are doing to their own surviving, or perhaps not surviving, world. For Cunningham, these deaths are the future, the legacy of the coming days. None of the dead disappears. Everyone comes round more than once (the formal repetition, or rhyming structure, of his novels is most simply his way of saying this). There is always a ghost in the machine: 'The dead returned in machinery', Lucas slowly understands, 'When we stand at a machine, we make ourselves known to the dead.' Cunningham's novels are a form of *Trauerspiel* (the German term whose translation should be, not 'tragedy', but 'mourning play'). Mourning becomes a form of accountability. The premature dead challenge the living to take their legacy – the bruteness of factory exploitation, the dissociated violence of young boys in the city, the hubris of technology – into the next generation, and, if need be, beyond. Again there is a political message: today's driven carelessness is destroying our tomorrow. Whitman's faith in immortality has been turned into a form of political reckoning. The one thing Cat believes in is that her son wasn't gone: 'That, and the workings of justice in a dangerous world.'

Do clones have souls? Or, to put it another way, do clones know that they are clones? In Kazuo Ishiguro's *Never Let Me Go* the flat, semi-detached, quality of the narrative voice is the novel's means of asking the question (since Ishiguro's narrators are nearly always like this, it feels as if a novel about clones is the perfect, logical, outcome of all the rest). Only at the end of the book do you realise that any difficulties you may have had as reader with Kathy, the teller of the tale – any withholding of empathy, slight uncomfortable mistrust, or even boredom – have turned you into an active participant in the struggle waged silently behind the scenes throughout the book, as the world first denies and then comes to recognise that it has created beings with their own inner lives who are painfully aware of what lies in store. Ishiguro's clones have been built to slowly discard their limbs to surgery, and then die – or in official-speak 'complete'. (There are shades here of the organ traffic in migrant labour of Stephen Frears's *Dirty Pretty Things*.) Cunningham's clones are designed to be propelled into infinite space, something it would be unethical to force on time-conscious humans. In both cases, the world's intent is both scientifically justified, and foul.

In the course of 'Like Beauty', the clone gets to meet his maker: 'We were hubristic', Simon's inventor tells him. 'We underestimated the complexity of the genome.' The first experimental simulos, he explains, were either suicidal, or ecstatic and murderous, rather like the child Cat saves in the previous tale. The first stab at artificial creation simply reproduces the extremes of human life. Whitman was thrown in to give Simon the rudiments of moral sense; he has also been programmed to start shutting down at the prospect of inflicting harm. He dreams, and has memory (again, only at the end of *Never Let Me Go* do you realise that Kathy's ability to recall her story, like the early slave narratives, is in itself proof of her soul). When it turns out to be impossible to know if clones have souls – 'Somebody in Texas invented and patented a soul-measuring apparatus' but it was disallowed by the courts – they are declared illegal, and must either hand themselves over to wither in prison cells, or be destroyed. Simon entwines his fate with a Nadian woman, Catareen, who, we discover, was also a rebel in her other world, one of a group of women condemned to death for withholding part of their harvest from the kings. 'The attitude of great poets', Whitman wrote in the preface to *Leaves of Grass* 'is to cheer up slaves and horrify despots.' In the burnt-out landscape of 'Like Beauty', Nadians and simulos are both threatened with death simply because they interfere with the 'accuracy' of the world. Cunningham's clone narrative is as fast-paced as Ishiguro's is deliberate and slow. His simulos know exactly who and what they are, and they are running away from their fate. This makes

Specimen Days the far more optimistic book. It is clearly meant to be a source of encouragement that science cannot control its own child.

Psychoanalyst Christopher Bollas once speculated on how different – and how much better – psychoanalysis might have been if Freud had remained true to one of his earliest moments: when he found himself up a mountainside listening to the random thoughts of a young hysterical girl. If psychoanalysis had not subjected the restlessness of the mind to the canon of interpretation. If it had stayed out of doors. 'Democracy', wrote Whitman in *Specimen Days*, 'most of all affiliates with the open air.' Cunningham's novel ends with Simon riding off across the grass into the mountains. If this is a cliché, it nonetheless makes a huge difference that the American myth of rugged individualism has been handed to the outcast and shorn of power. Cunningham, it seems, is finally placing his bets on one half of Whitman's vision which relies on the contemplative mode of nature and the inner life. Just before she dies, Simon had realised that Catareen had always harboured a 'privacy so deep it was almost inaudible, like the silence of a well'. It is one of many moments in the novel when the extraordinary quality of the writing lifts the bleakness off the page. 'I had not dreamed', wrote Anne Gilchrist in 1870 in 'An Englishwoman's Estimate of Walt Whitman', 'that words could cease to be words, and become electric streams like these.' This is Cunningham's most ambitious novel to date and, for me, his finest. *Leaves of Grass* is the text spoken by the characters, but he has named his novel after *Specimen Days* which, closing round the ecstasy of Whitman's poem, brings it back to ground: it was, as Whitman explains, written from the impromptu jottings of his 'gloomy experiences' of the war as he sat beside the corpses of the dead, and at Temple Creek where he recovered from the paralytic stroke that had prostrated him for several years. Folding one Whitman inside the other, Cunningham leaves open the question whether the ills of culture, his nation's capacity for desolation, can ever be redeemed by the poet's – or novelist's – vision.

*First published in the *London Review of Books*, 22 September 2005.

PART III

Men and Women in Dark Times

11

Continuing the Dialogue –
On Edward Said*

There is a strand in your thinking which is not, I think, well known. And that is the strand that makes a plea for peoples, however much history has turned them into enemies, to enter into each other's predicaments, to make what might seem at moments, if not an impossible, then certainly one of the hardest journeys of the mind. To be a literary critic – and you were as much a literary critic as political writer and activist – is, amongst other things, to enter into the mind of the other, to invite and even force your reader to see themselves in situations far from their own. So much so, indeed, that at moments it can feel like stretching the limits of the imagination beyond endurance to enter this other person's world. But this demand, for forms of understanding strained beyond the pitch of what is bearable, is – I believe – one of the things that you saw as crucial if there was to be any hope of changing the cruel deadlock of the Middle East.

'Why should the Palestinians make the effort to understand Zionism?' The question came from a young woman in the audience at one of the many memorials held for you, this one in London in November 2003 under the auspices of the *London Review of Books*. It was not your priority, responded Ilan Pappe. And Sara Roy simply and powerfully told the anecdote of how she had witnessed Palestinians flooding with joy onto the curfewed streets of the West Bank where she was living when the possibility of a Palestinian state was first acknowledged by Israel, while the soldiers stood by in silence and just watched. There will be understanding enough, I heard her saying, when there is justice.

They were of course both right: your preoccupation was with justice. In one of your most irate pieces about the Occupation – 'Sober Truths about Israel and Zionism', written for *Al-Ahram* and *Al-Hayat* in 1995, when the bitter reality of post-Oslo was becoming clearer by the day – you mince no words about the cruel asymmetry of the conflict and the peculiar injustice of the settlements: what they tell us about Israel as a nation, about Zionism as its founding idea. Once a piece of land is confiscated, 'it belongs to the "Land of Israel" ' and is 'officially restricted for the exclusive use of Jews'. Many nations including the United States, you allow, were founded on the confiscation of land, but no other country then designates this land for the sole use of one portion of its citizens. You are citing Israel Shahak, Holocaust survivor, founder of the Israeli League of Human Rights, 'one of the small handful of Israeli Jews who tells the truth as it is'.[1]

Earlier in the essay, you tell the anecdote of a Palestinian student at Birzeit University who, at the end of a lecture in which you were advocating a more 'scientific and precise' approach on the part of the Arab world to understanding the United States, raised his hand to say 'that it was a more disturbing fact that no such programme existed in Palestine for the study of Israel' (anticipating in reverse the young woman in London).[2] Shahak is your answer. Understanding Israel means understanding the discriminatory foundations of the nation state:

> Unless we recognise the real issue – which is the racist character of the Zionist Movement and the State of Israel and the roots of that racism in the Jewish religious law [Halakha] – we will not be able to understand our realities. And unless we can understand them, we will not be able to change them.[3]

And yet, to stop there is not, I believe – and I believe you believed – to go far enough. Your view was more complex. In fact you decried the UN resolution equating Zionism with racism as politically counterproductive: 'I was never happy with that resolution.'[4] Significantly, given your call for scientific precision in understanding, it was not *precise* enough: 'Racism is too vague a term. Zionism is Zionism.'[5] 'The question of Zionism', you said in conversation with Salman Rushdie in 1986, 'is the touchstone of contemporary political judgement.'[6] What did you mean?

Speaking at the memorial in November, I had cited what remains for me one of your most poignant pleas: 'We cannot coexist as two communities of detached and uncommunicatingly separate suffering' – the 'we' performing the link for which it appeals.[7] I cannot remember whether it was this quotation or my later attempt in the discussion to talk about Zionism that provoked the question of the young woman from the floor. But for me it is the peculiar quality and gift of your thought that you could make your denunciation of the injustice of Israel towards the Palestinians, while also speaking – without ever softening the force of that critique – if not quite *for*, nonetheless *of* the reality of the other side: what drove Israel, how it had come to be, what makes it what it is now.

Perhaps your best-known discussion of Zionism is the chapter in *The Question of Palestine* of 1979, which was your first extended analysis of this history, famously entitled 'Zionism from the Standpoint of its Victims'; the title unambiguously announces that your priority is to raise the plight of the Palestinians, at the time more or less passed over in silence, both in the world and for themselves. Yet that objective, on which you never wavered, is already here accompanied by interconnections and diffusions of another kind. It is here that the link between your literary and political thinking is key (the two roles passionately, intimately joined). 'The task of criticism, or, to put it another way, the role of the critical consciousness in such cases', you write in the course of the chapter, 'is to be able to make distinctions, to produce differences where at present there are none.'[8] To critique Zionism is not, you insisted then, anti-Semitic (an assertion that critics of Israel, especially post 9/11, are forced to make even more loudly today). It is, in one of your favourite formulae of Gramsci's, to make an inventory of the historical forces that have made anyone – a people – who they are. Zionism needs to be read. What is required is a critical consciousness that dissects the obdurate language of the present by delving into the buried fragments of the past, to produce differences 'where at present there are none'. It is not therefore a simple political identity that you are offering the Palestinians on whose behalf you speak, nor a simple version of the seemingly intractable reality to which they find themselves opposed. It is rather something more disorienting that confers and troubles identity at one and the same time (if the past is never a given nor, once uncovered, is it ever merely a gift).

For me, Gramsci's injunction always contained a psychoanalytic demand: 'the consciousness of what one really is [. . .] is "knowing thyself"', although such knowledge is hardly easy, as every psychoanalyst will attest.[9] I see this as your challenge to Zionism and Palestinian nationalism alike. By the time we get to 'Bases for Coexistence' in 1997, to this classic Freudian dictum, you have added the sentence I have already cited, which conveys another no less painful and difficult dimension: 'We cannot coexist as two communities of detached and uncommunicatingly separate suffering.' And then, against the grain of your own and your people's sympathies, 'There is suffering and injustice enough for everyone.'[10] (After this piece was published in *Al-Hayat* and *Al-Ahram*, you received your first hatemail in the Arab press.) Not just self-reflective, nor just internally unsettling, but perhaps precisely because it is both of these, such knowledge has the power to shift the boundaries between peoples. There can be no progress in the Middle East, I hear you saying, without a shared recognition of pain.

As I reread you today on Zionism, this strained, complicated demand seems in fact a type of constant. This may be of course because I personally so want and need it to be (as Brecht notoriously acknowledged when asked whether his interpretation of *Coriolanus* was true to Shakespeare's meaning – he was both 'reading *in* and reading *into*' the play). But it seems to me that – contrary to your detractors – you were always trying to do two things at once that you knew to be well-nigh impossible. As if you were requiring of all critics of Israel – whether Arab or Jewish, and without dissolving the real historical and political differences between the two peoples – to hold together in their hearts and minds the polar opposite emotions of empathy and rage (however reluctant the first, however legitimate the second for your people might be). Today the understanding of Zionism seems an even more crucial task than when you made the question the touchstone of political judgement nearly twenty years ago. I want to place the role of the critic as you defined it in 1979 together with the plea for a shared recognition of suffering of 1997, on either side of your answer to the Palestinian student at Birzeit. What then do we see?

Zionism has been a success. You said this many times. Shocking, if seen from the viewpoint of its catastrophe for the Palestinians, but true – even for those, such as David Grossman and Yaakov Perry, former head of Shin Bet, (to mention just two) who see Israel today as in a perhaps irreversible decline, in thrall to a militarism destructive of the Palestinians and of itself. Historically Israel has fulfilled its aims. You repeat the point in an interview with Hasan M. Jafri for the Karachi *Herald* as late as 1992: 'Zionism for the Jew was a wonderful thing. They say it was their liberation movement. They say it was that which gave them sovereignty. They finally had a homeland.'[11] But, as you laid it out so clearly in 'Zionism from the Standpoint of its Victims', Zionism suffers from an internal 'bifurcation' or even, to push the psychoanalytic vocabulary one stage further, splitting: 'between care for the Jews and an almost total disregard for the non-Jews or native Arab population'.[12] Not only unjust, this splitting is self-defeating for the Israeli nation. In the eyes of the Arabs, Zionism becomes nothing other than an unfolding design 'whose deeper roots in Jewish history and the terrible Jewish experience was necessarily obscured by what was taking place before their eyes'.[13] Freud of course spoke of the 'blindness of the seeing eye' (or in the words of Jean-Luc Godard, 'shut your eyes, and *see*'). Zionism, we could say, has done itself a major disservice. So fervently has it nourished the discrimination between Jew and non-Jew, the rationale of its dispossession of the Palestinians, that, while it may have seized the earth, it has also snatched the grounds for understanding from beneath its own feet.

The negative repercussions for Palestinian political consciousness have been no less, their own cause weakened by the failure to understand the *inner* force of what it is up against (as Lenin once famously remarked, you should always construct your enemy at their strongest point). The 'internal cohesion and solidity' of Zionism has completely 'eluded the understanding of Arabs'.[14] As has the 'intertwined terror and exultation' out of which it was born; or in other words 'what Zionism meant for the Jews'.[15] It is the affective dimension, as it exerts its pressure historically, that has been blocked from view. You are analysing a trauma – 'an immensely traumatic Zionist effectiveness'.[16] Terror, exultation, trauma – Zionism has the ruthlessness of the symptom (it is the symptom of its own success). Given this emphasis, your unexpected and rarely commented remarks on the 'benevolent', 'humanistic' impulse of Zionism towards its own people are even more striking (contrary to the opinion of some of your critics, there is no one- or even two-dimensionality here). On the colonial nature of the venture, and the cruel orientalism of how the Arab people were treated and portrayed, you never ceased to insist. But what if the key to understanding the catastrophe for the Palestinians, of 1948 and after, were to be found in the love that the Jewish people – for historically explicable reasons – lavish on themselves?

We have entered the most stubborn and self-defeating psychic terrain, where a people can be loving and lethal, and their most exultant acts towards – and triumph over – an indigenous people expose them to the dangers they most fear. For it is not just of course that Israel's conduct has made it impossible for the Arabs to understand her, nor that Israel has been blind towards the Arabs (in fact never true); but that she sees things in the wrong place: 'Everything that did stay to challenge Israel was viewed not as something *there*, but as something *outside* Israel and Zionism bent on its destruction – from the outside.'[17] Israel is vulnerable because it cannot see the people who – whether in refugee camps on the borders (the putative Palestinian state), or inside the country (the Palestinian Israelis), or scattered all over the world (the Palestinian diaspora) – are in fact, psychically as well as politically, *in its midst*.

Contrast this again, as you do repeatedly, with Israel as a nation for *all* Jewish people – this passionately inclusive, and violently excluding, embrace. Here time and place are infinite: 'If every Jew in Israel represents "the whole Jewish people" – which is a population made up not only of the Jews in Israel, but also of generations of Jews who existed in the past (of whom the present Israelis are the remnant) and those who exist in the future, as well as those who live elsewhere' – 'Israel would not be simply the state of its citizens (which included Arabs of course) but the state of "the whole Jewish people," having a kind of sovereignty over land and peoples that no other state possessed or possesses.'[18] This is in fact far worse than merely 'two communities of uncommunicatingly separate suffering', which might suggest indifference or ignorance of a more straightforward kind. This is a historically embedded failure of vision – multiply determined, and with multiple, self-perpetuating effects. In these early readings, you delve into the past, telling all the parties that the main critical, and political, task is to understand how and why.

I realise now that my writing on Zionism is an extended footnote to your questions, an attempt to enter into the 'terror and exultation' out of which Zionism was born, to grasp what you so aptly term the 'immense traumatic effectiveness' of the Israeli nation state. You mean of course traumatic for the Palestinians. I would add also for the Jews (exultation does not dispel fear). But I have also wanted to revive the early Jewish voices – Martin Buber, Hans Kohn, Hannah Arendt and Ahad Ha'am, some of whom called themselves Zionists – who sounded the critique, uttered the warnings that have become all the more prescient today. Somewhere, I believe, Zionism had the self-knowledge for which Gramsci and, through him, you, make a plea, although I know in the case of Buber and Arendt you feel they were not finally equal to their critique. Calling up these voices, torn from the pages of a dismissed or forgotten portion of the past, I like to think that – as well as rebuilding the legacy of my own Jewish history – I am also doing what you would have appreciated, fulfilling a very personal demand from you to me.

We did not of course always agree. I am sure that in the last analysis you believed that entering the Zionist imagination might be risking one identification too far (are you writing an apology? you once asked). I was preparing the Christian Gauss Seminars to be delivered in September 2003 under the title 'The Question of Zion', a deliberate echo of, and my tribute to, *The Question of Palestine*. When I was writing them last summer, you wanted to read them but I needed to finish them first. 'I might be able to help you', you said.

You were planning to attend the second lecture, but knowing by the time of my visit that you might not be well enough, I hurriedly emailed them to my neighbour here before I left so they could be sent to your personal assistant, Sandra Fahy, who was always so helpful, should the need arise. Then, as happens, something was wrong with the attachments so they could not be sent when – indeed unable to attend – you asked for them. I arrived at your apartment clutching a rapidly photocopied version when I visited you on the Sunday four days before you died. Amongst many other things, we talked about the dreadful, deteriorating situation in Israel–Palestine – a decline that had so cruelly tracked your illness over the past decade. 'I will read them this afternoon', you said at the end. You were admitted to the hospital the next day. It was of course the conversation I most wanted to have. I had held back in the blithe belief that our dialogue would be endless, that having defeated your illness so many many times before, you would go on doing so for ever. I will not have the gift of your response to the lectures. Which is doubtless why I have used this occasion to lift out of your work the inspiration and form of their imagining.

*First published in *Critical Inquiry*, vol. 31, no. 2, Winter 2005, special tribute to Edward Said: 'Edward Said: Continuing the Conversation'. All the contributors were asked to write as if continuing the dialogue. Only a few, possibly going beyond the intentions of the editors, took this literally, as I did here, I am sure out of my own need. I have chosen to keep the original format.

Notes

1 Edward Said, 'Sober Truths about Israel and Zionism', 1995, in *Peace and its Discontents* (New York, Random House; London, Vintage 1995).

2 Ibid., p. 126.

3 Ibid., p. 127.

4 'What people in the US know about Islam is a stupid cliché', 1992, interview with Hasan M Jafri, *Power, Politics and Culture – Interviews with Edward W. Said*, edited with an introduction by Gauri Viswanathan (London, Bloomsbury 2004), pp. 378–89.

5 Said, *The Question of Palestine* (New York, Times Books 1979; Vintage edition 1992), p. 112.

6 'A conversation with Salman Rushdie', 1986, in Said, *The Politics of Dispossession – the Struggle for Palestinian Self-determination 1969-1994* (London, Random House 1994).

7 'Bases for Coexistence', 1997, in Said, *The End of the Peace Process – Oslo and After* (London, Granta 2000), p. 208.

8 'Zionism from the Standpoint of its Victims', *The Question of Palestine*, p. 73.

9 Ibid.

10 'Bases for Coexistence', p. 207.

11 'What people in the US know about Islam', p. 378.

12 'Zionism from the Standpoint of its Victims', p. 83.

13 Ibid.

14 Ibid., p. 88.

15 Ibid., p. 60, p. 66.

16 Ibid., p. 83.

17 Ibid., p. 89.

18 Ibid., p. 84, p. 104.

Born Jewish – On Marcel Liebman*

Towards the end of his memoir, *Born Jewish*, Marcel Liebman writes:
'Questioning corpses is an obsession I shall leave to those for whom it is
a vocation. I have no faith in these false dialogues [. . .] I myself will settle for
questioning history.'[1] Liebman came relatively late to *Born Jewish*, his
intensely personal account of his life as a child in Nazi-occupied Belgium,
which was first published in French in 1977. By the time he wrote it, he had
written acclaimed studies of Lenin and of the Russian Revolution; he would
go on to write about Belgian socialism, a work incomplete when he died.[2]
In his obituary of 1986, Ralph Miliband describes him as: 'an independent
socialist and Marxist, critical both of social democracy and Stalinism in its
many forms'.[3] Fiercely independent, he never joined any party. But this did
not prevent him from leading a life of political engagement which included
negotiating with Anwar Sadat in 1967 for the release of hundreds of
Egyptian Jews imprisoned after Israel's victory in the Six Day War. And
he was an outspoken critic of Zionism. Liebman's life is haunted by the
ghosts of his childhood – notably that of his brother Henri who, at the
painful crux of his memoir, was deported to Auschwitz at the age of fifteen.
Miraculously, as *Born Jewish* repeatedly attests, Marcel and the rest of his
family survived, but the war 'corrupted' the peace and left its survivors
'stricken'.[4] The tribute he pays to his brother, here and in a sense in the
whole corpus of his writing, takes the form of a steady refusal to sacralise his
death, in favour of the task of the historian – to question and to go on
questioning history, so that its traumas never fossilise. History of this kind
does not involve forgetting, but nor does it involve 'cultivating' the
'memory of the harm'.[5] Zionism would make the fatal error of claiming
to speak for the dead Jews of Europe, affirming Jewish identity as an
absolute. For Liebman, the answer to racism is to denounce it, not to flee
behind a defensive, self-isolating barrier of being – and being only – a Jew
(hence the dedication here to 'Jews *and non-Jews*' in their common struggle

against Nazism). Amongst other things, Liebman's testimony stands as an extraordinary rejoinder to those who insist that Israel is the only, and definitive, answer to the genocide of the Jews.

One way of reading *Born Jewish* is as the story of the birth of political understanding. At the outbreak of the war, Liebman took from his father a fervent Belgian patriotism rendered complex, but somehow unmitigated, by the fact that they were a family of immigrant Jews (his father, born in Warsaw, had arrived in Antwerp as a young child, his mother, born in Oswiecim–Auschwitz, had lived in Zürich before marrying in Brussels at the age of thirty). As children they had been taught to hate Communism 'which we confused with a rejection of patriotism and a casting out of God'.[6] They abhorred Germany and fascism while being 'totally ignorant of its nature'.[7] As the net closed around them, no teacher at the school spoke of the war. When the announcement was made expelling all Jews, there was not a word of comment or protest. 'We were treated', writes Liebman, like 'frail, blind, befuddled children'.[8] Knowledge was 'dead knowledge', a 'blackening out' of political thought.[9] While the horrors of the war unfolded, there was a 'surfeit of talk about the great principles of morality' as 'mass graves were being dug and filled'.[10] Liebman's indictment of 'bourgeois humanism' could not be more severe and it extends beyond the war. When Marcel returns to the school in 1945 with his younger brother, only one teacher notices, let alone remarks on, the fact that Henri, the eldest of the three, is no longer there. At the time, writes Liebman, this 'cold passivity', or 'fatalistic resignation', which he now sees as 'aberrant', struck him as perfectly natural: 'the misfortunes of the war, including the most monstrous forms of racism, never did provoke my indignation at the time'.[11]

And yet there are moments in his account when we can see the kernel of political consciousness. In one striking anecdote from the time of Belgium's capitulation to the Nazis, the roof of the house in which the family were temporarily sheltering collapses. Although several occupants are smothered or emerge to be torn to shreds by shrapnel, all the Liebmans survive. For his father, this is proof – one he will appeal to for years to come – that their family has been chosen by God. For Marcel, such a God – who spares and destroys so indiscriminately, who saves his brother and then sends him to Auschwitz – can only be capricious. And what kind of God, as his father-in-law will later insist in quarrels with his father, would save one family while sacrificing another to such misfortune? There is something cruel in the idea of being chosen. Liebman's sense of social justice, and his critique of a too-assured Jewish identity, are inseparable. The germs of his socialism and his mistrust of Zionism are simultaneously born.

Near the end of his memoir, Liebman imagines his reader asking him

'What does it mean to you now to be a Jew?'[12] For Liebman, there can be no simple or straightforward – above all no absolute – reply. But if Zionism is one reason for his caution, this narrative also offers another in the dreadful story it relates of the part played by the Jewish Councils, or *Judenräte* as they are more famously known, in the deportation of the Belgian Jews (their role was essential in making those deportations voluntary). *Born Jewish* could be fruitfully read alongside Hannah Arendt's *Eichmann in Jerusalem* of 1963, whose account of the Jewish Councils' complicity with the Nazi genocide has frequently been dismissed or disbelieved; it provoked the most virulent hostility against Arendt at the time.[13] Liebman's memoir fleshes out her report with the lived substance of this complicity as it rebounds on the painful, if only partially grasped, experience of a young child. Although only 5 per cent of Belgian Jews had full citizenship, the committees were made up predominantly of Belgian nationals. Status, class and, it turns out, ethnicity are all decisive. These privileged, bourgeois Jews of Belgium despised the recent Jewish immigrants from Poland who they saw as another caste: 'Well, well!' one of them says to a poor Jewish woman with feeble command of the French language, 'If you ended up in Eastern Europe what would be wrong with that? [. . .] You'd just be going back where you came from!'[14] In this, as Liebman points out, the Belgian Jews were in harmony with their German counterparts, many of whom believed that Nazism would only be directed towards the lower orders and that they themselves would be spared. Among the most chilling parts of the memoir are the diary extracts of one 'S.V.', a prominent member of the Council, who welcomes the instruction from Berlin to 'clamp down on the Jewish problem' ('It seems to be just a matter of mixed marriages. In one sense that would be quite fair'), while lovingly detailing his trips to the opera and consumption of lobsters, as the Jews all around him were being deported or just struggling to survive: 'Let us try to be just as happy in the new peace.'[15] On the eve of liberation, as he senses the coming recriminations, he dismisses the Jews he betrayed as 'high and mighty [. . .] "foreigners" ' who 'have to be put in their place', 'jealous ones who've had a bad time of it': 'Does it need to be spelled out that [they] are the Jewish survivors of the genocide?'[16] Liebman is unsparing. None of these leaders are ever brought to trial or publicly condemned. When S.V. dies years after the war, he is still 'one of the most prominent leaders of the Jewish community in Brussels'. To the justification offered by one of their number – that old wounds should not be opened, that the Jews had suffered enough – Liebman simply asks: 'Which Jews?'[17]

'In this book', Liebman states after reporting the facts as known of the death of his brother, 'I have not asked any questions about myself.'[18] Liebman is not given to introspection – although the force of his narrative is no less for that. But the question of his brother's death is, decisively, Marcel's own question. And in the answers he provides to it, we can see taking shape the personal and political vision, the terms of analysis, or outlines of what – as historian and socialist – he was subsequently to become. 'Preserved from any social consciousness', 'taught fervour but not lucidity', Henri died first out of ignorance, a befuddled blindness which passed from the national conscious-ness into the schoolroom, depriving the children of this tragic generation of the tools for understanding, let alone resisting, what was happening to them.[19] But he also died as the victim of murderers and their numerous accomplices among the European bourgeoisie which had armed fascism, and then 'gazed without turning a hair' at the 'tortures inflicted on the Spartakus League in Germany, on the miners of the Asturias, on Guernica and on the German proletariat'.[20]

This moment in the memoir is something like a clarion call or political manifesto. It also has the profoundest relevance for us today. The issue, then as now, is not just the most glaring atrocities at which we can all be comfortably outraged, but the wider, often hidden, net of implication and complicity. For Liebman, understanding Nazism leads inexorably to the most basic truths of social inequality and exploitation under capitalism. To that extent, his brother is the victim of a murderous Nazism riding the back of a class system, whose deadly ramifications are simply exposed at their most treacherous by the behaviour of the notable Belgian Jews. While there is no limit to the ingenuity of his father in saving most of his family from the worst of fates (the book is also a tribute to his 'cleverness and clear head'),[21] nonetheless for the most part, you died in occupied Belgium if you had neither the money, privilege nor connections with which to protect yourself. S.V. is no aberration; he is representative. Death becomes a matter, not just of the race or caste, but also of the class into which you are born: 'If being Jewish was the worst of misfortunes, the plight of poor Jews brought them even closer to total strangulation and utter doom.'[22] Class distinctions were at once 'respected and reinforced' by the war: 'The fact that I was a child masked these distinctions from me, but it did not protect me from them.'[23]

It is one of the strengths of Liebman's writing that he can be so unerring in this analysis while at the same time acknowledging the point where understanding trails off into uncomprehending terror, where the most painful part of mourning trumps all rational thought. 'Against all reason', Liebman will strive to 'give solidity' to this brother for the rest of his life; he will struggle for an 'elusive and ungraspable' knowledge that that – the more he reaches out for it – 'disintegrates' in his mind.[24]

Towards the end of the war, Liebman is sent to the town of Schatlin where, on condition of disguising their Jewish identity to the other inmates and masquerading as Spaniards, he and a number of Jewish boys are taken in by the Jeunesse Ouvrière Chrétienne. This was one of many organisations sponsored by the Catholic Church that played a huge part in securing the lives of young Jews. Behind this move was the hand of the Comité de Défense des Juifs, a Belgian Resistance organisation, which is one of the heroes of the book. Resistance is key to Liebman's story. It is the other face of Liebman's preoccupation, not only with the fate of his brother, but also with that of his cousin Maurice. Henri dies because he takes a detour to visit a young woman on his way to the town hall to collect ration cards for some Jewish friends too afraid to venture out, instead of arriving at the crack of dawn when the Gestapo were less vigilant. But Maurice, in a gesture as brave as it is futile, gives himself up to the Nazis in order to join his recently captured parents and brother. Why? For Liebman, such 'poignant passivity' can be traced to the 'messianic dream and exaltation of martyrdom' that the Jews have historically taken from their experience of exile and persecution.[25] He does not judge Maurice; in many ways he admires him. But he is in no doubt that this 'profoundly noble and absurdly powerless' response to historical suffering played its part in the horrific destiny of the European Jews by giving murderers 'free rein, so that they became the unassailable perpetrators of an inevitable destiny'.[26]

To resist is therefore to answer that destiny with the fullest claim for another, potential, history. It is also, crucially, to recognise the affiliation between Jew and non-Jew. The strongest resistance came from the far-left Zionists, the Social Democrats of the Bund and the Communists – the last of the three assuming the most active role. Militants like the Communist Gert Jospa, one of the founders of the Committee for the Defence of the Jews, were men who in their social relationships and political choices were 'not particularist Jews cultivating and exalting their differences', but immigrants connected to Belgian working-class organisations, whose rootedness in local and political life, together with their distance from power and privilege, gave them a different sense of what cunning, well-orchestrated, action could do.[27] In the southern industrial city of Charleroi, the Jews joined with the militants of the far left to form the Jewish Solidarity of Charleroi, and compiled false lists of Jewish citizens for the Gestapo, depriving the Nazis of 'hundreds of their prey'.[28] At Malines, on the day of the Warsaw Uprising, a group of militants linked up with prisoners in the Dossin barracks to sabotage the twentieth transport of Jewish deportees to Auschwitz.

There is another subtext here. These moments read like a model for a revolutionary party at once able to seize its moment and organised (if the adventure at Malines had been more organised, they could have saved more). They offer, that is, a type of ideal political action based on a form of discipline that has not yet hardened into bureaucratic power. In his writings on Lenin and on the Russian Revolution, Liebman steers the most delicate course between the need for a revolutionary party that can take political control, and its inherent dangers (thus although he insists in *Leninism Under Lenin* that Lenin was 'thoroughly democratic in character' and the 'eternal enemy of nationalistic and bureaucratic tyranny', he nonetheless acknowledges that his belief in the vanguard contained the seeds of what was to come).[29] In *Born Jewish*, it is as if we are given flashes of political agency, at once organised and urgent, which – in the intensity, risk and necessary brevity of their moment – are never in danger of corrupting themselves. Against such moments, the privileged Jews of the *Judenrat* are like a party cut off from its base. Nor did any of the more traditional Jewish institutions, who proudly displayed 'the Jewish label in terms of either nationalism or religion', come anywhere near such achievements.[30] They were all trapped by a social isolation they chose for themselves and which 'the Nazi occupier criminally aggravated and exploited': 'The heroism of the Jewish partisans, acting in concert with non-Jewish partisans, is sufficient proof that it is not lack of courage which explains the passivity of the majority, but their marginal situation in Jewish society.'[31] Liebman's criticism is harsh. But because he offers this precise analysis of the social conditions – the isolation, and hence vulnerability – of the core of the *Judenrat*, he cannot be charged, as Arendt was charged, with lack of understanding.

There is an important history here. For Liebman, the disaster that befell Belgium in the 1940s must be traced back to the German occupation of the First World War, when socialism was sacrificed to patriotism, and previous links between socialists across national barriers crumbled in the face of a new militant nationalism. We only have one part of Liebman's second volume of his history of Belgian socialism, but it is a remarkable document that is in some ways the companion volume to, or hidden history of, *Born Jewish*. Before the war it had been possible to see capitalism as inherently belligerent – 'capitalism', as Jaurès once put it, 'brings war like a cloud brings the storm'.[32] But once the war was cast as the struggle of an innocent victim against an external aggressor, then all such analysis, together with any critique of the state as answerable for the horrors of war, was lost. In Belgium, the left flocked to the service of the 'sacred union' of the nation; of all the socialist parties of Europe, the Belgian Workers' Party – this is the fundamental reproach of Liebman's study of Belgian socialism – was the most complete in its capitulation to this ideal. 'All differences of opinion, all disagreements, all divisions' were suppressed and the nation became a family united 'in its hatreds' by a 'mixture of triumphalism, euphoria and the will to revenge'.[33] Belgium entered a time warp and 'the entire political life of Belgium was numbed by the fact of the occupation'.[34]

The worst ill, therefore, is self-idealising patriotism, or 'sacred egoism', a form of butchery since it justifies sending thousands of young men to their deaths.[35] Above all, this form of patriotism – which saved some of its harshest penalties for any fraternisation between enemy troops, while repressing the most graphic reports from the front – is a form of ignorance and isolation. Patriotism destroys thought. As they will be again in 1940, the Belgian citizens of 1914 are cut off from the forms of knowledge and understanding they need most. This is therefore far more than just a plea for the workers of the world to unite. It is at once a denunciation of pure nationalism, and a lament for what might have been other more generous forms of affiliation. In this account of Belgium as 'martyr country and innocent nation',[36] it is impossible not to discern a powerful analogy with Liebman's critique of Zionism – remember that the 'exaltation of martyrdom', as enshrined in Jewish history, was seen by him as playing a central part in his cousin's embrace of death. But it is also more than an analogy. In his writing on 1914, some of Liebman's harshest criticism is reserved for nations such as France and England who, even as they claimed democracy as the objective of the war (which would of course be the war to end all wars), were busily carving out new worlds, creating new nations, 'whose contours remained shrouded in the densest mystery'.[37] Israel will be one of the legacies – the Balfour Declaration allowing for the creation of a Jewish homeland in Palestine is issued in 1917 – the product of colonial omnipotence, and national grandiosity, steadily eroding the possibility of European socialism, and shadowed by the horrors of war.

For Liebman, Zionism is therefore colonialism, but it did not have to be. After an episode of fervent Jewish spirituality at Schatlin (he even briefly contemplates becoming a rabbi after the war), he is gradually alienated from the rigidity of traditional Judaism which he feels enclosing him after 1945, only to return to Jewishness 'through the roundabout route of politics'.[38] By then he is living in England and, hugely influenced by Ralph Miliband, is a Marxist. Alienated by the excesses of Stalinism, he eventually takes up the cause of Arab–Jewish rapprochement in the context of the Algerian war. A joint struggle against French colonialism might, he believed, offer the new Israeli nation a model for cooperation between the two peoples and unharness the new state from the West. What appals him right to the end is the unconditional support for Israel which he feels paralyses so many Jews; nor can he accept the demand Israel makes of all Jews to go to Palestine, an exodus which, in his mind, 'uproots', and 'maims' and 'leaves the field to the enemy'.[39] Jewishness must find itself in the connections between peoples, whether in the Diaspora or in Palestine.

To the end of his life, Liebman maintains these positions, while arguing for justice for the Palestinians. He does so undaunted even when, in public, he is shockingly compared with the worst of Belgian collaborators, accused in the room where his father died of precipitating his death (in fact, without sharing them, his father had defended his son's political views), and even of betraying his brother: 'How can you attack Israel and defend the Palestinians? Don't you think of your dead, your own people, your brother?'[40] 'On the contrary,' he concludes, 'I think of them very much.'[41] For Liebman, the best tribute he can pay his brother is to acknowledge that, in killing him, racism hacked out a void that cannot be filled. Not by statehood, nationality, or race – false icons of our times. The greatest danger is to 'beam' 'the blinding lights of yesterday's conflagration' onto the children of today: 'Leave my children – and yours', he pleads, 'to follow their own inclinations.'[42] Finally Liebman's appeal is for a Jewishness, not sealed behind walls of conviction, but open to the infinite possibilities of tomorrow.

*First published as the introduction to Marcel Liebman, *Born Jewish – A Childhood in Occupied Europe* (London, Verso 2005).

Notes

1 Marcel Liebman, *Born Jewish – A Childhood in Occupied Europe*, trans. Liz Heron (London, Verso 2005), p. 172. All quotes are taken from this edition.
2 Marcel Liebman, *The Russian Revolution – The Origins, Phases and Meanings of the Bolshevik Victory*, 1967, trans. Arnold Pomerans with a preface by Isaac Deutscher (London, Jonathan Cape 1970); *Leninism Under Lenin*, 1973, trans. Brian Pearce (London, Jonathan Cape 1975); *Les Socialistes belges 1914-18 – Le P.O.B. face à la guerre* (Fondation Joseph Jacquemotte, Vie Ouvrière 1986).
3 Ralph Miliband, 'Marcel Liebman', *Socialist Register*, 1987.
4 Liebman, *Born Jewish*, p. 158, p. 170.
5 Ibid., p. 174.
6 Ibid., p. 27.
7 Ibid.
8 Ibid., p. 28.
9 Ibid.
10 Ibid., pp. 28-9.
11 Ibid., p. 33.
12 Ibid., p. 172.
13 Hannah Arendt, *Eichmann in Jerusalem – A Report on the Banality of Evil* (New York, Viking 1963). For reactions to the book, see Elisabeth Young-Bruehl, *Hannah Arendt – For Love of the World* (New Haven, Yale University Press

1982, 2004), ch. 8, 'Cura Posterior – Eichmann in Jerusalem', and Anson Rabinbach, 'Eichmann in New York: The New York Intellectuals and the Hannah Arendt Controversy', Princeton University Library Chronicle, vol. 43, nos 1–2, Autumn 2001–Winter 2002.

14 Liebman, Born Jewish, p. 45.
15 Ibid., p. 50, p. 50, p. 53.
16 Ibid., p. 52.
17 Ibid., p. 99.
18 Ibid., p. 103.
19 Ibid., p. 105.
20 Ibid., pp. 104-5.
21 Ibid., p. 79.
22 Ibid., p. 63.
23 Ibid., p. 164.
24 Ibid., p. 105.
25 Ibid., p. 76.
26 Ibid.
27 Ibid., p. 177.
28 Ibid., p. 65.
29 Marcel Liebman, Leninism Under Lenin, p. 425, p. 433.
30 Liebman, Born Jewish, p. 177.
31 Ibid., p. 178.
32 Jaurès cited in Liebman, Les Socialistes belges, p. 4.
33 Ibid., p. 14, p. 52.
34 Ibid., p. 67.
35 Ibid., p. 57.
36 Ibid., p. 61.
37 Ibid., p. 36; on 1914 and its effects on international socialism, see also Liebman, '1914: The Great Schism', Socialist Register, 1954.
38 Liebman, Born Jewish, p. 169.
39 Ibid., p. 180.
40 Ibid., p. 172.
41 Ibid.
42 Ibid., p. 180, p. 179.

13

All Men Are Mortal –
On Simone de Beauvoir*

What makes a dictator? In the midst of Simone de Beauvoir's *All Men Are Mortal*[1] of 1946, the immortal Fosca stares at his political future after his son, Antonio, has died fighting for his native city. Impotent in the face of his son's death, confronted with a set of political options each likely to spell humiliation or ruin, he concludes, 'My son had died for nothing', and adds: 'There must be something I can do. But where? What? I now understand those tyrants who burn entire cities to the ground or decapitate a whole population to prove their power to themselves.'

Power at its most vicious is a riposte to powerlessness. Killing, not just a cause of death, can also be its frantic, grief-stricken, reply. Fosca is a conqueror with the blood of centuries on his hands. Because he is immortal, he can fight with impunity (he repeatedly dies and revives). Impervious to any ethics, he unleashes conquest as orgy; gutting cities, massacring peoples; looting, pillaging and raping sometimes without even declaring war: 'I was without law and could dispose as I please of poor human lives that were doomed to die.' Without law and without limit, Fosca dreams of – and comes close to – ruling the whole world: 'Nothing less than the whole world was worthy of eternity.' 'No one', he insists more than once in the novel, 'can govern without doing evil.' Later he says to the Emperor Charles V, 'Your only mistake was to reign.' If it is the fantasy of all rulers to transcend their own moment, such a fantasy, this novel suggests, is the true licence to evil (evil resides not on the outside, but at the very heart of power). Immortality sanctions the worst historical crimes. In *All Men Are Mortal*, Simone de Beauvoir immerses herself and her readers in horror. Barely out of the Second World War, she chooses to write a cautionary tale, not about the awfulness of death, but about the greater peril of being unable to die.

Fosca's female counterpart is the actress Regina to whom he tells his

gruesome tale. Regina – *Régine* in French, which makes her name a
virtual anagram for 'to reign' (*'reigner'*) – is imperious, manipulative and
cruel. Regina is the narcissistic woman *par excellence* who makes the fatal
mistake of assuming she can achieve transcendence through her own
person. 'The paradox of her attitude', de Beauvoir writes in her chapter
on the narcissist in *The Second Sex*, is that 'she begs to be valued by a
world which she deems worthless because only she counts in her own
eyes.' Existing solely in her own mirror, Regina cannot bear to sleep for
envy of those who remain awake; she so dreads her own mortality that
she will destroy anything, including her life's work, in order to feel alive.
Her nonchalance is a type of hate. The very idea that others could exist
without her is an affront. One taste of the other's autonomy fills her with
rage: 'Is there no way of preventing them from existing without me?
How can they dare?' For both Fosca and Regina other people are
dispensable. Worse, de Beauvoir seems to be suggesting, if people are
dispensable, you will have to dispose of them. To be careless about others
is in fact an intense, potentially brutal, form of connection. Narcissists are
tyrants. It is more than a moral platitude to suggest that being self-
centred is a crime. In different ways, both Regina and Fosca seek to
make the world their stage. *All Men Are Mortal* is a stunning indictment
of the delusion of omnipotence, but it also shows just how magnetic
monstrous people can be. Beautifully, Regina and Fosca deserve each
other.

Regina is drawn to Fosca when, after his long journey through the
night of the centuries, he has just emerged from an asylum. He appears a
broken man over whom she might exert total power, whom she might,
she muses, even cure. When she discovers he is immortal, she first toys
with the idea of her own immortality: 'With the tips of her fingers, she
stroked the narcissi in a vase on the table. "And supposing I, too, believed
I were immortal? The scent of the narcissi is immortal."' Realising the
dream is futile, she opts for the next best option. She will achieve eternal
life, go on living for ever, in his undying mind. 'He says that he never
forgets anything', she says to her lover, Roger. 'Then you'll be there,
pinned in his memory like a butterfly in his collection.' To live for ever in
the memory of an immortal man might just be the worst death sentence.
Later in the story, when one of the women who fall in love with Fosca
discovers his dreadful secret, he insists she will remain in his heart longer
than in the heart of any mortal man, 'No', she replies, 'If you were mortal,
I'd go on living in you until the end of the world, because for me your
death would be the end of the world. Instead I am going to die in a world
that will never end.' It is one of the strongest messages of de Beauvoir's

novel that you cannot be a lover – love or be loved – unless you know you are going to die.

All Men Are Mortal can be read as an existential counter-fable. In the present dispensation where women are always 'other' to the man, who takes the world as his measure, being a narcissist is one way for the woman to survive (being in love and a mystic are the two others offered in *The Second Sex*). For want of a collective, economic solution to the inequality of the sexes, the woman turns in on herself, becomes her own vain cause. Regina is a symptom of a failure at the heart of the polity. She pretends to exist for want of anything better. When she announces to her company of friends and admirers that she is giving up as an actress, it is her bid for authenticity: 'If in a single moment she were able to destroy both the past and the future, she would know for certain that that moment existed.'

Fosca on the other hand achieves a grandiosity which at moments looks like a parody, at others a fulfilment, of the dream of existential man endlessly reinventing himself. 'There is no justification for present existence', de Beauvoir writes in *The Second Sex*, 'other than its expansion towards an indefinitely open future.' Her statement could be a summary of Fosca's awful tale (he may not be free, but he created his own dilemma by freely choosing to take the potion of eternal life). That the man, unlike the woman, has the capacity to actualise such self-fulfilment in the world is, in this modern Faustian fable, both privilege and curse. Fosca is bored even in his dreams. In *Three Guineas*, her 1936 study of fascism, Virginia Woolf described modern man, whose crass apotheosis was Mussolini on parade, as a 'cripple in a cave'. As if on cue, de Beauvoir allows us to watch Fosca slowly shrink from the summit of his power – he goes from ruler to eighteenth-century scientist, to nineteenth-century revolutionary, to a man barely let out onto the street. In this historical stretch, there is an echo of another work by Woolf – her 1928 novel *Orlando* in which the central character famously sweeps through the centuries changing sex along the way. But de Beauvoir's novel is without whimsy. There is no androgynous fantasy here. The two sexes do not freely mesh and slide into each other. They are caricatures, trapped, confronting each other across the void of what a man and a woman can worst be for each other.

What redeems the novel – redeems the pair of them – is their insight. Since most of the novel consists of Fosca telling his tale to Regina, you could say that de Beauvoir has written the original novel of the psycho-analytic talking cure (the famous 'interminability' of analysis takes on a whole new meaning here). It is as if she could not quite bear to deprive her characters of her own voice. Regina knows deep down that narcissism is nothing if not self-defeating. Watching a group of women in a room, she observes 'with a sharp pang in her heart' that each one preferred herself to all the others: 'How can anyone have the audacity to believe', she wonders, ' "I alone have the right to prefer myself"?' And Fosca, faced with the death of Antonio, revolutionary comrade of 1848 – both name and scene are a reprise of the death of his first son – suddenly understands his fervour, his willingness to die for his cause: 'They were neither insane nor arrogant; I understood this now. They were men who wanted to fulfil their human destinies by choosing their own lives and their own deaths; they were free men.'

By sending her traveller through time, de Beauvoir can also use the occasion of her novel to chart the inexorable rise of capitalism, the ruthlessness of empire, the encroaching sovereignty of the machine. When Fosca arrives in the Americas in the sixteenth century he sees for himself what conquest has done to the Indians, 'a race of men so gentle that, being unused to weapons, they frequently wounded themselves on the Spaniards' swords'. He recognises in their vanished world the benign empire which, in his own better moments, he had himself wished to build: 'That, then, was the empire we destroyed, the empire I dreamed of establishing on earth and that I did not know how to build!' In 1946, de Beauvoir's political agenda was to foster a post-war socialism which would be the antidote to the worst of what man had done to woman and to man. It is a tribute to her vision that only once, with the hindsight of modern times, do you feel her prescience falter: 'He spoke of the future, of progress, of humanity [. . .] He conjured up images of a time when swift trains speeding along steel rails would break down the barriers raised by the selfish protectionism of nations. The world would then become an immense market-place which would provide the whole of mankind with its needs.' But the fact that in this new millennium the railroads have not undone the selfishness of nations, or that the global market has been so cruelly discriminating, trampling over more than half of the world's populations, only increases the relevance of her tale. In the very last line of the novel, when Fosca's story is over, Regina lets out 'the first scream'. More ambiguous in French, 'pousser le premier cri' is also the sound of the newborn. *All Men Are Mortal* suggests that acknowledging the role of vanity and omnipotence in the souls and the fate of nations might be the first stage in creating a new world.

*First published as preface to Simone de Beauvoir, *All Men Are Mortal* (London, Virago 2004).

Note

1 Simone de Beauvoir, *All Men Are Mortal* (London, Virago 2004), from which all quotations are taken.

14

Holocaust Premises: Political Implications of the Traumatic Frame – With Judith Butler*

Our title is 'Holocaust Premises'. I have spent some time musing on this title which is, I assume, like our subject, deliberately ambiguous and fraught. That the Holocaust could have become a premise – that is, a proposition which produces its own logical conclusions – is striking, or rather strikingly different from seeing it, for example, as unrepresentable atrocity, as un-assimilable or barely assimilable trauma in the way Judith Butler, citing Primo Levi, has so powerfully described: 'many survivors of war or other complex and traumatic experiences tend unconsciously to filter their memory [. . .] they dwell on moments of respite [. . .] the most painful episodes [. . .] lose their contours.' Suffering 'crystallises' as a story. Telling the story is crucial testimony to the event, but it can also lead – sometimes as a condition of survival she suggests – to the memory being lost.

The idea of 'Holocaust Premises' has a far more controlling ring to it than this, suggesting that the Holocaust casts its shadow over the future, not just as recurrent pain but as something that can dictate the logical or thinkable possibilities of what the future will be allowed to be. I think that this is what we mean by instrumentalisation of the Holocaust, the sense which I share with Judith Butler and others that the Holocaust is used by one strand of dominant discourse inside Israel, although not only inside Israel, as justification for the violence of state power. 'We must remember', Ariel Sharon said at the Jerusalem ceremony to commemorate the liberation of Auschwitz in January 2005, 'that this is the only place in the world in which we, the Jews, have the right and the power to defend ourselves with our own strength.' And, forgetting the liberators, forgetting we might say the occasion: 'We know that we can trust no one but ourselves.' Countering this way of thought, Israeli writer Shulamith Hareven writes in her 1986 article 'Identity: Victim': 'During the Second World War, not only did the world not remain silent, it lost more than sixty million men fighting Hitler. True they were not fighting because of us, and certainly they would not have offered aid for our sakes only. They were fighting against fascism in general [. . .] But the loss of more than sixty million men in a war does not exactly mean that the world sat by with its arms crossed. [. . .] Sixty million families suffered losses, and those of us who survived, including the small numbers of us then inhabiting Israel, survived because of them.'

As I thought about it, it seemed to me that the idea of 'premises' as diktat over the future might also do as a working definition of trauma. When I was studying Sylvia Plath a long time ago, and trying to understand the appearance of the Holocaust motif in her writing as something other than the opportunism of which she was accused, I read an article by German psychoanalyst Ilse Grubrich-Simitis on working with second-generation Holocaust survivors that has stayed with me ever since. She described how the language of these patients was characterised by a dull, thudding referentiality, with no mobility or play, as if they were saying – in a way only made clear after the most difficult and patient analytic listening – 'this *happened*', '*happened*' '*happened*' over and over again, to compensate for the silence, the psychic refusal to acknowledge the reality of the Holocaust, in the generation before. And in one of his most evocative articles, 'The Trauma of Incest' of 1989, psychoanalyst Christopher Bollas describes how trauma shuts down the mind of the patient. The problem is not believing what they say, but the fact that that is *all* they have to say, so that there is nowhere else left for them to go inside their minds.

We are talking then, not about the inability of the trauma to pass into speech, and its loss at the moment of articulation, but an endless appeal – as in court of appeal – to its reality, which then clouds the horizon to infinity, and brutally cuts down everything else that might be possibly thought or seen. 'The question is', Judith Butler asks, 'whether [the trauma] is mobilised for political purposes with the consequence of displacing the pain and losing the referent itself.' Perhaps, paradoxically, loss of the referent and its endless invocation can be one and the same thing. Perhaps invocation of the Holocaust in the public domain is a way of settling accounts with its psychic intractability, of trying to lay it to rest. To the further question she poses – does trauma act upon those who invoke it for political purposes, or is it pursued and orchestrated for its traumatising effect? – we would then indeed have to reply: both.

In November 2004, something in the nature of a national crisis was provoked inside Israel by the photograph of an Arab man being forced to play the violin at a roadblock. 'If we allow Jewish soldiers to put an Arab violinist at a roadblock and laugh at him,' wrote Yoram Kaniuk, author of a book about a Jewish violinist forced to play for a concentration camp commander, 'we have succeeded at arriving at the lowest moral point possible. Our entire existence in this Arab region was justified, and is still justified, by our suffering; by Jewish violinists in the camps.' The soldiers, he stated, should be put on trial not for abusing Arabs but for disgracing the Holocaust. As commentators were swift to point out, this episode caused far greater concern than the news in the same week of an army officer repeatedly shooting Iman al-Hams, a thirteen-year-old Palestinian girl, and then saying that he would have shot her even if she had been three. Or the report, also about the same time, of Chief of Staff Dan Halutz, who in 2002 had dropped a one-ton bomb on the house of Hamas leader Saleh Shehadeh, killing Shehadeh and fifteen civilians including eleven children, and who, asked how he felt about such moments, replied that he felt 'a light bump in the plane'. In discussion after the play *My Name Is Rachel Corrie*, performed in London in 2005, Corrie's father stated that his greatest anxiety was aroused when she told him not to worry because the army always aimed their bullets inside the houses low – he said that he knew, from his experience in Vietnam, that the bullet would ricochet to cause maximum damage and that the army was therefore out of control (Corrie was killed by an Israeli bulldozer as she was protesting the demolition of a Palestinian home).

The point is not to demonise the army. Occupying armies the world over inevitably corrupt and brutalise themselves. It is far more a question of seeing how – alongside this reality and often in strenuous denial of it – the Holocaust takes up its place inside the collective imagination as something which purifies – or must purify – the Jewish soul. The Holocaust, not just as Kaniuk states, the reason *for* the state; nor, as Sharon implies, the *reason of state*, but as redemption of the people. This is sacralisation of the Holocaust (which can lead, as Judith Butler points out, to a no less violent desacralisation, or downplaying of the Holocaust aimed to discredit what is felt to be its misuse). Commentators have also pointed out that to see the Holocaust in this way comes dangerously close to giving the worst catastrophe of Jewish history a type of divine sanction – implicit indeed in the term 'Holocaust', which endows the disaster with the status of an act of God. 'To name the Nazi genocide "the Holocaust"', writes Gillian Rose in 'Athens and Jerusalem: A Tale of Three Cities', 'is already to over-unify it and to sacralise it, to see it as providential purpose – for in the Hebrew scriptures, a *holocaust* refers to a burnt sacrifice which is offered in its entirety to God without any part of it being consumed.'

During the summer of 2005, as part of the preparation for a new course I was about to start teaching at Queen Mary, 'Palestine–Israel, Israel–Palestine: Politics and the Literary Imagination', I read about the Holocaust as it impacts on the new nation of Israel. For me, David Grossman provides the most brilliant exploration in fiction in his 1989 novel, *See Under: Love*, of how the Holocaust appeared as an object of shame for the founders of the nation after the war. Grossman's child hero, the boy Momik, has to dig deep into the cellar of his home to find the traces of the Nazi beast that his family will not talk about. He is the only one to rejoice at the arrival of his long-lost grandfather who had been presumed to have disappeared in the camps. But it was only reading around that novel, notably Idith Zertal's 1998 book, *From Catastrophe to Power – Holocaust Survivors and the Emergence of Israel*, and now more recently, her *Israel's Holocaust and the Politics of Nationhood* of 2005, that I realised that Grossman's story was in fact the tip of the iceberg. He was not only writing to bring the beast of Nazism out of the closet. He was also writing a literary exposé of the shameful treatment of survivors, a shame which Zertal persuasively argues was in many ways constitutive of the state.

The entry of the Holocaust into the national imagination was conditional, as discussed in Chapter 2. The annual day of commemoration, Yom Hashoah v'haGevurah, or Day of Destruction and Heroism, was declared in 1952 on the twenty-seventh day of the Hebrew month of Nisan, as close to the date of the Warsaw Uprising as religious laws relating to Passover would permit. 'The decade-and-a-half that preceded the capture and trial of Eichmann', writes Zertal, 'were marked, in Israel and in other countries such as France and the United States, by public silence and some sort of statist denial regarding the Holocaust' (a 220-page textbook of Jewish history published in 1948 contained one page on the Holocaust, but ten on the Napoleonic wars). Eichmann's trial ushered in a new phase because his arrest and the staging of the trial on Israeli soil could be seen in itself as a sign of the triumph of the nation over history. It was also intended to incorporate Israelis of non-European origin into a singular, narrative collective. 'I can testify for myself,' writes Zertal, 'a high school student at the time, and for my friends: the trial was an event of major influence for us. Although my father served as a soldier in Europe in World War II, worked with Jewish survivors after the war, and published a book about his war experiences; and although his entire family perished in the Holocaust, *he never talked about it at home. The trial was thus my first encounter with the horrors,* brought to us by the trial witnesses' testimonies that were broadcast live' (my emphasis).

There is of course no question of passing judgement on Israel for the slow, pained, process with which the horror came to be spoken, nor indeed for the need of the new nation to qualify the horror with the image of the resisting Jew. But part of the problem in Israel's relationship to the Holocaust is that the very gesture that welcomed the survivors to the shores of the fledgling nation, and used them – and 'used' is not too strong a word – as rationale for the state, also entailed a kind of hatred – and 'hatred' is also not too strong a word – of who and what they were. In his recent book on the tension between Diaspora and Israeli Jewry, *The Divided Self – Israel and the Jewish Psyche Today*, David Goldberg cites early youth leader Moshe Tabenkin on hearing of the fate of the European Jews: 'rejection of the Diaspora [. . .] now turned into personal hatred of the Diaspora. I hate it as a man hates a deformity he is ashamed of.' 'It will be hell if all the [DP] camps come [to Palestine]', Ben-Gurion was told by rescue operatives in Europe in early 1946, 'All this filth, just as it is, you [the Jewish Agency/Ben-Gurion] plan to move to Palestine?' Ben-Gurion never queried the use of the word 'filth', even as, as Zertal demonstrates, he expresses in his diary the deepest anguish at the plight of the survivors. But he silences the anguish. And in the meantime, although he himself on one occasion describes the camp survivors as 'holy', the rhetoric takes hold in public that *only the bad* could have survived. 'Had they not been what they were', he stated to the central Committee of his party four years after the war, 'bad, harsh, egotistic – they would never have survived'. (All quotes from Ben-Gurion taken from Idith Zertal, *Israel's Holocaust*).

Somewhere inside the nation's self-image, the survivors – the shame of the Holocaust that they represent – are interred. When, therefore, Ariel Sharon states: 'We must remember that this is the only place in the world in which we, the Jews, have the right and the power to defend ourselves with our own strength', it seems to me that such statements, their unswerving conviction, bear the traces of that repudiated past. Not to speak of the guilt of the new nation towards the Jews of Europe. 'If they [the survivors] arrive and perceive us as the prosecuted and they the prosecutors,' Ben-Gurion stated in a lecture to the farmers' youth movement after the war, 'we will have to bear it [. . .] even if it arouses anger and revulsion within us.' I read Ben-Gurion as offering a kind of self-diagnosis which opens up the link between anger, or even revulsion, and guilt. 'Us as the prosecuted' – could the *Yishuv*, and the new nation, be prosecuted – placed on trial – for its failure to save the European Jews? For Hareven, guilt is unavoidably part of the picture. A generation without grandparents transposed their loneliness and insecurity into the strongest, often self-denying, resolve. 'When the families who had remained abroad perished in the Holocaust, all these feelings became overlaid with a sense of guilt,' she writes in her 1988 essay 'Israel: The First Forty Years', 'the Guilt of Noah, it can be called, for Noah, too, according to the Scriptures, did not take his parents on the Ark.'

In his 2005 book, *The Suppression of Guilt*, Israeli former journalist and media analyst Daniel Dor shows how the Israeli media, of left and right, have equally produced a narrative of the conflict between Israel and the Palestinians in which Israel is never guilty and must not be blamed. Reading that statement of Ben-Gurion's, I am wondering if behind the suppression of guilt towards the Palestinians, as Dor describes it, there might not be another layer, which is the guilt of the Jewish people towards themselves. Redemption, therefore, might carry another meaning – not just redemption from catastrophe, but redemption from blame.

In our exchanges Judith Butler asked me if I would address the relationship between messianism and how catastrophe repeats itself over time. Following Gershom Scholem, I believe messianism, in its apocalyptic strain, to have been one of the defining instances of Jewish self-definition, and that it played its part in the language of the emergent Israeli state. Not exclusively – Zionism was crucially the movement of self-determination of the Jewish people driven by the urgencies of their history – but as its often-present shadow and only partially acknowledged accompaniment. Again reading for the new course at Queen Mary, I have understood from writers such as Sidra Ezrahi, Saul Friedlander and Adam Seligman the extent to which the Holocaust became part of a messianic vision. 'During the early statist period [up until the late 1950s] a commemoration day and commemoration sites were established,' write Friedlander and Seligman in their 1994 article 'The Israeli Memory of the Shoah', 'but it was only during the later phase that the Shoah became a central myth of the civil religion of Israel.' If the Eichmann trial and the 1967 war were a turning point, nonetheless the path had been laid long before, in the causal link established from the beginning between the destruction of European Jewry and the birth of Israel, combining both events in a new symbolic unity of catastrophe and redemption. The 1967 war opened a 'new phase' in which Arab hostility became equated with Nazism, and the Holocaust was mobilised for the first time to justify the policies of the state, but this move was 'inherent in the very symbolic logic which identified the Israeli state with the redemptive moment in history'. In his famous exhortation to Polish Jews on the eve of the Shoah, Ze'ev Jabotinsky proclaimed; 'What else I would like to say to you on this day of Tisha B'Av [the day of the destruction of the Temple] is whoever of you will escape from the catastrophe, he or she will live to see a great Jewish wedding – the rebirth and rise of a Jewish state.' 'The notion that we can use our enemies for our own salvation', Hannah Arendt wrote in a set of notes she prepared for a *Look* magazine interview in 1963, 'has always been the "original sin" of Zionism.'

The worst disaster becomes Israel's saving grace. In fact the link from the Shoah to state policy was laid down by Moshe Dayan at the time of Eichmann's trial: 'what is becoming clear at the Eichmann trial is the active passivity of the world in the face of the murder of the six million. There can be no doubt that only this country and only this people can protect the Jews against a second Holocaust. And hence every inch of Israeli soil is intended only for Jews' (cited in *Davar*, 1 July 1961, and reproduced by Zertal).

When Menachem Begin came to power, he suggested that the Shoah be commemorated on the day of the destruction of the Temple, instead of on the date which, binding the link between disaster and heroism, had been chosen to commemorate the Warsaw Uprising. His proposal was rejected by the Knesset. The redemptive link between the Holocaust and the resurgence of the Jewish people would remain, and still does. Pursuing this link, I discovered a document issued by the Cambridge University Centre for Modern Hebrew Studies in 1992 which consists of a translation of poems by Uri Zvi Greenberg, prophetic Zionist poet, to commemorate the centenary of his birth. Attached to two of the poems is a note from the translators explaining that although the poems were written in the early 1930s, they 'fittingly commemorate' the anniversary of both the Palestine Disturbances of 1936 and the Warsaw Uprising of 1943, which occurred on the same day. One of the poems, 'Beyond the Veil', contains these lines;

> And the brows of a people shamed shall grow horns of iron
> Wherewith they shall gore their foes.
> Their heels shall be brass and their foes a pile of olives
> For treading into a kingdom

The other poem, 'The Tower of Corpses', ends by speaking of 'the tower of corpses which my Jewish race will erect in the world'. The reprinting of these poems, and especially their attachment both to the Palestinian riots of the thirties and the Warsaw Uprising, both of which happened *after* the poems were written, seems a striking illustration of the way disaster turns into a hallowed identity which then knows no bounds. To defend itself, the nation will gore its foes and litter the world with corpses.

To end, however, on a more positive note, I offer two counter-instances from within the same narrative, one from outside Israel, the other from inside. First from inside. Before the disengagement from Gaza in the summer of 2005, one group of messianic settlers insisted that they would resist removal on the grounds that their allegiance was to the land, as divinely sanctioned, over the state. 'When the state behaves like a state of all its residents,' says one, 'and not as the Jewish state, the attitude towards it changes. I respect it as I do any other government, but it is no longer "the beginning of our redemption".' For one rabbi, however, Rabbi Fruman of Tekoa in Gush Etzion, he too would choose the land over the state, but for diametrically opposite reasons – in order to retain the links with the Palestinians amongst whom he has lived for so many years. There could, he speculates, be a new type of settlement as model for the future, no longer the dawn of redemption, but 'the dawn of peace'. Messianism is not singular. It can take unexpected paths and even undo itself.

The second is from Marcel Liebman, the Belgian socialist historian. I was privileged to write the introduction to his memoir of life in Nazi-occupied Belgium – *Born Jewish* – when it was translated for the first time into English in 2005 (Chapter 12 in this volume). His brother was deported to Auschwitz at the age of fifteen, while the rest of the family survived. He went on to become an outspoken critic of Zionism. Liebman could hardly forget the Holocaust. His adult life was wholly determined by the tragedy he witnessed as a young boy. But becoming a historian, he saw his role as a form of remembering that would not involve 'cultivating the harm'. Disaster must not be turned into an identity. In this he is very close to Shulamith Hareven who has written so eloquently on the danger for the Jews in Israel in defining themselves in perpetuity as victims. For Hareven, – to recall these lines cited in Chapter 2 – the lesson of the Holocaust should be: 'even if often in history, I have been the victim of others, I will never oppress those weaker than myself and never abuse my power to exile them'. The mistake is to 'define my uniqueness in terms of the past alone'. Unlike Hareven, Liebman did not go to Israel, was no Zionist, not even one with the humane and universalising qualifications which she brought to her place as an Israeli woman in the modern world. But reading him in this context, it seems that he may have been unable to identify with the new nation partly because he knew it would hold no place for grief.

For critiquing Israel and Zionism, Liebman was often accused of betraying the memory of his brother. But for him, the best tribute he could pay him was to refuse any redemption – national or otherwise – for his loss. Some disasters cannot be made good. In Liebman's story, memory of the Holocaust and its unassimilable trauma moves towards psychic pain and away from collective belonging. I share with Judith Butler a fear that, to date, these two have seemed to be incompatible. 'Has the discourse now taken on a life of its own,' she asks, 'one that grows at the expense of memory?' From the 1950s in Israel, personal memorials were slowly replaced by collective inheritance, public anniversaries supplanting the commemoration of the death of loved ones. In the redemptive, national, narrative, this one brother has no place. Idith Zertal ends her study of Israel's response to the Holocaust survivors with these words: 'Zionism's work of mourning (Freud's *Trauerarbeit*) for the Jewish catastrophe still remains to be done.'

*A revised version of a paper delivered, in dialogue with Judith Butler, at the opening session of 'Fear of the Other and the Israeli–Palestinian Conflict', a conference organised by the Faculty for Israeli-Palestinian Peace (FFIPP), London, 25 September 2005.

15

On Gillian Rose[*]

> There are achievements
> that carry failure on their back, blindness
> not as in Brueghel, but unfathomably
> far-seeing.
>
> Geoffrey Hill, 'In Memoriam: Gillian Rose'

Let me start with an anecdote. In the early 1990s, at a time when we were not especially – as we often were especially – in touch with each other, Gillian Rose, our cousin Braham Murray, artistic director of the Royal Exchange Theatre in Manchester, and myself all found our work drawn towards the Holocaust. I was trying to understand the place of the Holocaust in the poetry of Sylvia Plath, Braham was producing a version of *Macbeth* which he staged as performed by the inmates of a concentration camp, and Gillian was writing on Holocaust theology, notably in the works of Emil Fackenheim, whose vision of the modern state of Israel as legitimated by and redeeming the horrors of the Holocaust she refused.

I realise now that the three of us had been brought to this topic as a way of engaging a mostly unspoken part of our family history – on this, the lines that were running, strangely and unconsciously, between the three of us were clear. But there was something more. Plath was implicating herself in a history to which many critics felt she had no right. I was led to argue for the necessity – political and ethical – of the strained identification which, beyond her own lived experience, she was trying to make. Braham was blurring the ethical contours of history by forcing the inmates to perform, through Macbeth's burgeoning and finally uncontrollable violence, the reality of the evil, to which they as Jews were subject, on their own behalf. Gillian, at the beginning of a relationship to Judaism that would run through all her final writing, was, I think, making a not unrelated plea: that Auschwitz should not become sacred, its victims ideal innocents, its perpetrators unthinkable monsters, equally beyond the pale; nor should it be seen as absolute, unrepresentable, horror which can only therefore be countered by an equivalently absolute act of redemption by the Israeli nation state. Instead Auschwitz should found a new tale, or as she puts it in *Mourning Becomes the Law*, one of her last books, 'a new polity', 'a new prayer', one which demands 'a willingness to participate in power and its legitimate violence for the sake of the good. Not as sanctified, holy Israel, or any other *raison d'état*, but as the risk of recognition – the risk of coming to discover the self-relation of the other as the challenge of one's own self-relation.'[1]

In this complex, not easy formula, I read her as saying that Auschwitz obliges us to enter the reality of political and historical life, with no false innocence, bearing no redemptive offering for either state or human subjects; instead with a new recognition – a new tale, a new prayer – of the tormented, always difficult – 'difficulty' was one of her favourite words – the difficult relation that we have, of necessity, both to the reality of political power in which we must participate, to the others with whom we must negotiate, and to ourselves.

'If I knew who or what I were,' she writes in the opening lines of *Judaism and Modernity*, 'I would not write': 'I write out of those moments of anguish which are nameless, and I can write only where the tradition can offer me a discipline, a means to articulate and explore that anguish.'[2] Anguish and tradition, namelessness and discipline – these terms do not sit comfortably together. But for Gillian the challenge, intellectually and personally, was to hold these seeming opposites in some kind of relation, to let go of neither half of these antagonistic pairs. For her the only viable account of experience was one that 'persists in acknowledging the predicament': that we possess and lack our identity, are fiercely independent and utterly dependent, powerless and yet also endowed with, laying claim to, power. It was this account of experience – she called it *speculative* – that, she writes, 'has led me to Judaism'.[3] Gillian turned to Judaism, I hear her saying, as a way of articulating, at its profoundest, who and what she was, who and what we all – Jewish and non-Jewish – are. My question, then, is: what did Judaism mean for, and to, her? – partly because of the way my own thinking has gone in the last decade, partly as a way of continuing the silent conversation which began so many years ago between her, our cousin and me, a conversation in which I would also want to include our other sisters, Alison Rose whose fine writing has now brought her to a film script on Theresienstadt, and Diana Stone, whose understanding of Islam has always been accompanied by the profoundest consideration of Jewish history and thought, both of whom have also taught me much.

So what passage or pathways in and out of her own predicament did Gillian Rose's engagement with Judaism offer? Clearly, no simple identity, if identity at all. Judaism offered no point of arrival, no resolution, no redemptive consolation. 'Modern Judaism', she wrote, 'is most uncertain about itself.'[4] Judaism, as I read her, became the focal point through which her own anguish, and the anguish of modern political life, could be most productively approached and understood. For her, to be anguished was, I believe, the only psychic space worth living (perhaps her only option), certainly the only political place any of us can ever expect to occupy.

It seems to me that there is a line in her work of remarkable consistency, both logical, and political, also poetical, which relates the fate of Judaism to the fate of nations and of philosophy, with both of which she was so profoundly preoccupied. As she saw it, postmodernism was guilty of a refusal of reason which it identified as sublation or telos or phallocentrism (the list could be endless), together with a refusal of the empowerment of authority, a refusal which culminated as she saw it in a demonising version both of philosophy and of the modern city and state. Postmodern philosophy posits, as she saw it, a utopia beyond reason and coercion to which – cherishing ourselves as loving and ethical subjects – we can simply make our escape. For her this was the utmost evasion. There can be no such retreat outside the city walls of the modern *polis*. Even the wife of Phocion, in Poussin's famous 1648 painting – *The Ashes of Phocion Collected by his Widow* – gathering up the ashes of her husband outside Athens, is not, as the painting is often read, offering pure love against a corrupt authority which her gesture naively leaves behind. Rather she is reproaching the city for its lack of justice, making a demand on the very buildings that so forbiddingly rise up in the painting behind her act of grace. 'In these delegitimate acts of tending the dead,' she writes in her inaugural lecture at the University of Warwick, 'these acts of justice, against the current will of the city, women reinvent the political life of the community.'[5]

Increasingly, Judaism became the ground of this, her radical contestation of postmodern thought. Against Athens, a New Jerusalem was being erected as alternative touchstone, *alter ego*, of modern theory based on what she described as a 'dangerously distorted and idealised presentation of Judaism as the sublime other of modernity.'[6] Leaving aside for a moment the fact that Jerusalem today, in its violent contestation, can support no such idealisation, she was making another point. That such a vision traduces the history and theology of Judaism which demonstrates with startling vividness, and in a way from which we still have everything to learn, the relationship between power and ethics which modern theory wishes, disastrously as she saw it, to separate (there can be therefore no choice between ethical work and radical political critique).

Against the vision of Judaism as 'unchanging, without history', she offered us the early rabbis endlessly renegotiating 'knowledge and responsibility under their historically and politically changing conditions'.[7] Both Strauss and Levinas, as she saw it, misrepresented Judaism both as study and observance. The tradition handed down by halakhic Judaism 'obscures its tremendous plasticity' by seeming to subordinate it to the original revelation of Oral Law.[8] Contrary to any such subordination or fixity, Gillian saw the key to Talmudic argument as residing in its complex relation to a rationalism which it interrogated but never left behind, 'a rationalism which constantly explores its own limits without fixing them'.[9] It is because the Judaism of Strauss and Levinas is so static that it becomes trapped or 'staked' in opposition to modernity. Nothing moves. Nothing gives. This is to assign to Judaism a false, isolating and ahistorical innocence. Judaism and the Jewish community become 'sequestered': 'beyond rationalism, violence, the history of the world'.[10]

In what I believe to be one of her most important essays, 'Midrash and Political Authority', she offered us the Midrash endlessly devoted to the problem of constitutional law, making her appeal to the '*political* experience and wisdom of the Jews as embodied in their civic consciousness', to the Judaic body politic, massively neglected, she insists, in mainstream scholarship. Judaism cannot be construed as 'politics by other means', since it is rather '*politics per se*'.[11] Rabbi Akiba (or Akiva), the greatest rabbi of the Mishnaic period, whose method of preserving and interpreting the Oral Law made possible the later compilation of the Mishnah, was a 'consummate politician': the only rabbi of stature to oppose the Roman decree that prohibited study of the law and to give his support to Bar Kochba, the last attempt by the Jews to overthrow Roman domination.[12] What she seeks to avoid at all costs – 'correct' might be the more appropriate phrase – is a view of Midrash as a form of interpretative mobility beyond the reach of, and therefore safe from the crises and destitution of, political life – a simplification that amounts to using Midrash 'to deny one's own interest in power'.[13] To idealise the 'interpretative or discursive community' by denoting it as 'atoning criticism', or 'exilic writing', is to evade the 'difficulty of authority as such – the legitimation of domination and its coercive means'.[14] That the Jews have been an exilic, persecuted people has not for them dispensed with this problem, but placed the burden of its actualisation even more heavily on their shoulders, focusing its paradoxical nature all the more sharply: 'To oppose Midrash to the monolithic domination of reason would be to simplify the difficult history of Judaism and modernity; it would amount to using Midrash to deny one's own interest in power by idealising method and ethics beyond domination.'[15]

'Judaism and Jewish communities', she writes in *The Broken Middle – Out of Our Ancient Society* – the book I know she saw as her *magnum opus* – 'have always been more – not less – exposed to the equivocation of the ethical: the clash between meaning and configuration, the inversion of "generous" principles into outcomes of domination.'[16] Judaism, that is, has lived with especial intensity the problem of the relationship between authority – denied to the Jews by the outside world, all the more fiercely husbanded and enforced within their own polity – and ethics. It has demonstrated, and here I think we can hear her critique of Israel today, the point where an attempt to guarantee your ethical life precisely because you are, like Phocion's wife, an outsider, risks inverting itself into the most dangerous forms of self-legitimation and power. Judaism, wrongly idealised as sublime other, has in fact 'lived in fuller awareness than other polities of the ways in which the violence of non-legitimisable temporal and spatial boundaries rebounds into the collective and would-be sovereign definition of and commitment to the good.'[17]

This is not chosenness, privilege or redemption; but it does grant to the Jewish people a 'fuller awareness' of the tense, but always held, relationship between politics and ethical life. To ignore this equivocation, to use one of her favourite terms, is to snatch the Jewish people and Judaism from their history.

Always hovering within sight of this analysis is the legacy of Auschwitz – 'the difficulty of thinking in the wake of disaster'.[18] Gillian was invited to participate in the Symposium of Jewish Intellectuals on 'The Future of Auschwitz', initiated by the Polish Commission for the Future of Auschwitz, a symposium that met first in Oxford in 1990 and then in Krakow and Auschwitz in 1992. 'It is possible,' she writes in 'The Future of Auschwitz', her essay on those meetings, 'to mean well, to be caring and kind, loving one's neighbour as oneself, yet to be complicit in the corruption and violence of social institutions.'[19] The challenge is not therefore how to think responsibility 'beyond knowledge', which is to isolate the trauma in the domain of the unspeakable and tear it out of history; nor to see the Holocaust as the logical consequence of modernity's instrumental reason, which places it beyond the reach of ethics altogether (the pure culmination of the unstoppable march of history). Instead, once again, it is the breach between morality and legality – between the inner realm of being and our outer institutions – 'that depraves us'.[20] The question for her was not therefore 'Could *I* have done this?', which plunges ethical life into pure interiority, a realm of the soul dangerously sequestered from the world; but

'How easily could we have allowed this to be carried out?', which leads to a more political form of awareness: 'a questioning of our sentimentality as modern citizens, protected in all "innocence" by the military might of the modern state'.[21]

We are always implicated in power, and we are never pure. There is no outside of the city and its laws. 'No one and no community', she writes, 'is exempt from the paradoxes of empowerment.'[22] This was not an apology for statehood, but a laying bare of its anguish. In just one of the moments in her writing which left me gasping at the prescience of her thought for today, she wrote, 'The city, like the nation-state, implies the bounded political entity, but especially the breaches in its wall.'[23] When she wrote these words, there was no wall, or 'security barrier', in Israel snaking itself through Jerusalem cutting off the Palestinians from their dream of statehood. Over the past few years, as my own thinking has brought me to Israel and Zionism, I have so often wanted to talk to her, to hear what she would have said. I have wanted to ask her: how do you stop coercion, as the unavoidable shape of all legitimacy and law, from brutalising itself? Is there a way of wresting from Jewish history and thought 'a new polity', 'a new prayer', to counter the worst of Israel's present-day dominion? Today, I, we, still terribly – still terribly, after these ten years – need her reply.

*A revised version of the presentation delivered at the memorial for the tenth anniversary of the death of Gillian Rose. With Rowan Williams, Howard Caygill, Maggie Gee, chaired by David Held, ICA, London, 9 December 2005.

Notes

1 Gillian Rose, ' "Would that they Would forsake Me but observe my Torah": Midrash and Political Authority', in *Mourning Becomes the Law* (Cambridge, Cambridge University Press 1996), p. 100.

2 Rose, 'Introduction', *Judaism and Modernity – Philosophical Essays* (Oxford, Blackwell 1993), p. ix.

3 Ibid.

4 Rose, 'Is There a Jewish Philosophy?', in *Judaism and Modernity*, p. 18.

5 Rose, 'Athens and Jerusalem – A Tale of Three Cities', in *Mourning Becomes the Law*, p. 35.

6 Ibid., p. 26.

7 'Is There a Jewish Philosophy?', p. 17.

8 Ibid.

9 Ibid.

10 Ibid. p. 18.

11 'Midrash and Political Authority', pp. 77-8.

12 Ibid., p. 84.

13 Ibid., p. 96.

14 Ibid., p. 80.

15 Ibid., p. 96.

16 Rose, 'New Political Theology – Out of Holocaust and Liberation – Levinas, Rosenzweig and Fackenheim', in *The Broken Middle – Out of Our Ancient Society* (Oxford, Blackwell 1992), p. 270.

17 'Midrash and Political Authority', p. 89.

18 Rose, 'Introduction', *Mourning Becomes the Law*, p. 9.

19 Rose, ' "The Future of Auschwitz" ', in *Judaism and Modernity*, p. 35.

20 Ibid.

21 Ibid., p. 36.

22 'Introduction', *Mourning Becomes the Law*, p. 5.

23 Ibid., p. 10.

Index

234 THE LAST RESISTANCE

Warsaw Uprising 3, 5, 204, 217, 220
Warschawski, Michael 35
Weil, Simone 10–11, 12
Weizmann, Chaim 43, 48, 95, 104, 107
Wertzberger, Naftali 131
West, Paul 9, 143–5
West, Rebecca 166
White, Katherine 171, 176
Whitman, Walt 9, 182–6, 188–9
Winnicott, D.W. 163–4
Woolf, Virginia 120, 174, 184, 211
Wulff, Moshe 7

Yad Vashem see Holocaust and
    Heroism Remembrance Law
Yaday, Maayan 39–40, 41, 45
Yediot Ahronot 58
Yerushalmi, Yosef 76, 79, 83, 85
Yizhar, S. 47

Zangwill, Israel 49
Zealots 126
Zertal, Idith 3, 6, 52, 217, 222
Zionism 193–9, 219–22

anti-Semitism and 195
Arendt on 44–5, 220
as flawed 13–14
Freud on 17–18, 22, 48–9, 74, 76
Hareven on 50–56
Jacob de Haan and 6–7
Labor 95
Liebman on 200–202, 204, 206–7
London Zionist Conference (1945) 5
Palestine and 193–9
socialists and 204
Zangwill on 49
Zweig on 27, 30, 34
see also Israel; Jabotinsky; Judaism;
    Moses
Žižek, Slavoj 32
Zuckerman, Anton 4–5
Zuckerman, Yitzhak 3
Zuckerman, Zivia Lubetkin 3
Zweig, Arnold 6–9, 17
    on de Haan 25–6
    De Vriendt Goes Home 26–8, 33
    Freud and 18–25, 28–9, 31–36, 76
    on Zionism 27, 30, 34